STANDARD LOAN

Teaching and Learning in Physical Education

Teaching and Learning in Physical Education: A social psychological perspective

Gordon L. Underwood

Christ Church College
Canterbury
and
Institute of Social and Applied Psychology,
University of Kent

 The Falmer Press

(A member of the Taylor & Francis Group)
London · New York · Philadelphia

UK   The Falmer Press, Falmer House, Barcombe, Lewes, East Sussex, BN8 5DL

USA   The Falmer Press, Taylor & Francis Inc., 242 Cherry Street, Philadelphia, PA 19106-1906

© G. Underwood 1988

First published 1988

British Library Cataloguing in Publication Data

Underwood, Gordon L.
  Teaching and learning in physical
  education.
  1. Schools. Curriculum subjects : Physical
  education. Psychological aspects
  I. Title
  613.7′071

  ISBN 1-85000-422-6
  ISBN 1-85000-423-4 Pbk

Library of Congress Cataloging in Publication Data

Underwood, Gordon L.
  Teaching and learning in physical education.

  Bibliography: p.
  Includes index.
  1. Physical education and training—Study and
teaching.   2. Physical education and training—Study
and teaching (Secondary)—England.   I. Title.
GV361.U53   1988   613.7′07′1242   88-24388
ISBN 1-85000-422-6
ISBN 1-85000-423-4 (pbk.)

Jacket design by Caroline Archer

Typeset in $10\frac{1}{2}/12$ Bembo by
Mathematical Composition Setters Ltd, Salisbury.

Printed in Great Britain by
Redwood Burn Limited, Trowbridge, Wiltshire

Contents

List of Tables and Figures

Tables

Acknowledgements

This book has taken several years to complete and I am indebted to many people who have sustained and motivated me during this time. In particular I wish to express my appreciation to Professor Geoffrey Stephenson, Director of the Institute of Social and Applied Psychology, University of Kent, for his constant encouragement and guidance throughout this period. His perceptive comments are in evidence at every stage of the investigation and his advice has been greatly appreciated. I also wish to thank: Mr Geoffrey Edmondson, Specialist Inspector, Kent Education Authority, who has given me constant support in my research work for many years; Dr Stephen Bird, Lecturer in Movement Studies at Christ Church College, Canterbury, who gave so freely of his time to discuss statistical interpretations; Mr Michael Holliday, Senior Lecturer, Loughborough University of Technology, for his advice on statistical procedures; and the teachers and pupils in the schools who took part in the study for their generous cooperation. I am also indebted to my colleagues and friends in lecturing, advising and teaching who have influenced my thinking over a long period of time. Finally, I should like to thank my wife, Beryl, for her constructive criticisms on the original draft and for her unwavering support.

Foreword

The contribution of physical education to general psychological well-being is a lively research issue, and it is, therefore, appropriate that the research reported in this book should have been carried out within the framework of the University of Kent's Social and Applied Psychological research programme. In this study, techniques of observation and data analysis developed within social psychology have been systematically employed in a unique study of teaching and learning involving 2000 or so pupils in the 4th year of fourteen secondary schools. Video-recording, questionnaires and interviews were employed in what is the most extensive study yet of pupil-teacher interaction in physical education in this country.

Based on sound observation and sophisticated data analysis, the book conveys well the realities of physical education lessons in schools. What makes for good and effective physical education? That was the key question addressed by Gordon Underwood when he embarked five years ago on this research. In pursuit of the answer he examined pupils' perceptions and evaluation of their lessons, the teachers, 'philosophies' and preparation, the organisation of the curriculum and of the department concerned, and he observed in precise detail the interaction of pupils and teachers in class. The results of the study are fascinating and certainly not as everyone would have expected. For example, lessons do not have to be popular to be positively appreciated, the teaching techniques of male and female teachers do not differ as expected and departmental organisation really does matter. Teachers and students of physical education and movement studies will find the route by which these and many other conclusions are reached an interesting and enjoyable reading experience and of immediate benefit to their teaching. Social psychologists and educationalists more generally will also be intrigued and gratified by a number of the findings. Particularly important, in my view, is the discovery that pupils who are taught in the well-organised, efficient and enthusiastic departments of physical education, develop a consensus about the benefits or otherwise of the work they do. Moreover, their views are critical and discriminating.

If the recommendations of a recent report (*Sport and Young People:*

Partnership and Action: School Sport Forum, The Sports Council, 1988) sponsored by the British government are accepted, it is likely that at least 10% of the new national curriculum will be allocated to physical and sports education. It is especially important that informed discussion of present practices in physical education should take place. Gordon Underwood has a broad experience of teaching in schools and colleges, and is already well-known as a researcher in this area. The book makes an important contribution to our understanding of the process of effective physical education and will decisively influence future research in this and related areas, besides encouraging and shaping what is best in current practice.

Professor Geoffrey Stephenson
Director
Institute of Social and
Applied Psychology

1
Introduction

The main aims of this book are to investigate the ways in which teachers teach physical education and examine the effects teaching strategies have on pupils' behaviour in lessons. A secondary, but nevertheless important, aim is to consider pupils' perceptions of their learning in the subject. Most teachers aspire to be efficient and effective in their teaching and would readily subscribe to Nixon and Locke's (1973) comment that 'So long as the skills of sports and games remain part of the heritage transmitted by the schools, children deserve to encounter these skills under optimum conditions for successful mastery.' Nowadays the subject has been expanded to cover the whole range of human movement and includes many other activities such as dance and gymnastics, but the ideal of Nixon and Locke is still relevant and exactly how it may be achieved is dependent upon a number of interrelated variables.

Purposes of Physical Education

Of primary interest is the fact that the educational process in secondary schools sets out to achieve rather broad aims related to the optimal development of the personality of each child. Although this underlying philosophy will influence all decision-making in schools, each school has a great deal of autonomy in deciding how this will be achieved. All subjects in the curriculum should make some contribution to these broad aims consistent with the philosophy of the school. Without exception, physical education forms part of the curriculum in all schools in this country, and Meek (1986) suggested that it accounted for approximately 10 per cent of the secondary school timetable. Inevitably, some of the aims and objectives of physical education which teachers hope to achieve will overlap with the aims of other subjects. The development of moral attitudes would permeate all aspects of school life and physical education would contribute towards this end through an understanding and concern for others in

1

activities such as games, outdoor activities and dance. Another example would suggest that the ability to observe, analyze and evaluate is not the sole prerogative of physical education but that these abilities would also be cultivated in the scientific subjects. The recent upsurge of interest in health-related fitness programmes has also led to a number of interdisciplinary topics taught by the science and physical education departments in a number of schools. On the other hand some aims may be unique to physical education, for example, the development of motor skills in athletics, games, gymnastics and swimming or an understanding of sportsmanship. Irrespective of whether the aims are specific to physical education or interrelated with other subjects, the physical education departments in all schools have a responsibility to attempt to achieve these aims to the best of their ability for all children. This inevitably involves teachers deliberately setting out to change the behaviour of the learners. Under these circumstances, the aims of the subject assume considerable importance. It is therefore pertinent to identify the aims of physical education and whether or not there is a consensus of opinion about what the subject is trying to achieve. In a review of over 200 articles and texts Kane (1974) suggested there were nine long-term aims which appeared most frequently in the literature. These were the development of motor skills, self-realization, leisure-time activities, emotional stability, moral development, social competence, organic development, cognitive development and aesthetic appreciation.

A sample of physical education teachers in England and Wales (N = 888) were asked to place the above aims in rank order and the results indicated that male and female teachers differed in the importance they attached to these nine aims. For example, male teachers ranked the development of leisure-time pursuits and organic development higher than female teachers, whilst the reverse trend was apparent for emotional stability. In a recent enquiry into the state and status of physical education in schools in England and Wales published by the Physical Education Association (1987), the same aims were ranked by a smaller sample of heads of physical education departments (N = 218). Again the development of motor skills was the highest ranked overall aim and, apart from one aim, similar results were reported to the 1974 study. The exception was the importance now attached to physical development (previously named organic development) which had risen from seventh to second ranked overall position. In a separate analysis for the male and female teachers, the males ranked physical development first (previously ranked fourth), and the females ranked this aim third (previously ranked eighth). This significant change must largely be attributed to the importance now being attached to health-related fitness programmes in the physical education curriculum and the substantial publicity and publishing in physical education journals that has occurred during the last four years.

Further differences in the perceived aims of male and female teachers was also highlighted by Underwood (1983) when interviewing sixteen heads of physical education departments (eight males and eight females). The five most frequently mentioned aims were skill acquisition (six males and six females), recreation for leisure (seven males and five females), organic fitness (seven males and three females), socialization (two males and six females) and enjoyment (three males and five females). Apart from the obvious fact that several teachers in the sample of sixteen did not even mention these aims when asked 'What are the main aims you hope physical education achieves in your school?' there were differences in emphasis, particularly in relation to organic fitness which was again stressed by the male teachers and socialization by the female teachers. Of particular interest was the inclusion of enjoyment. It would be difficult to justify the inclusion of physical education in the curriculum solely on the grounds of enjoyment, but it was obviously an important ingredient for many staff and an essential outcome of their teaching. Apart from the above five aims, eighteen other claims were made for the subject, but none was mentioned on more than three occasions. Another finding from this study was that the men made eleven claims for the subject whereas the women referred to twenty possible aims. Thus the female teachers in this sample felt that physical education had a more wide-ranging effect than their male colleagues.

The information presented from the above three studies suggested that female teachers gave a different emphasis to some of the subject aims. Additionally, they appeared to make many more claims in a wider range of aims. Whilst there are similarities, there are also some important differences which will be reflected in the emphases given to the teaching of different aspects of physical education in different schools. Although there are broad and similar guidelines for the subject, there does not appear to be an agreed consensus of opinion. Thus a broad spectrum of aims is apparent, with male and female teachers in different schools giving the subject different emphases.

Planning the Physical Education Curriculum

In a national survey related to the planning and implementation of the physical education curriculum in secondary schools, Underwood (1983) obtained further evidence from a questionnaire completed by 572 heads of physical education departments in England and Wales that there were inconsistencies in planning. For example, one of the conclusions stated that in mixed schools where there were male and female staff, half the departments planned the school physical education programme together, whereas the other half planned separately. In view of the differences in aims between males and females which have been identified, it would appear that two different philosophies about the purpose of the subject may be operating within the same school. In the event of mixed work where boys and girls combined to participate in activities such as badminton, hockey or trampolining, then the aims and objectives may be different. There is nothing wrong with this as any physical education teacher has to cater for differing needs and abilities, but these differences need to be recognized and planned for by the staff beforehand.

A second conclusion was that teachers communicated the short-term objectives more frequently than the long term aims. Indeed, more than half of this large sample only occasionally told their pupils what they were ultimately trying to achieve in the five or more years that were devoted to physical education. Thus pupils' perceptions of physical education may not be clear and indeed may even be different from the teachers' perceptions.

Apparently, most heads of department do not regularly and systematically evaluate their original aims. Indeed evaluation was a rather neglected aspect of planning and was given very little emphasis. This being the case, how can teachers know whether they have achieved what they set out to achieve? Obviously there are subjective means through personal observations and these are important, but more sophisticated and clearer methods are necessary.

A fourth conclusion relevant to the present study was that not all the aims proposed by curriculum theorists were considered to be important by practising teachers. This again points to discrepancies between what teachers think or hope is being achieved and what is actually being achieved. Not only will there be variations between schools but also, as has already been indicated, differences between male and female teachers within a school.

There appeared to be a number of inconsistencies in the planning and execution of the physical education programme in secondary schools. In an analysis of nearly 100 syllabuses, Underwood (*ibid*) indicated that staff were not particularly good at setting out their aims and objectives in written form and as a result there may well be a loss of efficiency and direction to the programme. Support for this viewpoint was recently provided by Flanagan (1985) who highlighted five current issues in physical education which he, as the Staff Inspector for Physical Education at the Department of Education and Science (DES), considered to be worthy of note and action. These were that:

(i)   the curriculum should be planned as a whole;
(ii) progress needs to be monitored;
(iii) there is a need for coherence and progression;
(iv) there is a need to avoid unnecessary repetition and discontinuity;
(v)   there is a need to have better defined objectives for subjects, remove clutter in course content and make better use of the time available.

The above concerns suggest that 'all is not well' within physical education and that in some instances the autonomy which is given to each school has resulted in some lack of clarity and direction. This not only applied to the planning of the physical education curriculum but also to the manner in which it was taught.

Teaching Strategies

In spite of these differences and inconsistencies in the purposes of the subject, all teachers will have some aims and objectives which they hope to achieve and these are mainly communicated to the pupils during the lessons in the gymnasium, swimming pool, dance theatre or on the games field. It is at this point that the 'transaction' takes place and is the main link between the teachers' aspirations and the pupils' outcomes. During a five-year period in a secondary school, a pupil could expect to spend approximately 350 timetabled hours being actively involved in the physical education programme. When one considers that, during the course of a career in physical education the number of teaching hours amounts to approximately 50,000, it is surprising that there has been so little research conducted in this country on this central activity.

It is pertinent therefore to consider the role and function of the physical education teacher in a lesson or series of lessons. The teacher is a key figure in as much that the programme is planned in order to facilitate learning. Not only will he decide on the objectives to be achieved but he will also organize the learning experiences in the most efficient way in an attempt to ensure that optimal learning takes place for every child in the class. During the course of the lesson he will observe the children working and the quality of these observations should have a direct relationship to the task that has been set. On the basis of these observations, decisions will be made concerning the length of the practices, the type of feedback to be given, whether to direct comments to individuals, groups or the whole class as well as a host of other functions. Physical education lessons are conducted at a very rapid pace as substantiated by Hurwitz's (1978) review of

5

eighty-three lessons. He reported that, on average, teacher functions do not last longer than ten seconds and that pupil functions last an average of twenty seconds. Thus the teacher plays an important and central role in the conduct of the lesson.

The current climate of 'educational accountability' inevitably impinges on physical education and involves an evaluation of the effectiveness of teacher and pupil behaviour. As has already been indicated, there is a broad spectrum of aims in physical education and it would be difficult to make an accurate evaluation in every area. A distinction can be made within the aims ranging from overt to covert. Overt aims would include the acquisition of motor skills and the development of fitness levels where it is comparatively easy to identify short-term objectives leading to the achievement of these aims. In contrast, covert aims would be concerned with such ideals as emotional development and aesthetic appreciation where the identification of objectives is much more difficult to define. Obviously, it is much easier to make an evaluation in an overt area and the development of strength and endurance which can be accurately monitored by computer programme would be a good example. Conversely, it would be extremely difficult to measure the development of personal control or the understanding of aesthetic judgements. Thus within physical education, it may not be possible to 'be accountable' for everything that the teacher does but he must be able to account for what he does.

Professional teaching skills are not innate. They are learned and consequently are capable of being developed and improved over a period of time. Teaching is both an art and a science. As an art, one would be concerned with individuality, creativity, improvization and flair, and every support should be given to develop these aspects, whereas the scientific aspects of teaching would be more related to lengths of practice, time on task and prespecified presentation. There is, of course, a place for both forms of teaching in the repertoire of any teacher.

A teacher's subjective rating on a lesson, scheme of work or total curriculum can often be remarkably accurate and acceptable. However, there are times when it may be very inaccurate and influenced by personal prejudices. If the evaluation of a component is to act as a form of feedback of information for the future, it needs to be as accurate as possible, otherwise future decisions will be made based on false data. Thus subjective ratings may sometimes be lacking in reliability and validity. More objective ways are now being used to provide additional information. For example, lessons are being subjected to event recording, time sampling and duration recording. Thus the behaviours of teachers (for example, organizing or providing instruction) or pupils (for example, time on task or waiting), can be systematically observed, recorded and analyzed. This kind of data collection can give high reliability and over the past decade a number of systems have been developed which have contributed a significant amount of information concerning the behaviours of teachers and pupils in physical education settings. Many of these systems have been incorporated into a text by Darst *et al* (1983) and the works of Anderson (1980) and Siedentop *et al* (1982) are also noteworthy.

It is, therefore, during the lessons that teachers impart and pupils assimilate the underlying philosophy of physical education. Considering the importance of this phase, it is somewhat surprising that little research work in this country has examined the teacher and pupil in a naturalistic setting. Inevitably the behaviour of one is reflected in the behaviour of the other and the two are inextricably linked.

A number of questions arise from the above comments. For example, how much time is spent by the teacher:

— preparing for motor activities;
— giving instructions;
— organizing equipment;
— helping individuals;
— allowing pupils to practise;
— being involved or standing back and observing?
— Do teachers use the same teaching strategies regardless of the nature of the practical activity, for example, in games and gymnastics?
— Are there any differences in the ways in which male and female teachers approach and execute their teaching?
— What effect does the behaviour of the teacher have on pupils' behaviours in a lesson?
— What effect does the teacher have on pupils' attitudes to the subject?
— Are pupils' perceptions of the subject congruent with the teachers' aims?

These are important questions to which, in this country, we currently do not have sufficient information to be able to give definitive answers. Indeed Tinning (1983) intimated that discussion of what teachers do in the practical setting is nothing new but that detailed information about what actually takes place is comparatively new. Some information and guidelines are available from other parts of the world which are extremely helpful. However, it is sometimes difficult and often inappropriate to interpret data from one culture and transpose the results into another culture. Indeed this can sometimes prove to be misleading.

It is clear that it is necessary to make some kind of appraisal and observation of the teaching of physical education in a naturalistic setting. This notion was supported by Locke (1977) who stated,

> If teaching behaviour is thought to be a factor of importance in determining the production of educational outcomes, then there is only one way to study it and only one place to study it. That way is by observing teaching directly where it occurs, in the place where the action is, inside the black box.

These pertinent comments heralded an upsurge of interest and the publication of numerous research studies in physical education which examined the teaching and learning effects in a naturalistic setting.

2
The Development of Systems of Observation

Historical Development

Many of the early observation systems focused on the verbal behaviour of the teacher and/or the pupil/s with a marked emphasis on the classroom setting. It was recognized that the quality and quantity of the teacher-pupil interaction was an important key to the understanding of effective teaching and one of the first attempts to examine this relationship took place in the late 1930s. Anderson's classic study in 1939 examined teacher pupil relationships between teachers who were classified either as dominative (characterized by giving directions, expressing their own ideas or knowledge and justifying their own position) or integrative (accepting pupils' ideas and feelings, and praising and encouraging) and kindergarten children. He established twenty three distinct categories based on the observation of teachers' behaviours which could be placed into either the dominative or integrative pattern of teaching. The dichotomy of teaching styles was undoubtedly a forbearer and influenced many of the later studies (for example, Flanders' (1970) direct and indirect teaching styles).

At the same time, another classic study was published by Lewin, Lippitt and White (1939) who investigated the social climate under three different types of leadership, viz. authoritarian, democratic and laissez-faire. Different leadership styles produced different social climates which in turn influenced individual and group behaviours. For example, there were more instances of aggressive behaviour under authoritarian leadership. These attempts to observe and control the 'climate variable' as well as placing different verbal behaviours into category systems were influential in shaping subsequent work.

The concept of climate or psychological atmosphere was further developed by Withall (1949) who devised a technique to measure the social-emotional climate in the classroom. This was done by placing the statements of the teacher into one of seven categories which ranged from teacher to learner-centredness. During this period, consideration was given

9

to the types of behaviour which were most effective and it was recognized that flexibility in the teacher's behaviour was important in dealing with each individual situation.

As systems developed, they inevitably built on each other and distinctions between systems became blurred. The work of Flanders in the 1960s was a landmark in the field and culminated in the Flanders Interaction Analysis System (FIAS) in 1970 which was devised to enable an observer to record and analyze the verbal behaviour of the teacher and the pupil. The system incorporated all teacher–pupil interactions into ten separate categories, seven of which were devoted to teacher talk, two to pupil talk and one to a 'catch all' category. The teacher talk was further sub-divided into direct (for example, lectures or gives directions) and indirect influence (for example, praises or accepts pupils' ideas). The dominant behaviour was then recorded every three seconds on to a prepared chart and it was thus possible to glean information about the sequence of the behaviours and their frequency. It is important to note that FIAS only recorded the verbal behaviour of the teacher and the pupils and the assumption was made that this was an adequate sample of the teaching in the classroom. Whilst accepting that verbal behaviour is a vital part of the teaching-learning process, to concentrate solely on this aspect would be to ignore many other elements which are equally, if not more, important. This is especially true in physical education where much of the 'dominant behaviour' would be the physical activity of the pupils. To ignore this aspect would provide only a partial picture and exclude the process of learning through movement in physical education lessons.

Multi-dimensional Systems

In 1970 when Flanders published his book entitled *Analyzing Teaching Behaviour*, he dedicated it to 'those thoughtful social scientists whose accomplishments will someday make what is written here obsolete by pushing far beyond this progress report to create new understanding of the teaching-learning process'. FIAS proved to be a forerunner in the field for obtaining quantitative data and many of the new systems adapted Flanders' original ideas and categories (for example, Dougherty, 1970; Melograno, 1971; Goldberger, 1974; Rankin, 1975; Heinila, 1979; and Underwood, 1980). However, the system most frequently used in many research studies was the Cheffers Adaptation of FIAS (1972) known as CAFIAS. This imaginative adaptation was specifically developed for use in physical education settings and enabled behaviour to be categorized as verbal, non-verbal or both. In addition, he increased the range of teaching agencies to the teacher, other students, or the environment, as well as coding whether the class was working as a whole, in groups or individually. The number of categories devoted to pupil behaviour was also increased substantially which enabled a broader spectrum to be recorded.

Flanders was correct in predicting that his system would soon be out-dated and the 1970s saw a proliferation of descriptive-analytic techniques about the behaviours of teachers and pupils which could be used in a variety of physical settings. The major systems developed during this period have been brought together in a book by Darst *et al* (1983) entitled Systematic Observation Instrumentation for Physical Education. The results from the research studies which utilized these systems provided a great deal of objective data about the teacher and pupils' behaviour. Teachers were observed in naturalistic settings and the amount of time devoted to such functions as observing, describing and providing feedback were recorded. Similar procedures were also used for recording the amount of time pupils spent in such behaviours as on-task, listening to instructions or off-task. Batchelder and Cheffers (1976) suggested that these systems could be used for the following purposes:

(i)   to describe current classroom practices;
(ii)   to modify teacher behaviour;
(iii)   to provide a tool for the analysis of teaching;
(iv)   to give feedback about one's own teaching;
(v)   to train student teachers;
(vi)   to discriminate between patterns of teaching;
(vii)   to determine the relationships between various classroom behaviours and student growth; and
(viii) to help in projecting future teaching patterns.

It would be naive to suggest that information from these observation systems could provide complete answers to the above issues. However, they should provide a source of illumination to some of the problems and give some insight into the process of teaching and learning. Hopefully this would make the teaching process more informed and effective in achieving its objectives.

It is clear that teaching is a complex and diverse activity. To measure any behaviour in just one dimension would be too simplistic. Recognizing this, a number of wide-ranging studies were attempted. One of the most significant of these studies was conducted by Anderson at Teachers' College, Columbia, in the 1970s. He initiated a number of complementary investigations examining different aspects of the teaching of physical education in the USA. Initially, eighty-three physical education lessons were videotaped which provided a constant source of reference. Forty were examples of current practice in elementary schools and the remainder were from secondary schools. (The project has subsequently become known as the Videotape Data Bank Project). Examples of the kind of research carried out by this group were Fishman's (1974) procedure for recording augmented feedback, and Laubach's (1975) system which objectively and sequentially described the behaviour of selected pupils in physical education lessons. Anderson's (1974) contribution to this project was to develop a system which allowed an observer to describe the professional functions of physical education teachers. A multi-dimensional approach was used which comprised six dimensions, each being divided into a number of sub-categories. The six dimensions were concerned with 'what' the teacher did (interactive function), the extent to which the teacher carried out the function or shared it (function subscript), the means of communication (mode), to whom the teaching was aimed (direction), the subject content (substance), and the length of time devoted to the behaviour (duration). The system was specifically designed to analyze videotaped lessons and necessitated a digital time clock being imprinted on the film. This enabled an accurate record to be made of the many teacher functions that physical education teachers engage in. Apart from the potentially high reliability and validity of the system, one of its major strengths was that it measured each teaching act in a number of different ways and was truly multi-dimensional.

Running parallel with the VDBP was the development of a number of observation systems under the direction of Siedentop at Ohio State University. These were mainly used in the training of students to become teachers of physical education but they were also utilized for in-service training. The OSU Teacher Behaviour Rating Scale and the Data Collection for Managerial Efficiency were typical of this work. (For details of these and other systems developed at Ohio State University see Darst *et al* (1983), Part 2, pp 126–95).

Academic Learning Time — Physical Education (ALT-PE)

Until the development and application of these systems in the 1970s, Paese (1982) reported that

> There was no evidence of what students were learning or if learning was actually taking place. Also there was no data on the type of teacher behaviours which effected student performance, and, of course, no data on how students were spending their time during physical education class.

As a result of this still inadequate picture of the dynamics of teaching, further developments were made based on the Beginning Teacher Evaluation Study (BTES) which focused on the relationship between the pupils' contact with appropriate curricular content (Berlinner, 1979). Three types of instructional time were identified, viz., ALLOCATED TIME referred to the amount of time a teacher gave for learning a particular subject matter, ENGAGED TIME or time-on-task related to the time a pupil was involved with the subject matter, and ACADEMIC LEARNING TIME (ALT) was the time spent on tasks when the pupils experienced a high success rate. Thus Berlinner stated,

> The variable used in BTSE research is the accrued engaged time in a particular context area using materials that are not too difficult for the student. This complex variable is called Academic Learning Time (ALT). Although the relationship is probably not linear, the accrual of ALT is expected to be a strong positive correlate of achievement.

As a result, ALT becomes an intervening variable between teaching (the process) and pupil achievement (the product) and is defined as the amount of time a pupil spends in relevant instructional activities at an easy level of difficulty.

This research approach provided a slightly different emphasis in the focus of attention. In the past, teacher behaviour had been the primary focus and pupil behaviour had been secondary. Now the two were seen as being inextricably linked and an ALT system was devised specifically related to physical education which was named ACADEMIC LEARNING TIME — PHYSICAL EDUCATION (ALT-PE). The first system for collecting ALT-PE data was devised by Siedentop, Birdwell and Metzler (1979) and used interval recording techniques. One of its strengths was its recording of live teaching situations which was consistent with Siedentop's (1983) statement that '... the best hope for continuing research productivity is to keep our research firmly rooted in the realities of teaching'. The system was later revised by Siedentop, Tousignant and Parker in 1982 and had two levels of decision-making. The first focused on the class in its context and the second on the involvement of the learner.

ALT-PE has been widely used by researchers in the 1980s and particularly at the University of Victoria, British Columbia, Canada. A progressive programme of research involved videotaping over 100 physical education lessons and the results of some of these studies were reported by Howe and Jackson (1985). Of particular interest is the chapter by McLeish who presented an overall view of this project. In it, he stated,

In studying teaching efficiency, we start from three basic assumptions; (i) we must control our intuitive understandings by collecting comparative data for systematic study: data must be collected in the classroom environment — in physical education, in the gymnasium; (ii) in examining the data we must concentrate on actual behaviours and pay no regard to teachers' intentions, nor to declared objectives, unless stated so that we can check if they have been achieved or not; (iii) we accept as a basic principle that classroom learning is unlikely unless students have the opportunity to learn.

Again there is strong support for studying teaching-learning through direct observation and that learning is related to the number and type of opportunities that pupils are given to learn a motor task.

The learning of motor skills in ALT-PE seems to centre on the ability of the pupils to practice at an 'easy level of difficulty' and as a result produce a high success rate. Subject matter which is too difficult will result in many failures and if this continues for any length of time will lead to avoidance or modification of the situation. A similar situation will obtain if the task is too easy and does not challenge the pupils. Usually this results in a loss of motivation. In the learning of motor skills, a balance has to be struck between the practice and the enjoyment of well-established skills and the challenge of mastering more difficult or more complicated aspects of the same or a new skill. In the achievement of most skills, the learner often has to go through difficult and uncertain phases. In 1962, Fuchs referred to the progression-regression hypothesis which suggested there were times when rapid progress was made as opposed to other occasions when there was a regression to previous and lower levels of skilled performance. Earls (1983) also suggested that '...a child's regression to the practice of a less advanced movement pattern is not generally conducive to motor development'. Thus, achievement in the psychomotor area can be elusive and often prove to be frustrating. This suggests that once improvement and learning has taken place, the skill should be practised and the learning consolidated. If this is done, an element of 'overlearning' is involved. Arranging the environment for pupils in physical education lessons to practise at an optimal level of efficiency is therefore an important element which is encompassed in the ALT-PE system.

The above discussion has pointed to the importance of the qualitative aspects of practice time and that pure quantitative recording may only give a partial insight into pupils' time-on-task. There is strong support for the suggestion that a combination of the two might be the best way to examine the teaching-learning process.

3
Teacher and Pupil Behaviour in Physical Education

Teacher Behaviour in Physical Education

In their introduction to the book *Social Psychology of Teaching*, Morrison and McIntyre (1972) clearly emphasized the complex interactional nature of the teaching-learning process when they stated,

> Teaching is both familiar and intriguing; something that most of us engage in during our everyday lives as professional teachers, but at the same time a difficult set of processes to analyze, hard to describe, and clearly complex and often subtle in its effects upon those we are attempting to teach.

This quotation probably applied mainly to classroom subjects but at the time was equally true of physical education. During the last fifteen years there have been a number of significant advances in our understanding of the teaching-learning process in physical education but the complexity remains. In reviewing the literature for this book, two main criteria have been used in the selection of texts and articles. The first was that the majority of the studies should focus on the teaching of physical education in a naturalistic setting rather than in a laboratory or artificial situation. By doing this it was intended to establish as high a level of validity as possible in making inferences from the review. The second criteria was that the empirical procedures and findings were relevant to the teaching of physical education. However, this did not preclude studies from other subject areas which were relevant to the investigation.

Teaching Behaviour in Lessons

Teachers obviously have a central role to play in the planning and implementation of all physical education lessons. Not only must they

15

decide what they intend to teach, but also in a manner which they hope will be effective. Anderson and Barrette's (1978) report on teacher behaviour in twenty elementary and twenty secondary classes in the Videotape Data Bank Project (VDBP) has provided the most detailed and in-depth study about how teachers actually teach. They reported teachers spending 36.9 per cent of the lesson on active instruction which included preparatory instruction and providing different types of feedback to pupils, 21.2 per cent on observation when the teacher stood back from the class and silently observed pupils performing motor activities, 20.4 per cent on managing pupils and the environment which involved providing and dealing with equipment and organizing pupils, and 16.9 per cent on instruction related activities which mainly comprised officiating, leading exercises and partici- pating as a performer in an activity. As a result, the teachers in this sample spent approximately 95 per cent of their time on interactive functions. In a comparison of the teaching behaviours at the elementary and secondary level there were few differences. Indeed Anderson and Barrette reported, 'There was little evidence in virtually all analytical areas provided for in the System to substantiate the notion that teachers at the elementary and secondary levels spend their time very differently.' Thus, a remarkably similar teaching profile emerged. It was also clear that most of the functions were carried out solely by the teacher (77 per cent) and that 'talk' was the most significant mode of interaction and communication. It is interesting to note that the teachers rarely listened and that teacher demonstration was, on average, used less than six times in a lesson. Approximately one-third of the time was spent addressing one pupil and a slightly larger fraction of the teachers' behaviours were directed towards a group or the whole class.

In summary, it can be seen from the above data that the teachers were highly interactive and spent a large proportion of their time involved in active instruction and silently observing pupils working. The teacher did most of the talking, almost to the exclusion of other modes of communi- cation. Any suggestion that physical education teachers frequently use personal performance to demonstrate skills to pupils was not supported in this study.

The lessons were conducted with many frequent changes of direction. On average, pupils changed what they were doing three times every minute, while the teacher made six changes in function every minute. This supported Hurwitz's (1978) contention of a 'fast paced, constantly chang- ing' environment. The pattern of lessons was characterized by the teacher giving instructions and directions, followed by clearly defined movement responses by the pupils in practice situations.

Cheffers and Mancini (1978) applied the CAFIAS system to the eighty-three videotaped lessons and a summary of their results indicated the following:

1   Minimal differences were detected in category usage, interaction parameters or in interaction patterns between male and female teachers and between elementary and secondary teachers.
2   Teachers used lecture and the giving of directions as their overwhelmingly predominant mode of teaching.
3   By comparison with the total recorded teacher behaviours, virtually no acceptance of students' feelings and ideas, praise or questioning behaviours were recorded by the sample of teachers.
4   Very little genuine student initiated activity was recorded.

The similarity between the teaching behaviours of male and female teachers in elementary schools lends some strength to the argument for coeducational classes. Indeed, in this country almost all physical education classes in the primary school are mixed whereas relatively few schools teach with mixed physical education classes in the secondary school. But perhaps the most important observation is the prevalence of the traditional teacher-dominated teaching model and the absence of pupil-initiated ideas. The non-acceptance of pupils' ideas and feelings, and the absence of praise and questioning, suggests that the interaction is nearly all in a one-way direction and may not be encouraging enough contribution from pupils.

Teaching Behaviour of Male and Female Teachers

The VDBP indicated that male and female teachers adopted similar teaching patterns in physical education. Some qualified support for this was given by O'Sullivan (1985) in an analysis of the teaching of eight male and eight female students training to become physical education teachers. Both groups were equally effective in the conduct of their classes but there was a statistically significant difference at the 5 per cent level in the amount of time pupils spent on-task. Lessons taught by the female physical education students allowed significantly more time for pupils to be engaged in motor activity. However, this may well have been due to the nature of the content of the lessons and the fact that the dance lessons taught by the female teachers had an exceptionally high motor component of 73 per cent in one lesson rising to 95 per cent in another. This compared with a mean score of 21.6 per cent for a soccer lesson. Obviously the dance lessons distorted the results and enabled statistical significance to be reached. Hickey (1985) also found similar results. In an analysis of the teaching of six male and six female practising physical education teachers, the male teachers had

significantly more off-task behaviour whereas female teachers had signif-
cantly more on-task movement behaviour. In spite of these differences, he
concluded there were 'almost no sex differences in style and effectiveness of
teaching'. Again, the differences that were noted may be attributed to the
type of activity being taught. It would be perfectly reasonable to expect
greater levels of non-movement time and off-task organizational behaviour
in such activities as tennis, gymnastics and athletics, and greater amounts of
on-task movement behaviours in dance and fitness lessons. Thus the
independent variable of the physical activity being taught is an important
one. In simplistic terms, similar levels of activity can not be expected in
activities which make contrasting demands on pupils. To illustrate this, the
pupils' motor involvement in a lesson on pole vaulting would be markedly
different from a lesson aimed to develop cardiorespiratory fitness.

A research project carried out in Finland in 1983 by Varstala *et al*
examined the relationship between the teachers' teaching behaviour and the
pupils' learning behaviour in 262 physical education lessons. This study did
reveal some differences in that female teachers used more time to explain
the content of the lesson and less time observing and supervising pupils'
performance than their male colleagues. These results were consistent
regardless of the activity being taught or the objectives being pursued (for
example, motor skills or fitness levels). The consequent result of this was
that girls spent more time in a cognitive phase following the teacher's
explanations, and the boys had more time-on-task in the physical activity.
Obviously the behaviour of the teacher had an effect on what the pupils did
and because of this close interrelationship, they recommended 'not to talk
about teacher behaviour and teaching separately from pupil behaviour and
learning, but instead to talk about teaching-learning behaviour together'.
One longitudinal study by Cheffers and Lombardo (1979) observed four
elementary teachers twice a day for twenty days. They concluded that each
teacher's behaviours and interactions varied minimally during this period
and that the traditional, non-humanistic teaching styles prevailed. As well
as this, they found significant differences between the male and female
teachers in 60 per cent of all the CAFIAS parameters used in the study. Of
particular interest were the following findings:

1 Male teachers contributed more verbally and gave more directions.
2 Female teachers made greater use of verbal questioning and pupils
   contributed more in female classes.
3 Pupil-initiated behaviour was higher in classes taught by female
   teachers.
4 There was more off-task behaviour in classes conducted by male
   teachers.

5   Male teachers used more non-verbal criticism.
6   Male teachers gave more non-verbal information (i.e. demon-
    stration).

Although this study was conducted with a small sample of elementary
teachers, there was an earlier suggestion by Cheffers and Mancini (1978)
that there was minimal differences between the teaching behaviour of
elementary and secondary school teachers. Therefore these results may be
applicable to the secondary sector. If this is true, the above findings suggest
that pupils are able to make a greater input to lessons taught by female staff
in relation to initiating behaviour and personal contribution. Male teachers
appeared to be more directive and experience greater levels of off-task
behaviour. They also demonstrated motor skills more frequently than their
female colleagues which again pointed towards a more direct type of
teaching approach.

In a recent study carried out in England, Spackman (1986) devised an
observation system based on Anderson's (1974) work to describe teacher
behaviour and used it to analyze nineteen videotaped lessons. The lessons
were taught by eleven teachers and embraced eight different physical
activities, viz. netball, hockey, badminton, gymnastics, swimming, rugby
football, volleyball and basketball. Some intra-individual variations in the
teaching behaviour of three male teachers was reported, together with
some significant differences between male and female teachers in the
management and teaching of games. However, in the overall analysis,
Spackman stated, 'male and female teachers across all the activities and age
groups did not show any significant differences in their managerial and
teaching behaviours examined collectively.'

In summary, the results appear to be equivocal and there is no clear cut
answer to the question 'Are there any differences in the manner in which
male and female teachers conduct their lessons?' The actual content of
teaching behaviour appeared to be similar but the proportion of time spent
in each category may differ. Sometimes it was difficult to make comparisons because different studies used different observation systems and
there was often an overlap of categories or definitions. Some of the
recorded differences can certainly be attributed to the different activities
being taught, but there was often less variance within the same activity. A
variety of schools, variously called primary, elementary, junior and senior
high, and lower and upper secondary have been mentioned in the review.
Although there was some consistency in teacher behaviour irrespective of
the age range being taught, there were also some differences reported. The
literature certainly points to the need for more information in this area
which addresses some of the variables mentioned above. In particular, an

investigation in which the research design allowed each male and female teacher to teach two different types of activity would give some insight into some of the questions that have been identified above and enable some comparisons to be made.

Management

Physical education classes invariably involve a large number of pupils in a great deal of movement and activity. Reference has already been made to the fast pace and high interaction in these kinds of lessons. Efficient management techniques are imperative if lessons are to progress smoothly. Anderson and Barrette (1978) reported American teachers spending approximately 20 per cent of their time in managerial behaviour which mainly involved organizing, providing equipment and discipline. An even higher percentage of management time (27 per cent) was reported by Spackman (1986) in her study of English physical education teachers. Obviously management is an essential element of effective teaching, especially in physical education where there can often be an element of danger. In the planning of group apparatus in gymnastics for example, the teacher must ensure that safety is the first priority and that pupils do not use the apparatus until it has been checked. However, as Pieron (1983) pointed out, 'these behaviours do not have a direct educational effect on the learner'.

Feedback

In physical education, the teacher often plays an important role in providing information and feedback to the pupils about their performance. Feedback refers to the information a learner receives in his or her attempts to learn a motor skill and is an important variable in the learning process. Since Trowbridge and Cason's classic study in 1932 on a line-drawing experiment which suggested that detailed information about a performance provided the best information for the learner to adjust subsequent performance, there have been a number of experiments to support this contention. For example, Bilodeau, Bilodeau and Schumsky (1959), in a hand dexterity task, found that no learning took place unless there was some information given to the learner about the nature of the errors.

The two types of feedback normally referred to in the literature are intrinsic and extrinsic. Intrinsic feedback refers to those aspects of feedback which are inherent in the activity. An obvious example would be the games player who can see if the ball hits the target area. Equally important is the intrinsic feedback a performer receives from the proprioceptors in the body which relay information about the position and movement of body parts from the muscles, tendons, joints and vestibular apparatus. It is from these sources that a performer receives personal information about the 'feel' of a movement in such activities as a vault in gymnastics or a dive in swimming. This feedback provides valuable information that can effect future performances and the attention of the learner should be drawn to this during the learning process. In contrast, extrinsic feedback is usually provided by other means either during or after a motor performance. In an educational context this is mainly provided by the teacher through verbal comments, but non-verbal means are also possible. Comments can also be made which refer to all or part of a movement.

It is not suggested that intrinsic and extrinsic feedback are mutually exclusive, as this would be far from the truth. Both forms can be valuable in all movement activities but will vary according to the requirements of the task and the nature of the situation. One of the main purposes of feedback is to establish a 'perceptual trace' of the correct response (Adams, 1971) in every performer. This enables them to make a comparison of current performance with the trace that had been established during previous trials. Obviously the establishment of the correct trace is vital from the outset otherwise false comparisons will be made.

The various forms of feedback are an essential component of learning and a valuable aid for the teacher. Its importance is perhaps best summed up by Schmidt (1982) who suggested there were four ways in which it could help produce learning. These were that, 'It acts as guidance. It acts to form associations between response parameters and resulting action. It acts as a reward or punishment. And it acts in a motivational role.'

Feedback therefore appears to be an important variable in the learning and performance of motor skills and the teacher of physical education has many opportunities to observe and react to pupils' performance. It has already been established that teachers spend a great deal of time in a lesson observing pupils (over 20 per cent in the VDBP) and it would be reasonable to assume that the larger proportion of this would be spent watching pupils attempt skills and subsequently allowing them to provide some kind of feedback. In a review of research studies on extrinsic feedback, Pieron (1983) reported that its occurrence was extremely variable and ranged from less than 10 per cent in some studies (Stewart, 1980) to approximately 25 per cent in others (Anderson and Barrette, 1978). Thus there appeared to be a great deal of variation in the teachers' reactions to pupils' performances. In an analysis of the distribution of occurrences of types of feedback in eighty-one physical education lessons, Fishman and

Tobey (1978) reported that the most commonly-used method was auditory and directed at one pupil. Very little feedback was given to the class as a whole. Information about a performance is usually pertinent to the particular performer and it might be inappropriate to give the same feedback to a class of thirty children. They also found that nearly all the feedback was equally divided between concurrent (during the perform-ance) or terminal (immediately after the completion of a task) feedback. This would be consistent with good practice and effective teaching as a long period of delay after a performance, especially when other trials intervene, would make the feedback less relevant. Of particular interest in Fishman and Tobey's study was the incidence of feedback which had no specific reference but which was positive and included statements such as 'Well done' or 'Getting better.' Presumably these were given for moti-vational reasons which is one of the purposes of feedback identified by Schmidt. Nearly half the comments made by the teachers could be placed in this category. However, the quality and value of this type of reinforcement was questioned by Imwold *et al* (1984) and referred to it as being 'non-genuine'. Regardless of the number of times feedback is administered, the quality of the response is of equal importance. To a large extent this will depend on the quality of the teachers' observation and their ability to provide relevant feedback. Inevitably this will be influenced by their knowledge of the subject and the learner. In a study with elementary pupils on the immediate effects of instructional variables, Earls (1983) found that most of the teachers' comments referred to the end result or motor output of the performance rather than to the way in which it was performed. The same trend had not been apparent in Fishman and Tobey's study who found that 34.7 per cent of the feedback was directed to part of the movement. These, and other studies (for example, Pieron and Devilliers, 1980; and Pieron and Dèlmelle, 1982) suggested that most of the teachers' comments appeared to be directed towards the performance of the motor skill. Using an information processing approach to the acquisition of skill, Whiting (1969) and Marteniuk (1976) both refer to a model which identified the three interrelated aspects of input, decision-making and output. All skills, and in particular 'open' skills where the environmental factors are continually changing, are dependent upon the performer attending to the relevant cues in the environment, making a decision about the action to take, and ultimately sending messages to the muscles in the body to initiate action. If the wrong perceptual cues are processed in the first instance and the performer attends to unimportant features of the display, then there is no possibility that the motor output will be either appropriate or correct. In such a case, the teacher would have to direct the pupil's attention to the perceptual components at the input stage of the decision-making process to effect improved performance. In a study which similarly stressed the importance of prior aspects of motor performance, Hoffman (1983) referred to primary and secondary errors. For example, the secondary error of a twisting action in a back somersault from the 1 metre diving board could be attributed to the primary error of the head turning slightly during the initiating movement. It therefore appears that many poor motor performances may be due to input and/or primary errors. In view of this it is surprising that so much of the teachers' feedback is directed towards the motor or output aspects.

Once a pupil has been given feedback about a performance, it is then necessary to practise the skill again to ensure a change has been effected. With large numbers of pupils in a class it is doubtful whether the teacher is able to spend enough time with any one pupil to make sure this happens. Also, there may be occasions when the teacher and the class watch a pupil or group of pupils performing. This can often be followed by other pupils demonstrating their skills. (A successive showing of group work in gymnastics would be an example). If these are shown at the end of a period in order that refinement and alternatives can be suggested and further practice can take place and there is no time left for practice, this obviously defeats the purpose of the exercise.

There appeared to be a great deal of variance in the use teachers made of feedback in their teaching. There was little mention of the development of intrinsic feedback in the studies and extrinsic feedback was almost solely related to the motor aspects. The use of this powerful variable in the teaching process is a complex issue and in two short 'experimental teaching units' by Yerg in 1977 and 1982, which revealed contrasting results, she compared the data in 1983 to support this complexity in relation to the teacher's understanding of the skill and the ability of the learner to profit from this. She concluded, 'that to be effective, the teacher must understand the learners, the tasks and the learning process in order to appropriately provide practice and feedback in facilitating learning'.

In spite of the overwhelming support for the value of feedback in teaching, there does not appear to be a consistent and informed use of this important variable in physical education.

Environmental Factors

The teaching of physical education appears to take place in a dynamic environment and the teacher needs a variety of alternative methods available in order to be able to adapt to the changes. Support for the contention that teaching is complex and complicated came from Jensen

(1980) who likened teaching to Poulton's (1957) idea of 'open and closed skills'. The concept of open and closed is determined by the temporal and spatial demands of the environment. In an open skill such as the playing of a team game, the successful player 'discriminates and chooses a movement or strategy almost automatically as he adjusts to the changing environmental display'. The act of teaching would appear to require similar abilities to those of the successful performer in open skills. There is a need to identify changing elements in the situation, decide what to do and then carry them out efficiently. These are essential ingredients of effective teaching.

Overview

Earlier in this review of literature, it was suggested that 'all is not well' within physical education in this country. A similar concern was expressed by Locke in 1983 in relation to the teaching of physical education in North America. He stated,

A small but growing body of observational evidence from qualitative studies, and the cumulative picture revealed in the studies of ALT-PE suggest that many physical education teachers do not:

1   plan lessons in advance;
2   adapt lessons to the needs of individual pupils;
3   provide positive reinforcement for learning;
4   provide adequate opportunity for practice of skills;
5   provide enough vigorous activity to contribute to fitness;
6   prevent waste of time on managerial tasks;
7   provide prompt and specific feedback for practice trials;
8   hold students accountable for execution of practice trials;
9   provide clear models of the desired learning;
10   maintain a warm and positive social atmosphere in class.

This is quite an indictment of physical education teaching in North America and the literature review does give some substance to these charges. Whether or not the same or similar charges can be made against the teaching in this country appears to warrant some serious consideration. As in most issues, there is another side to the argument and most physical education teachers could be classed as dedicated, effective and keen members of the teaching profession with a genuine concern for the pupils they teach. Many attend numerous in-service courses in an effort to improve their teaching skills for the ultimate benefit of the children.

However, this does not mean that they can not become even more effective and they need to be alerted to these issues and to consider ways to overcome them if they apply to their teaching in their school.

Pupils' Behaviours and Perceptions in Physical Education

Most teachers think they know how pupils spend their time in physical education lessons. Usually this is based on a global impression of the activity of the whole class and Underwood (1978), using this impressionistic approach, recorded levels of motor activity as high as 65 per cent. However, these may not be entirely accurate and it would be more sensible to concentrate on one or a few pupils over extended periods of time or record accurately the behaviour of all class members at a particular moment. This would result in a more sensitive measure.

Any form of motor activity is not acceptable. It must be related to the objectives of the lesson and 'quality practice' should be aimed for. Activity which does not meet these demands is likely to be irrelevant. If measures are taken in the ways outlined above then it is likely that the amount of purposeless activity will be greatly reduced. This then raises questions about what pupils are doing in the remainder of the lesson under the management strategies. Obviously lessons in which pupils spend less time in organizational and instructional situations will give them more opportunities to practice their motor skills.

If there is a high proportion of non-movement time then this may have an adverse effect on one of the most important aims of the subject which is to develop appropriate levels of physical fitness. This aspect can only be developed through progressive training procedures.

Pupils' attitudes towards physical education are largely formed from their curriculum experiences and their relationships with the teacher and other pupils. Thus a supportive socio-emotional climate is an important prerequisite for effective learning.

The literature review which follows examines some of the research related to these issues.

Motor Involvement

A number of different methods have been used to describe and examine the behaviour of pupils in physical education lessons. In the main, they have either focused on the behaviours of individual pupils or on the whole class. Obviously the activity that pupils engage in is central to the learning process and is what Pieron (1983) referred to as the 'mediating link to learning'. In a subject that is so allied to the physical, it is somewhat surprising to find that most of the lessons are characterized by 'non-movement' behaviour. Indeed in an observational study of 193 elementary school children in twenty different classes, Costello and Laubach (1978) reported that 63 per cent of the lesson was characterized by non-movement for example waiting or receiving information. Of the remaining time, only 27 per cent was spent in movement activity which was linked to the objectives of the lesson. McLeish's (1985) analysis of 104 lessons suggested that appropriate practice of motor skills averaged out at 25 per cent. Similar proportions were also found by Pieron and Haan (1980) in the observation of 300 pupils in secondary schools, and by Dodds, Rife and Metzler (1982) in a review of nine studies in a range of schools in a variety of activities. One study which produced higher percentages of movement activity was conducted by Varstala *et al* (1983) in Finland and reported an average of 48 per cent for time-on-task. No details were provided about the quality of the pupils' time-on-task and may well have included all time spent in a motor-engaged category. This could account for this high score.

Overall, there is a surprisingly low motor involvement and it is relevant to ask what the pupils are doing during the remainder of the lesson which comprises the majority of the time. There will obviously be occasions when pupils are listening to explanations and watching demonstrations of the skill to be learned and these are essential elements of the learning process. However, there will also be other times such as waiting for a teacher to give instructions, waiting to take part in an activity or off-task behaviour which could be regarded as 'unproductive time'. These may well be occasions when little or no learning is taking place and could occupy as much as a third of the lesson according to Pieron (1983).

Global totals which make assessments of all the pupils in a class may give an important general indication of what is happening, but may not be completely accurate. It is true that it is possible to indicate the number of pupils involved in physical activity at any one moment in time, but this would only provide part of the picture. It may also be necessary to examine the nature of the activity in relation to the ability level of the pupil. Thus practising movements which are too easy or too difficult may not be having a positive learning effect.

Merely quantifying the amount of time a pupil spends 'on-task' may be misleading. There is evidence from Tousignant and Brunelle (1982) that there are differences in the quality of pupils' time-on-task. Using qualitative observation techniques of 127 physical education lessons, they analyzed pupils' responses to tasks set by the teacher and identified four different categories of behaviour. The first category included those pupils who performed the task as required. The second embraced pupils who experienced a low rate of success and modified the task 'to avoid failure or boring repetitions of easy responses'. The third category was named deviant off-task behaviour which interrupted the lesson, and the final group included pupils who avoided participating as much as possible without drawing attention to themselves. They were appropriately named 'competent bystanders'. Confirmation for this last grouping has also been provided by Griffin (1984 and 1985) who placed pupils into 'hanging back' and 'invisible players' categories'. These referred to pupils who deliberately missed their turn, allowed others to push in front, or who stopped and just failed to make contact with the ball. Much of this was done quietly without bringing attention to themselves. Tousignant and Brunelle clearly revealed that there were differences in the ways in which pupils respond to a movement task. The obvious implication of this is that immediately after a task has been set, teachers should always spend a short time observing the class moving to ensure pupils are working to the task requirements. Once the class is working within an acceptable framework then it is important that pupils stay in this context. This may be easier said than done as it would be impossible to monitor the behaviour of every pupil in such diverse activities as group work in a gymnastic lesson or creative dance. However, it would be easier in situations where the pupils are engaged in the same activity such as front crawl in swimming. As Placek and Randall (1986) succinctly remarked, teachers were inclined to 'focus on the nature of the group activity, without regard for the level of successful involvement of individual students'.

By far the most frequently used method for examining the involvement of the learner in physical education has been the ALT-PE system devised by Siedentop *et al* (1982). Two main categories were identified, namely Not Motor Engaged and Motor Engaged. The latter category only included those motor activities which were related to the objectives of the lesson and differentiated between motor appropriate and inappropriate behaviour. Motor appropriate only included those behaviours in which the pupil practised a motor skill at an 'easy level of difficulty', or, put another way, the pupil experienced a high rate of success. Following an analysis of over 100 videotaped lessons, McLeish (1985) suggested that a number of basic principles had been established. These were that:

(i)   learning is maximized in direct proportion to the number and type of opportunities to learn;
(ii)   pupils learn best by concentrating on practising the desired skill; or
(iii) by observing others perform it; and

27

    (iv)   pupils should practise at an 'easy level of difficulty'.

In relation to the first point, McLeish is almost suggesting a linear relationship between learning and time-on-task. This could never be the case as it is always necessary for a teacher to 'feed in' information at regular intervals during the learning process. A lesson which allowed 100 per cent time-on-task with no instruction or suggestions from the teacher would, in an educational context, be seriously flawed. Comments from the teacher, the organization of guided and progressive practices, and the provision of feedback are all essential components of the learning process. Without them, learning would be reduced. It is more likely that the relationship is curvilinear and that most learning would take place when there is some control exercised by the teacher. Exactly how much control is impossible to say. It will depend on the nature of the task and the ability level of the pupil.

Some pupils may need to spend time thinking about ways of overcoming problems in a gymnastic sequence on apparatus, whereas others may need to tackle the problem through trial and error. Activities which are mainly concerned with physiological conditioning or the establishment of techniques in skills, such as back crawl in swimming, will obviously involve longer periods of time on the activity than practices associated with initial confidence activities in the water. Whilst there is some truth in McLeish's first statement, it does perhaps need some qualification.

There is no doubt that the correct practice of a skill is the most important variable in the learning process. Without some form of movement, there is unlikely to be any improvement. However, it is important to stress that the practice must be consistent with the later requirements of the skill. Practising the wrong movements will have a detrimental effect at a later stage. Many children learn breast stroke with a screw kick in the leg action which is not only difficult to eradicate but will seriously impede future development.

If the third principle which suggests that pupils learn through observing others perform the skill is true, then it would be expected that teachers would frequently use some form of modelling. As stated earlier, teachers rarely used personal demonstration in their teaching. Of course pupils can learn through watching a performance from the teacher or other pupils, but it does often need the teacher to isolate specific elements of the performance for the pupils to watch. Thus the help the teacher gives the children to attend selectively to the vital components of the skill is important. The modeling of a skill does assume that there is a pre-specified way in which it should be performed — a dive from the 3 metre board or a double somersault on the trampoline would be examples. In contrast, teachers often set pupils open-ended tasks where the end result is not pre-determined. Examples would include creating a dance to a piece of music where each pupil's response would be different, or creating a synchronized swimming routine. In these instances, an important part of the educational process is for the pupils to invent their own movement patterns and not copy someone else.

The final principle of practising at an 'easy level of difficulty' is sound and requires pupils to practice close to their present level of ability. In the main they should be successful, but there will be occasions when they experience failure. This contrasts with practices which are too easy and do not challenge, and practices which are so difficult that pupils constantly fail. Levels of aspiration should be set within achievable limits. In physical education lessons, some concern was expressed by Earls (1983) when he criticized teachers for using progressive practices which were often too far apart and unrelated. Specifically, he stated,

> After inadequate time or poor quality work in progressive skill development, students are placed in competitive games where the primacy of results and the complex demands of performance almost ensure that most of them will substitute less desirable movement patterns. A child's readiness is frequently violated by the leap from single drills to complex games.

Although these comments were made in relation to a research study with elementary school children up to the age of 10 years, the same may be true of some of the teaching at the secondary level. The author's experience in observing physical education lessons would suggest that it is quite common for pupils to be placed in movement situations where they do not have sufficient experience to draw on to participate effectively. This particularly applies in the teaching of games when a quantum leap is sometimes made from small unopposed practices to full-sided competitive games, and in gymnastics from the solving of tasks on the floor to complicated groupings of apparatus.

Whilst accepting that McLeish's statements have a strong element of truth in them, some qualification is appended to these four rather broad statements.

Fitness

As well as the learning of motor skills, another major aim of physical education as stated by both theorists and practitioners, is the development of fitness levels. If lessons are characterized by approximately one-third physical movement, is this sufficient to develop cardiorespiratory efficiency which is an essential component of physical fitness? One study which addressed itself to this problem was conducted by Verabioff (1983) with 9 and 10-year-old children in Canada. There were twenty-six children in the sample — thirteen of each sex. Using telemetry to monitor the heart rate, the results were used as an indicator of the level of intensity of the activity. In order to achieve any improvement in the cardiorespiratory system, Verabioff suggested it was necessary to achieve recordings of at least 150 beats per minute. Rarely was this figure exceeded and the periods of activity that were in excess of this target were too short to have any training effect. Two of the conclusions from this study were that physical education classes 'are generally inactive and activity intensity is not sufficient to have a training effect'. Support for this lack of activity intensity was provided by Armstrong (1984) who reviewed the physical activity patterns of school children in England and concluded that the evidence indicated 'that habitual activity is seldom of high enough intensity to promote cardiovascular health'.

Further support for the low physical commitment came from Peckman *et al* (1986) who made an evaluation of a daily physical education programme in Australia. The lack of success in some schools was attributed to the fact that 'the duration of activities and their intensities often remained unchanged all year rather than increasing in line with progressive overload principles'. Fitness levels can only be maintained if a minimum level of intensity is reached and held for a period of time. To improve on these levels it is necessary to increase the intensity gradually and this requires fairly precise and constant monitoring. If a multi-gym is available it is possible for pupils to devise accurately and adjust their own training programmes once the teacher has shown them the principles for determining training loads.

Another study which investigated the physical activity patterns of 11- and 16-year-olds in England was carried out by Dickenson (1986). The sample consisted of 500 boys and girls from six comprehensive schools and he reported that between 80 and 85 per cent did less than five minutes vigorous activity on any one day and that apart from a brief increase for boys between 14 and 15 years, inactivity accelerated with age.

These studies appeared to question whether teachers understand the principles of, and motivation for, fitness. One of the rationales for the Health Related Fitness programmes in schools in this country, 'to encourage an active life style' does not appear to have permeated these groups of secondary school pupils.

Enjoyment

In an evaluation of the physical education curriculum in Finnish schools, Telama *et al* (1983) reported that pupils did not find the subject physically demanding and that physical education lessons were 'a pleasant experience' for most pupils. Under these circumstances it was not surprising that many pupils enjoyed their physical education lessons. Indeed there is evidence from Placek (1983) which suggested that the most frequent measure of success for both teachers and students in training was the pupils' enjoyment of the lesson. In this country, Coe (1984) provided further support for the enjoyment factor when she asked 11 and 12 year old pupils in two middle schools, 'Do you enjoy physical education?' Ninety-seven per cent of the boys and 92 per cent of the girls replied in the affirmative. Such responses would be congruent with the aims of those teachers interviewed by Underwood (1983) who considered enjoyment to be one of their important aims. However, justification for the subject can not be made solely on the grounds of enjoyment. There is an old sporting adage which says 'No pain, no gain'. This applies firstly in a physiological sense that in order to achieve high performance levels, much of the physical training is hard and there are many occasions when it is necessary to work close to the 'pain barrier'. Secondly, in the process of achieving full mastery of a skill, progress is not always overtly obvious. There are times when the learner feels that he or she is not making progress and on these occasions may be reverting back to lower performance levels. It is as if the skill has an elusive quality. These are times when there is no immediate enjoyment and further practice has to be undertaken in order to consolidate the skill learning that has taken place. In these instances, the sense of achievement is delayed until full mastery is achieved. Thus to pamper to the teachers' or the pupils' desire to enjoy the lesson may be to deny pupils the ultimate reward of optimum achievement levels in skilled performance.

Self-fulfilling Prophesy

It might be reasonable to assume that the aspirations of pupils, their work rate and their attempts to achieve skill will be linked to the expectations of the teacher. However, the research findings differ slightly. In their book entitled *Pygmalion in the Gymnasium* Martinek, Crowe and Rejeski (1982) extol the self-fulfilling prophesy in which pupils perform in accordance with the teacher's expectations. The authors refer to studies in physical education settings which indicated that 'high achievers' were given more practice time and praise and were treated more warmly than 'low achievers.' Pieron (1982) also found high achievers had more opportunity to participate and because of this, there was an expectancy that the performance gap between these two groups would widen. In examining the amount of time high, average and low skilled pupils spent in motor appropriate behaviour in volleyball, Wuest *et al* (1986) suggested that low and averaged skilled pupils had less opportunity to participate actively than the highly skilled pupils. Because the better performers practice more often, it would be reasonable to expect this group to make more rapid progress. In contrast, one study by Shute *et al* (1982) revealed only small differences in the motor appropriate category for high, medium and low achievers. Overall there does appear to be some support for the notion that physical education teachers treat more able pupils differently than the less able. Teachers need to be aware of this and develop their sensitivity to cater equally for the needs of all pupils — possibly through four factors identified by Martinek *et al*. These were the establishment of a warm socio-emotional climate; the provision of equal amounts of feedback to all pupils, the teaching input to be equal to the true potential of the pupils; and the encouragement of greater motor output for all pupils.

Learning Opportunities

Motor output in particular will inevitably be linked to the opportunities a pupil is given to practise skills and the advantage he or she takes of this time. In 1983, Graham reviewed the results of five mini experimental teaching units in which teachers taught closed skills (a novel golf task or gymnastic tasks) to small groups for periods of time ranging from 9 to 40 minutes using a process-product design. The most important result relating to the utilisation of time was that 'Students who learned more had teachers who provided them with more time to practice the criterion skill. Students who learned less spent more time waiting, listening, managing and organizing than their counterparts.' Perhaps the key point is practising 'the criterion skill'. It is essential that pupils do practice the specific task set by the teacher which is consistent with the objectives of the lesson. Another study by Grant (1980) used judges' ratings of teacher effectiveness of the instructional process and reported pupils on-task behaviour was three times longer in classes taught by 'more effective' than 'less effective' student teachers. Similarly, Phillips and Carlisle (1983) reported on the teaching effectiveness of 'most' and 'least' effective teachers based upon pupils' improvement after ten volleyball lessons. The general trend of this study indicated that the most effective teachers used more of their teaching time to present materials and provide performance feedback. They also appeared to manage the time more efficiently and as a result, pupils spent less time in management activities. A different grouping of teachers by Mancini *et al* (1983) made a comparison of low and high 'burn-out' secondary physical education teachers using the ALT-PE methodology and found that pupils in low burn-out teachers' lessons spent 48 per cent of their time in the motor appropriate category as opposed to 25.7 per cent for the high burn-out group. Naturally this reflected in longer periods of time pupils spent in the interim, off-task and waiting categories of high burn-out teachers. Thus the enthusiasm and efficiency of the teacher is reflected in the behaviour of the pupils and will inevitably influence learning opportunities.

Although outside the educational context, McKenzie (1986) examined the behaviour of elite athletes (national volleyball players) in practice sessions and found that players of this calibre spent over half (54.2 per cent) of their time in motor appropriate behaviour. This study is useful because at this level of performance, elite atheletes are likely to be working at a high level of productivity and efficiency and may provide a guideline for other working groups in volleyball.

The opportunity to 'motor engage' pupils does appear to be an important element in effective teaching, and Dodds *et al* (1982), in a paper which summarized the results of 9 ALT-PE studies stated, 'Because of the expressed motor performance focus of physical education, ALT-PE(Motor) is now considered the best evidence of students' opportunity to learn in physical education.' Even stronger support for this contention was given by McLeish (1985) who, having observed 104 videotaped lessons, concluded that, 'the central feature of effective teaching in physical education is time-on-task as measured by the proportion of time devoted to task-practice-motor easy'.

Physical education lessons appear to be characterized by much longer periods of 'not motor engaged' than 'motor engaged'. The evidence cited above appears to suggest that an increase in the amount of time pupils spend in motor appropriate behaviour could show increased levels of learning. A number of intervention strategies have been used to facilitate the class organization, increase and encourage higher levels of pupil activity and eradicate inefficient practices. Dodds *et al* (1982) reviewed five studies in this area which, with one exception, all showed that it was possible to increase substantially the motor component in the lesson — sometimes with as much as a three-fold increase. Recently Borys (1986) reported mean percentage increases in practice time from 17.8 per cent to 31.7 per cent after several intervention workshop sessions. However, she did warn against being too prescriptive from these results because of the influence of other variables such as the complexity of the subject matter, levels of pupils' ability and fitness levels.

There have been a few correlational attempts to examine the relationship between motor involvement and pupils' achievements from process-product studies. Dodds *et al* (1982) summarized these and, in the main, reported a low positive correlation which indicated that an increase in the motor component did result in increased levels of learning. Only one of the studies in this review conducted with swimmers did not fit into this pattern.

Although there are a few exceptions the majority of the evidence does suggest that the movement time in physical education lessons could be increased and that if intelligent use is made of this time, then more efficient learning could occur. As has already been argued, the relationship between time-on-task and learning is not linear, nor is there an optimal amount of practice time regardless of the activity. Gymnastic lessons which incorporate the use of large apparatus for group work will obviously have to devote a large proportion of time to handling apparatus, whereas a swimming lesson based on schedule work will have much less organizational requirements. Thus, not only will the content and organization of the lesson affect the movement time, but the subject content itself will also be a variable. The general trend is for team sports to have a higher and gymnastics a lower engagement time for pupils, as evidenced in studies by Costello and Laubach (1978) and Pieron and Haan (1980).

Attitudes in Physical Education

Developing favourable attitudes to a subject is a laudable aim for most physical education teachers and often appears as a stated aim in many syllabuses. An attitude implies a pre-disposition to act and Triandis (1971) suggested that 'Attitudes involve what people think about, feel about, and how they would like to behave towards an attitudinal object.' Thus there would appear to be three interrelated elements, namely, the cognitive, affective and action tendency components. In relation to physical education, the cognitive component would include the beliefs a pupil had about the value of the many different activities which comprise the subject. These could vary considerably and possibly incorporate a very favourable attitude to the necessity to learn to swim but an aversion to fitness training. The affective or feeling component refers to the emotions a pupil experiences connected to an activity. Personal satisfaction derived from mastering a complex motor skill such as a twisting somersault on the trampoline would obviously induce feelings of satisfaction, whereas forcing pupils to take part in a cross country run in inclement weather against their will would probably develop feelings of antagonism. Finally, the action tendency implies that a pupil who has a favourable attitude will willingly take part. This will not merely include the physically gifted who enjoy developing their physical prowess but also those who are less able who enjoy taking part. An indicator of the strength of this component can often be gauged from the number of pupils who participate in the extra curricular programme in school.

Attitudes are not innate but are developed from social learning situations. Consequently, pupils will be influenced by the variety of experiences they have in physical education and from their contacts with the teacher and their peers.

In a review of fifteen studies of teacher effectiveness in classroom subjects, Locke (1979) reported that 70 per cent of the studies linked higher levels of academic achievement with positive attitudes, whereas in the remaining 30 per cent, teaching behaviour can be positively linked to pupil learning but is 'negatively associated with student attitude'. It must be emphasized that these findings related to classroom subjects and might not necessarily apply to the teaching and learning in physical education but further information in this area is warranted.

Determinants of Attitudes

In an attempt to identify the causal determinants of pupils' attitudes towards physical education, Figley (1985) used a critical incident technique with 100 college students and asked them to describe incidents in their school life which had made a favourable or unfavourable impact. From the 266 reported incidents, two major features were identified as having the most influence on the development of positive and negative attitudes. These were named curriculum content and teacher behaviour. Positive experiences in the curriculum referred to involvement in specific practical activities as well as the opportunity to participate in a variety of new activities at some stage in the programme. Negative experiences were mainly related to the content and the respondents described many of the activities as being 'irrelevant, repetitive, formal and shallow'. Curriculum content was also found to be important in a study by Evans (1983) who investigated the attitudes to physical education of 221 fifth-form girls in an upper school in England and reported positive attitudes for the majority of the practical areas — especially badminton and swimming. The notable exceptions to this were gymnastics and cross country running. Option schemes were popular and the majority of girls enjoyed working in mixed groups.

As expected, teaching behaviour will influence attitudes and in Figley's study, the presence or absence of reinforcement was the most important single factor. The ability of the teacher to praise pupils' efforts and raise self-esteem were the most frequently mentioned in the promotion of positive attitudes. Conversely, lack of reinforcement embraced occasions when the teacher did not recognize effort, made unfortunate comparisons with the more able pupils or suggested pupils were not trying. It was not surprising that exposure to these kinds of experiences had a negative effect. The personal characteristics of the teachers and the manner in which they reacted to the pupils were also influential. Thus humanistic mannerisms which included a natural and fair approach to the relationship were preferable to ones which were autocratic and uncaring. In turn, these would inevitably have an effect on the learning atmosphere. These studies strongly support the contention that the formation of attitudes in physical education is inextricably linked to curriculum experiences and the manner of pupils' interactions with the teacher.

What is not clear is whether the attitudes that are engendered are a reflection of the learning that has occurred. The relationship between pupils' attitudes and their perception of learning may not always be in a positive direction. As Locke (1979) pointed out, it is possible to have a poor attitude yet still feel that worthwhile learning had taken place. Conversely, it would be possible to have a positive attitude to the subject but consider that very little learning had occurred.

Relationship Between Teachers' and Pupils' Perceptions

Teachers often state the aims they hope to achieve through their teaching and it would be revealing to examine the relationship of these aims with pupils' perceptions of their learning in physical education. The recent Physical Education Association report (1987) enquired into the teachers' perceptions of the effects of 30 outcomes and/or values of the physical education curriculum on the pupils. A factor analysis based on the inter-correlations of these items revealed six main factors, viz. social awareness and responsibility; general physical development; enjoyment in participation; general interest in school; self awareness, and general movement ability. It is somewhat surprising that the teachers attached greater importance to the social awareness and responsibility factor than to the physical development of the child. In an overall comment, the report stated, 'these effects would seem to reflect physical education teachers' broad educational ambitions and achievements for their pupils'. Whether or not pupils would have similar perceptions of their own learning is purely speculative at this stage and commends itself to further detailed analysis.

4
Methodological Priorities and Emerging Issues in Research in Physical Education

There is no doubt that 'A teacher is a person engaged in interactive behaviour with one or more students for the purpose of effecting change in those students. The change, whether it be attitudinal, cognitive or motor, is intentional on the part of the teacher.' This statement by McNeil and Popham in 1973 emphasized the enormous moral responsibility that teachers shoulder in their attempts to influence the development of boys and girls in the secondary school. Physical education teachers are an integral part of the teaching profession and along with teachers of other subjects, play an important role in pupils' personal development.

Direct Observation of Teaching

There has been surprisingly little research conducted in this country which describes the process of teaching in physical education and provides detailed information about the teachers' functions. What is clear is that teaching is multi-dimensional in nature and any attempts to measure 'the teaching act' must reflect this. There is strong support for the direct observation of teaching in situ and the 'naturalistic approach' seems to permeate much of the research. The technological advances in videotape recording techniques have made it possible to make accurate recordings of 'life in the gymnasium' and allow detailed and repeated viewing to take place. It has also enabled the reliability of the observations to be enhanced. These techniques appear to be particularly appropriate for the study of teaching in physical education and commend themselves for serious consideration in the research strategies for the current investigation.

Quantitative and Qualitative Control

One of the difficulties in quantitative research appears to be the problem of comparing 'like with like'. Lessons which are as diverse as educational gymnastics involving large apparatus and rugby with a high proportion of games playing will obviously have different formats. This points to some form of control over the types of lesson being compared at some stage in the investigation. Averaging out scores of codings over a large number of lessons in different activities needs to be done with caution and any inferences from such procedures can only be tentative and made with a great deal of careful thought. As Anderson (1983) pointed out,

> adding up the codings for the day, the week or for the entire sample population can yield nothing more than a shadow of shadows. Those of us involved in the coding and quantification of human experience naturally find it painful to confront the extraordinary reductionism we engage in ... a very meagre representation of the richness of realities.

Again, it would appear that a complete picture of the interactions in physical education lessons can only be gained through a variety of approaches such as quantitative methods which produce global totals, and qualitative approaches which identify important features of the teaching-learning process. This suggests that methods such as interviewing and talking to pupils and teachers may be relevant and provide valuable insights into the issues to be investigated. Extended observation in a number of schools could also provide a series of case studies which would illuminate the problem.

Academic Learning Time — Physical Education

During the last five years there has been a great deal of research information on teacher and pupil behaviour revealed through ACADEMIC LEARNING TIME — PHYSICAL EDUCATION. In particular, the motor appropriate category of practising skills at an 'easy level of difficulty' which will ensure a high level of success appears to be an important element in the learning of motor skills. It may not be sufficient merely to quantify the time spent in this category but some qualitative control is also necessary. This points towards identifying and following one student for an extended period of time.

Department Organization

In many schools it appears that physical education is divided into two departments with separate responsibility for the boys' and the girls' programmes. As well as having their separate autonomy, the female teachers often place a different emphasis on some of the aims of the subject and in some cases may even have different aims. The time when teachers transmit their philosophy and achieve their aims will be mainly through the contact that occurs during lessons. Whether or not these fundamental differences in aims will have any effect on the teaching styles of male and female teachers warrants investigation. It is quite unique for a subject to be divided in this way and there is no other subject in the school curriculum which adopts this administrative arrangement.

Management of Lessons

All teachers should provide a rich environment which is conducive to pupil learning. Physical education lessons appear to be characterized by a great deal of 'non-movement' because of the emphasis teachers place on preparing pupils for motor activity. The proportion of time teachers devote to these and other managerial tasks needs probing. Inextricably linked to this is the amount of time pupils are given to practise motor skills. If excessive time is spent on managerial tasks, then there is proportionately less time for motor activity. There is support for the contention that more effective teachers provide more opportunities for pupils to spend time-on-task and this warrants attention. The motor appropriate category which enables pupils to work at a level with a low rate of error also appears to be significantly important.

Lesson Themes

Identifying a consistent theme in a lesson does provide continuity and progression and is considered to be good teaching practice. The literature review has suggested there may be times when lesson themes in physical education are not apparent and as a result, pupils may have difficulty in understanding the relationship between the different parts of the lesson. This may be due to the fact that the parts are unrelated or it may be because the gaps between the progressions are too large. Thus lesson themes and their continuity need further analysis.

Development of Fitness

The development of organic fitness is a common aim for physical education. However, it does appear that the physical is being somewhat neglected both in the amount of time devoted to physical practice and the intensity of the physical workload. It is probably beyond the scope of the present study to monitor accurately the cardiorespiratory responses of pupils in lessons, but it may be possible to examine the extent to which fitness is incorporated into the physical education curriculum and equally importantly, the understanding pupils have of the principles which underpin the different components of fitness.

Feedback

Providing feedback to pupils about the effectiveness of their motor performance does appear to be an important part of the teachers' repertoire of teaching skills. To be effective, this feedback must relate to key aspects of the movement which will enhance future performance. The proportion of feedback which has no specific reference and merely consists of a positive motivational statement may be quite high and warrants further investigation.

Enjoyment

Enjoyment appears to be an important aim for nearly all teachers of physical education and they are anxious to ensure that pupils enjoy participating in the subject and consider it to be an essential ingredient of their teaching. This suggests a concern for all pupils regardless of their levels of ability and may well be reflected in the working atmosphere created in lessons as well as in the opportunities that are offered to pupils to participate in the extra-curricular programmes.

Pupils' Perceptions of Learning

Apart from a few small scale studies, there have been remarkably few attempts to probe pupils' perceptions of their own learning in physical education. This would appear to be an important area worthy of further investigation as it would give some indication of the relationship between the teachers' perceptions of the effects participation in physical education activities may have on pupils, and the pupils' perceptions of the subject. Such an attempt would make a link between the process of teaching and the end product, and provide some valuable insights.

Secondary Age Range

Most of the discussion has focused on teaching and learning in the secondary school. There were two main reasons why it was decided to concentrate on this particular age range. The first was that it was a natural development to the author's (1983) global study on the planning and implementation of the physical education curriculum in the secondary school which had identified a number of areas for further research and in-depth analysis. The second reason was that the teaching experience of the author had been in secondary education either as a teacher or as a lecturer training students for this age range. It was felt that this background and experience would provide greater insight into the issues under consideration. There is remarkably little hard evidence about the teaching behaviours of physical education teachers in secondary schools in this country and the effect their teaching has upon pupils' behaviours. This study will attempt to provide insight into some of these issues.

5
Analysis of Videotaped Lessons

At this stage it seemed sensible to conduct a carefully controlled pilot study which examined some of the issues that had been identified in the literature review. The justification for the methodology used in the pilot study emanated from the recommendations made in the previous chapter which identified methodological priorities in research in physical education. Perhaps the most important recommendation which influenced the design of this investigation was the suggestion that the research should be conducted in a naturalistic setting. This obviously meant observing the teaching of physical education as it actually happened. With the development of portable videotape recorders it was therefore possible to make an accurate and permanent record of the teaching-learning process. It also had the added advantage of establishing high levels of coder reliability through the replay facilities. Because of the complexity of teaching, a multi-dimensional observation system was considered to be the most appropriate method with which to conduct an analysis. It was important that the design of the pilot study should implement these considerations. An additional advantage was that this form of recording would also enable a record to be made of the pupils' behaviour in lessons.

The nature of the activity being taught appeared to be a variable and the value of comparing and contrasting the teaching behaviour in the same and different types of activity appeared to be warranted. The sex of the teacher was another variable under consideration and needed to be incorporated into the design.

Thus a preliminary study which embraced all these methodological considerations would provide a sound basis from which to examine some of the educational issues which had been highlighted. These included the amount of non-movement time in lessons, the importance of motor appropriate practice, the management of the lesson, the type of feedback provided by the teacher and the nature of the pupils' behaviour.

Procedures

Following the above recommendations, an attempt was made to make as accurate a record as possible of the behaviour of teachers and pupils in physical education lessons through videotape recordings of what actually happens in the gymnasium and hall. This subsequently allowed the tapes to be played several times and was conducive to multiple methods of analysis. The imprinting of a digital clock on the tapes ensured that recordings were always made at the same time.

The sample consisted of three men and three women secondary school physical education teachers who each took a lesson of educational gymnastics (an individual activity) and basketball or netball (a team activity) with a first, second or third year class. Diagrammatically this may be represented as follows:

Table 1: Design of pilot study: Diagrammatic representation

	Individual Activity	Team Activity
3 male PE teachers	Educational gymnastics	Basketball
3 female PE teachers	Educational gymnastics	Netball

All lessons were indoors. The gymnastic lessons were conducted in fully equipped gymnasia with ample apparatus. The games lessons were conducted in either a sports hall or a gymnasium. Because boys and girls mainly play different games, it was not possible to select the same activity. However, there were certain similarities between basketball and netball to make the comparison acceptable.

Coding Teacher Behaviour

For the purposes of this research a method was needed which would allow for an accurate description of what the physical education teacher does when he or she is teaching and also allow for comparisons to be made between different teachers and different types of lessons. After reviewing the literature, it was decided to use Anderson's Descriptive Category System. A summary description of the system appears in appendix 1.

There were several reasons why this system was chosen. Firstly, in its development it had the specific intent to produce a method which would allow for a 'professionally meaningful' description of the behaviour of a teacher in a physical education setting and thus had particular application to the present study. Secondly, a multi-dimension approach was used which ensured that four different codings were made for each sample or unit of behaviour. These identified the purpose of the teacher's interactive behaviour, the extent to which the teacher carried out the function himself or shared it with others, the ways in which the teacher interacted with the pupils, and the person or group to whom the teacher behaviour was directed. The width and depth of the method would go a considerable way to ensure adequate coverage of the teaching process. Thirdly, the system was developed as a research tool to 'accurately describe videotaped teaching behaviour' and thus had obvious application to the present study.

All systems which attempt to describe interacting behaviour will have their limitations and Anderson's Descriptive Category System is no exception. Certainly there will be aspects of the lesson which will not be recorded. Two of the most obvious examples relate to the affective tone of any conversation and the meanings that intonations play in understanding language, and also whether the feedback that is provided is positive or negative and the amount of technical information that is included. Another inherent disadvantage is that there is a tendency to derive static information from a highly interacting and fluent situation. Teaching physical education is a very dynamic activity and the recording of these events into predetermined categories may not capture the reality of the situation. It may sometimes be difficult to decide exactly where to place some types of behaviour and this has been highlighted by Walker and Adelman (1976) in relation to verbal exchanges. In this type of analysis only quantitative information is produced and there is no indication of the qualitative nature of the verbal behaviour. It is important to recognize and acknowledge these limitations from the outset and bear them in mind when interpreting the results.

Using Anderson's Descriptive Category System

After considering the advantages and limitations of Anderson's system, it was decided to use the system but to incorporate a sampling procedure which would ensure an accurate recording at a specified time. A time sample of four recordings per minute at a specified second was considered to be an adequate representation of teaching behaviour. Preference was given to a randomly selected sample for each minute rather than recording every 15 seconds. By using this method it was hoped to avoid recording the same teaching behaviour of any cyclical pattern that might be adopted. Through reference to random number tables four specific seconds in each minute were identified. Thus the four categories of function, subscript, mode and direction were recorded on each occasion. This resulted in sixteen instances of teaching behaviour per minute and approximately 750 recordings for each lesson. For the pilot study of twelve lessons, over 9000 instances of teaching behaviour were recorded.

Coding Pupil Behaviour

Although much of the emphasis of the study was on the teacher, it was felt that the teaching behaviours would have a significant effect upon the behaviour of the pupils. As most of the pupils in every class were shown clearly on the videotape, it was decided to record their movements in the various physical education settings.

Academic Learning Time — Physical Education (ALT-PE)

ALT-PE had been developed in the early 1980s as a process measure of teaching effectiveness. Siedentop, Tousignant and Parker (1982) refer to the system as being conceptualized at two levels. The first is the context level which refers to general and subject matter content, while the second level involves observations of individual learner involvement and judgments are made about each pupil's behaviour under the headings of 'not motor engaged' and 'motor engaged'. Each of these two main classifications is further subdivided into five and three sections respectively and these were identified as follows:

Not Motor Engaged	Motor Engaged
Interim	Motor appropriate
Waiting	Motor inappropriate
Off-task	Supporting
On-task	
Cognitive	

A definition of each of the categories is to be found in appendix 2.

The coding manual suggests that recordings of what each pupil is doing can be taken every three minutes by scanning the class in a live situation. This also enables other contextual aspects to be recorded in the intervening period. As the lessons were on videotape and playback facilities were available, it was decided to use a group time sampling procedure every minute. This involved recording the behaviour of each pupil in one of the learner categories outlined above. Thus, at the end of every minute, the videotape was stopped and the behaviour of every pupil in camera was recorded on prepared sheets. This procedure was carried out for each of the twelve lessons in the pilot study.

Reliability of Coding Teacher and Pupils' Behaviour

Teacher Behaviour

Anderson's Descriptive Category System contains a large number of categories and was primarily constructed for use by researchers. Because of its diversity and the fact that interpretations had to be made by an observer about the placing of teaching behaviours into pre-specified categories, it was essential to test the reliability of the coding. In other words, it was necessary to ensure that the codings reached satisfactory levels of agreement when measured by different observers or when measured by the same observer on different occasions.

In a review of methods used to establish reliability of data recorded in a natural environment using interval techniques, Hawkins and Dotson (1975) recommend the use of the scored-interval (S-I) method. They state that,

> In S-I agreement, all intervals in which neither observer scored the behaviour as occurring are ignored in calculating agreement scores. Only an interval in which both observers recorded the presence of the behaviour is counted as an agreement.

Thus the S-I method of determining reliability is a very rigorous one as a comparison of each separate observation by category is included in the calculations. It therefore appeared to be eminently suitable for use in the present study and would give a rigorous level of reliability for each category. One weakness of the system is that S-I scores can become highly variable when the number of comparisons is small and this must be taken into consideration when interpreting the results. Usually low scoring samples are ignored and in the present sample it was decided that reliability would not be calculated for categories which received a total of sixteen scores or less over the four lessons (i.e. an average of four occasions per lesson). The formula for calculation the S-I level of reliability was:

$$\frac{\text{Agreement}}{\text{Agreement} + \text{Disagreement}} \times 100 = \% \text{ of Agreement}$$

Siedentop *et al* (1982) referred to levels of agreement which reached 75 per cent or above as being 'excellent'. Four of the twelve lessons were analyzed a second time by the initial observer after an interval of two months, thus establishing a measure of intra-observer reliability. Of the seventeen categories examined in this way, twelve were well in excess of the 75 per cent level of agreement and five fell slightly short of this figure. An overall assessment of the reliability for the complete system would suggest that highly satisfactory levels of intra-observer agreement were reached. In addition, inter-observer overall reliability levels of 81.8 per cent for the interactive function, 81.5 per cent for the function subscript, 83.1 per cent for the mode and 88 per cent for the direction for the three netball lessons were established and reported by Miller (1986).

Pupil Behaviour

An intra-observer reliability score for one of the lessons based on a three months interval between recordings resulted in an overall reliability score in excess of 90 per cent. Only one of the categories (waiting) fell below the 75 per cent level and this may partly be attributed to the small number of fourteen recordings.

Results and Discussion

For the purposes of analyzing the teachers' behaviours, two main methods were used. The first utilized descriptive statistics for each category in the system for the male and female teachers and for the games and gymnastic lessons. The second used an analytic approach using chi-square to examine the similarities and differences between the teaching behaviours of male and female teachers in the different activities.

Teacher Behaviour

The average percentage recording in each category of the four dimensions of Anderson's Descriptive Category System for the twelve lessons in the pilot study is set out in the following sections.

Interactive Function

The average percentages for each category which identified the purpose of the teachers' interactive behaviour is set out in table 2.

Table 2: Interactive function: Category percentages

Interactive Function	%
1 Organizing	13
2 Preparatory instructing	22
3 Providing equipment	10
4 Concurrent instructing	9
5 Officiating	1
6 Spotting	1
7 Leading exercises	1
8 Intervening instruction	18
9 Observing performance	13
10 Participating	0
11 Other interacting (motor)	6
12 Administering	0
13 Codes of behaviour	1
14 Other interacting	2
Non-Interactive Intervals	
15 Dealing with equipment	2
16 Other non-interactive	1
Non-Discernible Intervals	
17 Insufficient audio/video	0
18 Absent from gymnasium	0

The first and most obvious observation on table 2 is that eleven of the categories received 2 per cent or less. However, only the two categories of participating and administering received 0 per cent in the main interacting section. Two other categories namely insufficient audio/video and absent from gymnasium also scored 0 per cent but these were in the non-discernible intervals section and indicated satisfactory recording levels with the teacher present all the time. Preparatory instruction which prepared pupils for activity was the most used category with a score of 22 per cent. This meant, on average, nearly a quarter of every lesson was spent by the teaching providing information and this might be regarded as excessive. A substantial amount of time was also spent during (concurrent instruction) and after (intervening instruction) motor performance giving feedback and average scores of 9 per cent and 18 per cent were recorded in these two categories. There is substantial support in the motor skills learning literature (for example, Singer, 1980; and Schmidt, 1982) on the advantages of the performer receiving positive feedback. Subjectively, most of the feedback was supportive and positive but the analysis did not distinguish between positive and negative types of comment. Organizational factors (13 per cent) and providing equipment (10 per cent) were two areas where almost a quarter of the lessons were related to organization as opposed to instruction and again this might be considered to be excessive. It was pleasing to see that the teachers did stand back and observe what was taking place in the lessons and they did this for 13 per cent of the time. The ability to observe the motor performance of pupils is an essential ingredient of good teaching. What is observed and the comments relevant to that performance is also important but the analysis procedures in this study did not capture that information. The only other category to receive a substantial percentage was other interacting (motor) which was mainly concerned with the handling of apparatus — especially in gymnastic lessons.

All the other eight categories received 1 per cent or 2 per cent and these were officiating, spotting, leading exercises, establishing or enforcing codes of behaviour and other interacting. Just because they were not used by this sample of teachers does not mean that they are unimportant. In fact quite the reverse is true because a low score on enforcing codes of behaviour indicated that there were few disciplinary problems in any of the classes. With the present-day philosophy of using problem-solving approaches in educational gymnastics where the task is set by the teacher and each pupil solves the task in a way commensurate with his or her physical and creative ability, it is unlikely that there would be much spotting (supporting) by the teacher and this proved to be the case. Non-interactive intervals also received a low percentage and the few codings that were made related mainly to the teacher dealing with equipment.

Subscript, Mode and Direction

No interaction can be carried out in isolation and consideration must be given to the subscript (who) carries out the interaction, the mode (how) and the direction (to whom). Percentages for these three functions are set out in tables 3, 4 and 5.

Over two-thirds of the interactive functions were carried out by the teacher alone with 31 per cent being shared. There was no indication that the teacher ever delegated in this area. The dominant mode of interaction was talk (63 per cent). What is not separated out are those occasions when

Table 3: Subscript categories: Average percentages

Subscript	%
1 Does	68
2 Shares	31
3 Delegates	0

Table 4: Mode categories: Average percentages

Mode		%
1	Tasks	63
2	Listens	3
3	Observes	20
4	Demonstrates	7
5	Uses St. Demo.	5
6	Uses aids	0
7	Signalling device	0
8	Written material	0
9	Manually assists	1
10	Participates	0
11	Performs task	0

Table 5: Direction categories: Average percentages

Direction		%
1	One student	22
2	Group/class	60
3	Comb. 1 & 2	19
4	Other persons	0
5	Comb. 1, 2 and 4	0

talk was used with another mode such as demonstration. A computer analysis of such combinations of behaviour would have been helpful. Demonstration by either the teacher and/or pupils was used by most teachers. All teachers spent time observing as a mode of behaviour but it was surprising that there was such a small recording (3 per cent) for the listening category. The remaining categories were not used apart from manually assisting pupils (1 per cent). In relation to the direction of the behaviours, 60 per cent was directed towards a group or class, 22 per cent to one pupil and the remainder to a combination of these two categories.

Teaching Behaviour — Male and Female

Apart from presenting a descriptive account of what happens when teachers teach physical education in a secondary school, an attempt was also made to ascertain the nature and degree of teaching differences between male and female teachers. In examining the differences within the interactive function, the following results were obtained.

Table 6: Male and female teachers: Raw scores, average percentages and chi-square analysis for interactive function categories

Interactive Function		M-n	F-n	M%	F%	χ^2	p
1	Organizing	90	201	9	16	25.30	<0.001
2	Preparatory instructing	243	228	23	19	6.15	<0.05
3	Providing equipment	110	128	11	10	0.00	N.S.
4	Concurrent instructing	112	91	11	7	6.82	<0.01
5	Officiating	5	12	0	1	1.24	N.S.
6	Spotting	17	0	2	0	—	—
7	Leading exercises	11	3	2	0	—	—
8	Intervening instruction	171	241	16	20	2.28	N.S.
9	Observing performance	160	140	15	11	6.57	<0.05
10	Participating	4	0	0	0	—	—
11	Other interacting (motor)	56	96	5	8	4.55	<0.05
12	Administering	0	4	0	0	—	—
13	Codes of behaviour	13	18	2	1	0.06	N.S.
14	Other interacting	8	34	1	3	11.05	<0.001
Non-Interactive Intervals							
15	Dealing with equipment	24	19	2	2	1.36	N.S.
16	Other non-interactive	7	10	1	1	0.02	N.S.
Non-Discernible Intervals							
17	Insufficient audio-video	6	3	1	0	—	—
18	Absent from gymnasium	2	2	0	0	—	—

Interactive Function

In an overall chi-square analysis of items 1–14, a highly significant difference (p < 0.001) was revealed which indicated that there were a number of differences in the ways in which men and women teachers taught physical education. It was therefore important to identify where these differences were occuring.

The number of codings, average percentages and chi-square analysis for each category of the interactive function is set out in table 6 and it is clear that some differences may exist between the teaching behaviours of male and female physical education teachers. For example, the latter spend almost twice as much time (16 per cent to 9 per cent) organizing pupils in their lessons. In addition, they also devoted more time to intervening instruction. On the other hand, the men teachers recorded higher percentages in preparatory instruction (23 per cent to 19 per cent) and concurrent instruction (11 per cent to 7 per cent). Perhaps the most surprising result was that male teachers spend a greater proportion of their time in observation (15 per cent to 11 per cent).

Subscripts

With regard to the function subscript dimension the results are set out in table 7.

Table 7: *Male and female teachers: Raw scores, average percentages and chi-square analysis for function subscript categories*

Subscript	M-n	F-n	M%	F%	χ^2	p
1 Does	709	778	71	65	2.75	N.S.
2 Shares	288	416	29	35	5.81	<0.05
3 Delegates	0	0	0	0	—	—

Clearly, male and female teachers carried out the function themselves for the majority of the time. An examination of the categories within the interactive function would suggest that the majority of them would be carried out by the teacher alone. Most teachers would expect to deal with organizational aspects, provision of equipment, feedback and observation themselves. Only when it came to the teacher and pupil sharing in the execution of a function was there a statistically significant difference ($p < 0.05$) and females were more likely to elicit the assistance of pupils. Effective use can be made of sharing techniques such as questioning when providing feedback or giving preparatory instruction and it may be that female teachers use these techniques of involvement more frequently than their male counterparts. Neither group of teachers ever delegated the carrying out of a function to the pupils and this appears to be a totally neglected method where pupils learn from one another in aspects of reciprocal teaching.

Direction

The results for the direction of the teachers' behaviours is set out in table 8.

Table 8: *Male and female teachers: Raw scores, average percentages and chi-square analysis for direction categories*

Direction	M-n	F-n	M%	F%	χ^2	p
1 One student	207	260	21	22	0.20	N.S.
2 Group/class	573	707	57	59	0.22	N.S.
3 Comb. 1 and 2	217	229	22	19	1.71	N.S.
4 Other persons	0	0	0	0	—	—
5 Comb. 1, 2 and 4	0	0	0	0	—	—

No significant differences were apparent between the groups of teachers with regard to the direction of their behaviour. This suggested that male and female teachers adopted the same teaching strategies in this sub-section. At least one-fifth of the behaviours were pointed towards one pupil with the majority of the remaining behaviours directed to groups or the class. This would appear to be a fair balance as it allows for the major interactive functions to be directed towards groups yet still catering for the individual aspect of the relationships which are so important in physical education.

Mode

The methods of communicating the interactions are set out in table 9 together with the results for each category.

The main mode of communication was 'talk' but the chi-square just failed to reach statistical significance. It was not surprising that verbal behaviour was the most common method of communicating instructions and information in physical education. Regardless of the activity, all lessons in the gymnasium and sports hall are usually highly interactive. Children are often working individually or in a group, apparatus and equipment has to be provided and comments made regarding the appropriateness of the pupils' motor performances. All situations of this kind provide opportunities for verbal behaviour from the teacher.

It appeared that the teachers talked a lot but listened very little. There was no significant difference between male and female who, on average, listened to pupils' comments on only three or four occasions in each lesson. Nevertheless, this mode of behaviour was rarely used and prompted two comments. Firstly, very little use is made of question and answer tech-

Table 9: Male and female teachers: Raw scores, average percentages and chi-square analysis for mode categories

Mode		M-n	F-n	M%	F%	χ^2	p
1	Talks	684	891	60	66	3.42	N.S.
2	Listens	36	48	3	4	0.18	N.S.
3	Observes	258	243	23	18	6.36	<0.05
4	Demonstrates	112	64	10	5	21.89	#0.001
5	Uses St. Demo	36	82	3	6	10.48	<0.01
6	Uses aids	0	0	0	0	—	—
7	Signalling device	2	8	0	1	—	—
8	Written material	0	9	0	1	—	—
9	Manually assists	14	10	1	1	1.06	N.S.
10	Participates	2	0	0	0	—	—
11	Performs task	1	1	0	0	—	—

niques and this may be a weakness in teaching method. It is sound educational practice to encourage children to think about their movement activity and to respond to direct questioning. Secondly, the teachers may be so involved in their teaching and the children so engrossed in their activity that the pupils do not initiate questions to the teacher. Although listening is an infrequent occurrence, the suggestion that teachers are always talking to individuals and groups in a highly interactive teaching situation is partially off-set by the fact that the next most used category was 'observes' and this was statistically significant ($p < 0.05$) and indicated that males spent more time observing pupils than females. This is consistent with the trend of observing performance in the Interactive Function. Why this should be the case is not clear at this stage.

The most significant difference ($p < 0.001$) occurred in the 'demonstrates' category. Males were more likely to give a personal demonstration to the group whereas female teachers tended to use pupils demonstration far more ($p < 0.01$). This may possibly be attributable to the long-standing tradition within the male physical education profession that high levels of personal performance are encouraged and with it a belief that personal demonstration provides a visual display that can assist pupil learning. Female teachers on the other hand prefer to involve the pupils in demonstrations and this could be more effective as it may provide a more acceptable motivational level for children to see one of their peer group performing an activity. However, this is a tentative interpretation.

None of the other categories in this dimension received enough recordings to warrant analysis or were not statistically significant.

Teaching Behaviour — Individual and Team Activities

Another aspect to be considered in this study is whether or not teachers adopt the same teaching style and strategies regardless of the activity being taught. The purpose of this section is to ascertain whether there are any differences in teaching styles and behaviours related to the teaching of an individual type activity (educational gymnastics) and a team activity (basketball or netball).

Interactive Function

In examining the differences within the interactive function, the following results were obtained (table 10).

Table 10:   *Games and gymnastics: Raw scores, average percentages and chi-square analysis for interaction function categories*

Interactive Function		Ga-n	Gy-n	Ga%	Gy%	χ^2	p
1	Organizing	187	104	18	8	38.28	<0.001
2	Preparatory instructing	264	207	25	17	18.71	<0.001
3	Providing equipment	24	214	2	17	122.23	<0.001
4	Concurrent instructing	99	104	9	8	0.52	N.S.
5	Officiating	16	1	2	0	—	—
6	Spotting	0	17	0	1	—	—
7	Leading exercises	5	9	0	1	0.25	N.S.
8	Intervening instruction	177	235	17	19	1.42	N.S.
9	Observing performance	160	140	15	11	6.18	<0.05
10	Participating	2	2	0	0	—	—
11	Other interacting (motor)	40	112	4	9	22.95	<0.001
12	Administering	4	0	0	0	—	—
13	Codes of behaviour	18	13	2	1	1.36	N.S.
14	Other interacting	20	22	2	2	0.00	N.S.
Non-interactive Intervals							
15	Dealing with equipment	10	33	1	3	8.07	<0.01
16	Other non-interactive	10	7	1	1	0.67	N.S.
Non-discernible Intervals							
17	Insufficient audio/video	6	3	1	0	—	—
18	Absent from gymnasium	2	2	0	0	—	—

A chi-square analysis of items 1-14 revealed that there were some highly significant differences (p<0.001) between the teaching behaviours in games and educational gymnastic lessons. To some extent this is to be expected as the nature and organization of the subjects varies according to the differing demands.

For example, the teachers spent significantly more time (p<.001) in organizational behaviour and preparatory instruction when teaching games. A total of 43 per cent was devoted to these first two categories in games as opposed to 25 per cent in gymnastics. It appeared that more information was given and greater control exercised in games. This may have been because the skills and responses in games were often pre-specified and the teachers spent a great deal of time explaining and providing information.

The most significant difference occurred in the providing equipment category where a much larger proportion of the time was spent getting the environment and equipment ready for motor activity in gymnastics.

No significant differences were revealed in the concurrent and intervening instruction categories. Just over a quarter of the teaching time was spent giving feedback and information during and after performance although there was a greater preference for post-performance feedback.

This essential ingredient of teaching appeared to be used equally by teachers in both areas and suggested a consistency in teaching style.

There was a greater occurrence of observation in games lessons and this was significant at the 5 per cent level. The reasons for this are not immediately apparent. It could be that a greater proportion of the games lessons was spent in motor activity and this would have given more opportunities for observation. However, this is speculative at this stage.

The other interacting (motor) category was used far more by the teachers in gymnastics than in games and was highly significant ($p < 0.001$). This could largely be attributed to the time that was spent putting the apparatus back into the equipment rooms and would not be due to differences in teaching style.

Dealing with equipment was significantly different ($p < 0.01$) in gymnastic lessons and could be attributed to the teachers getting out, adjusting or retrieving equipment. As intimated earlier, the exact positioning of equipment in gymnastic apparatus work is essential to the satisfactory completion of many tasks and teachers did spend time making minor positioning adjustments once the pupils had set out the apparatus.

None of the other categories showed any significant differences and six categories were not used sufficiently often to be included in the analysis.

Subscripts

There were some significant differences in the personnel who carried out the function during the teaching of games and gymnastics and these are presented in table 11.

There was a greater likelihood ($p < 0.01$) that the teachers would carry out the function themselves (does) when teaching games. This may again be related to the more formal nature of the games teaching in the sample and the structure of the lesson, the precise skills to be learned and the timing of the feedback. An even greater statistical difference ($p < 0.001$) appeared in the shares category where the gymnastic teaching indicated that the teachers were more likely to carry out the function with the aid of a pupil or pupils. This may indicate more frequent use of questioning in

Table 11: Games and gymnastics: Raw scores, average percentages and chi-square analysis for function subscript categories

Subscript	Ga-n	Gy-n	Ga%	Gy%	χ^2	p
1 Does	745	742	74	63	8.98	< 0.01
2 Shares	267	437	26	37	19.02	< 0.001
3 Delegates	1	1	0	0	—	—

activities where the children were being encouraged to think creatively, as well as involving pupils in teacher-pupil demonstrations of motor performance. The delegation of functions in this sub-section were virtually non-existent.

Direction

The results for the direction of the teachers' behaviours is presented in table 12.

No significant differences were revealed in this analysis and indicated that teachers spend approximately the same proportion of time directing their interactive behaviour to one student, groups or class in games as in gymnastics. This may suggest that teachers adopt the same teaching strategies in this dimension regardless of the type of activity. However, this is a very tentative suggestion at this stage as the category definitions are rather crude and lack precision in some instances. For example when the teacher is observing the class, category 3 is always used as it is impossible to decide whether one student, a group or the whole class is being observed. This inevitably tends to distort the accuracy slightly.

Table 12: Games and gymnastics: Raw scores, average percentages and chi-square analysis for direction categories

Direction	Ga-n	Gy-n	Ga%	Gy%	χ^2	p
1 One student	194	262	19	23	3.06	N.S.
2 Group/class	617	663	61	58	1.04	N.S.
3 Comb. 1 and 2	200	227	20	20	0.00	N.S.
4 Other persons	0	0	0	0	—	—
5 Comb. 1, 2 and 4	0	0	0	0	—	—

Mode

The results for the modes of communication are set out in table 13.

Teachers appear to talk a lot and listen very little when teaching games and gymnastics. The statistical analysis showed no significant difference between the two activities. As expected verbal behaviour was the dominant mode. The fact that hardly any listening was taking place suggested that the interaction was almost entirely a one-way process from the teacher to the pupil(s).

There were significant differences ($p < 0.01$) in the observes category which indicated that teachers attended silently to the behaviour of other

Table 13: Games and gymnastics: Raw scores, average percentages and chi-square analysis

Mode		Ga-n	Gy-n	Ga%	Gy%	χ^2	p
1	Talks	743	832	61	65	2.17	N.S.
2	Listens	37	47	3	4	0.66	N.S.
3	Observes	211	290	17	23	9.39	<0.01
4	Demonstrates	147	29	12	2	82.27	<0.001
5	Uses St. Demo.	75	43	6	3	9.35	<0.01
6	Uses aids	0	0	0	0	—	—
7	Signalling device	10	0	1	0	—	—
8	Written material	0	9	0	1	—	—
9	Manually assists	1	23	0	2	—	—
10	Participates	2	0	0	0	—	—
11	Performs task	1	1	0	0	—	—

people more in gymnastics than in games. The reverse trend was apparent in the observing performance category in the interactive function sub-section (table 10). This apparent anomaly may have been accounted for by the teachers spending more time observing in other categories. For example, standing back and watching pupils carry and place the large apparatus in gymnastic group work, both in the assembling and dismantling stages, could well account for these results.

The largest differences appeared under demonstrates ($p < 0.001$) and indicated that a much greater emphasis was being placed on personal demonstration by the teacher in games than in gymnastics. This may be due to the pre-specified nature of the skills to be performed in games and the ability of the teacher to show them to a high standard. The involvement of the pupils in demonstrations was also statistically significant in games lessons ($p < 0.01$) which again pointed to the greater use of this form of demonstration.

None of the other categories had sufficient raw scores in one of the variables to warrant statistical analysis. The use of manual assistance was used on a number of occasions in gymnastics but hardly at all in games. This was almost entirely due to the teacher 'standing-by' to assist in the performance of gymnastic vaults such as an overswing off a long box or a rotating jump from a trampette.

Pupils' Behaviour

The recording procedures resulted in a total of 5810 pupil behaviours and their distribution is presented in table 14.

The results do represent an accurate account of pupil behaviour in

Table 14: ALT-PE: Pupil behaviour during physical education lessons by sex and activity

Not Motor Engaged	%Men	%Women	%Games	%Gym	%All
Interim	4	2	3	3	3
Waiting	12	16	14	13	14
Off-task	1	1	1	0	1
On-task	14	14	8	21	14
Cognitive	42	48	48	42	45
Motor Engaged					
Motor appropriate	28	19	26	21	24
Motor inappropriate	0	0	0	0	0
Supporting	0	0	0	0	0
N =	2559	3251	2889	2921	5810

physical education lessons and indicated a consistently high commitment to cognitive aspects which ranged from 42 per cent to 48 per cent. Waiting and on-task behaviour each accounted for 14 per cent but there was a much greater range for the latter category (8 per cent to 21 per cent). The motor component of the lessons averaged out at just below a quarter at 24 per cent but again there was a considerable range, the girls and the gymnastic lessons at the lower end and the boys and the games lessons at the higher end. There were a few recordings for off-task behaviour and none for motor inappropriate and supporting.

It must be pointed out that category systems which rely on an observer's interpretations can sometimes be misleading. Concern was felt about the absolute validity of the results for a number of reasons. Firstly, the data revealed a periodic picture rather than a continuous account of life in the gymnasium or sports hall. Secondly, the results are cold, impersonal and quantitative and give no indication of the nature or qualitative aspect of any of the behaviours. For example, some children were totally involved in trying to achieve the objectives of the lesson whereas there were others who had a minimal commitment and they have sometimes been referred to as 'competent bystanders'. Children classified in this category would stay within the managerial requirements set by the teacher but work at a minimum level and avoid being involved to any great extent. To identify pupils who fall into this category at a specific time is quite difficult. A third reason centred on the cognitive category. When all the children were sitting in front of the teacher listening to an explanation it was recorded as cognitive. The assumption being that the pupils were listening and understanding. However, if they were not paying attention and the explanation was beyond them then they should have been recorded as off-task. There was no way of knowing when and if this was ever the case. Fourthly, some concern was felt over the distinction between motor appropriate and motor inappropriate behaviours. The definitions centred on the level of difficulty of the task. Thus motor appropriate behaviour refers to the time a pupil spends practising a motor skill at as easy level of difficulty. Anything that is too easy or too difficult should be coded as inappropriate. Without knowing the skill levels of each individual pupil, it was not possible to assess capabilities and thus judge the degree of difficulty. Lastly, there were occasions when pupils were waiting for a turn in a queue and this would obviously be scored under the waiting category. Observation of one pupil showed him to be mentally rehearsing and practising a shooting skill without a ball. In this instance, the waiting time was being put to effective use as was evidenced by the pupil's later performance.

There is little doubt that ALT-PE will vary according to the nature of the activity being taught. Lessons involving high quality individual work such as sprinting or pole vaulting would obviously have a lower work rate commitment than an activity which was less physically demanding and more continuous in nature. In this study it was not surprising that a higher percentage of time was spent in the motor appropriate category for games than gymnastics because of the different organizational and apparatus requirements. However, this does not explain the differences between lessons taught by males and females where the boys were involved in motor appropriate behaviour for 28 per cent of the time whereas the girls were only involved for 19 per cent of the time. Whether or not this is a consistent trend in all teaching warrants further attention. Research in Finnish schools by Telama *et al* (1982) does give some tentative support to this suggestion. What was clear in this pilot study was that lessons taught by males had a higher motor content for the pupils with more 'time-on-task'.

The percentages that are presented in table 14 refer to all the pupils who were in view of the camera at a particular time. To make global interpretations from these results may be slightly misleading. Clearly, pupils react to learning situations in a variety of ways and to infer that increased amounts of motor appropriate behaviour will automatically result in more learning for all pupils would be to ignore the individual nature of human learning. Similarly, to infer that more 'time-on-task' will result in greater learning would also be incorrect as the relationship is probably not linear but more in the shape of an inverted 'U'. However, this could vary with the pupils level of ability and/or the nature of the teaching strategies adopted. Thus pupils with a low level of ability might benefit from much practice of simple tasks in a highly-structured teaching situation whereas more able performers may need more time to think and assimilate complicated strategies in loosely structured conditions. There is some tentative support for his idea from Griffey (1983), but further research which specifically investigates this hypothesis is necessary. However, this probably falls outside the boundaries of the present study. Nevertheless, the importance of the objectives of the lesson cannot be ignored.

In spite of all the reservations, it was felt that ALT-PE data did give a more valid account of pupil behaviour than the previous attempt described under the heading 'engaged time'. The system did include thousands of recordings of actual pupil behaviour and in spite of some difficulties of category interpretation, they did reflect what was happening in physical education classes. It was certainly felt to be more appropriate to use this method of measuring pupil involvement in the future. Since the behaviour of the children must be related to the teachers' behaviour, it might be possible to establish links between the two.

Considerations for the Main Study

The main purpose of the pilot study was to discover if the methodology that had been adopted would give a valid indication of how physical education teachers taught their subject in secondary schools and its effect on pupils' behaviour. In addition, comparisons were made between male and female teachers teaching an individual and a team activity. It was felt that the pilot study had achieved its original intentions and certainly had ecological validity. At this stage, some aspects were highlighted for further investigations and these are now summarized with a view to incorporating them into the main study.

Teacher Behaviour

The use of Anderson's Descriptive Category System gave an indication how secondary school teachers taught physical education. The system was adapted to record the teachers' behaviours at four specified precise moments during every minute of teaching and this adaptation produced over 9000 examples of teaching behaviours. All these recordings were made over a time sample of four recordings per minute at a specified second, but in the achievement of precision, the total continuity and length of the interactive functions were sacrificed. In order to examine this sequencing, it would be necessary to carry out a separate analysis. On balance, the more accurate recording is considered to be preferable. However, the use of the system is dependent on the use of VTR as it was specifically designed to analyze videotaped lessons. If videotaping is not used, an alternative system for measuring teachers' behaviours will be necessary.

It is clear from the results presented so far that some aspects of the analysis have proved to be of greater importance and significance than others. For example, within the eighteen categories of the interactive function, ten were rarely used viz: officiating, spotting, leading exercises, participating, adminstering, codes of behaviour, dealing with equipment, other non-interactive, insufficient audio/video and absent from gymnasium. In fact, they accounted for only 7 per cent of the teachers' functions and would appear to play a comparatively minor role in the repertoire of teachers' behaviours. It would therefore seem sensible to place greater emphasis in the main study on those categories which were used more frequently and which indicated statistically significant differences between male and female teachers and games and gymnastic lessons. Thus the focus of the study narrows to the following eight categories: organizing, preparatory instructing, providing equipment, concurrent instructing, intervening instructing, observing performance, other interacting (motor) and other interacting. Within each of these categories different issues have emerged and these are highlighted briefly. On the basis of these results, consideration will be given for further and more detailed analysis.

Organizing

Teachers spent a considerable proportion of their time organizing pupils but significantly more time was spent on this function by female teachers and in games lessons. Whilst recognizing the importance of efficient organization, some teachers appear to be more effective in this aspect. In addition, more time is spent on organizational aspects in certain types of lessons. There would appear to be a need to analyze the content and amount of time spent in this function.

Preparatory Instructing

This category was the one most frequently used by both males and females (22 per cent). However, it was used significantly more by male teachers and in games lessons. There is a suggestion that the time allocation may be excessive and this warrants more detailed analysis through an inspection of the length and content in an attempt to examine efficiency.

Providing Equipment

Significantly more time was spent in gymnastic lessons. This was an expected result, but an examination of the time allocation of 17 per cent is warranted.

Concurrent Instructing

This form of instruction was used significantly more by male teachers and in gymnastics. An examination of the different types of concurrent instruction (for example, auditory, tactile or descriptive) and whether they are directed towards an individual, a group or a class is indicated. A prepared check list would be suitable for this purpose.

Intervening Instruction

Although no significant differences were revealed between male and female teachers and games and gymnastic lessons this is a very important category and was used for almost one-fifth of all teaching behaviours. A breakdown of the types of feedback, for example positive or negative, or whether it referred to the movement or its outcome, would be valuable and could be obtained through recordings on a prepared check list.

Observing Performance

Males spend more time observing the motor performance of pupils than their female colleagues but this was only significant in games lessons. In addition, significantly more time was spent by both groups of teachers observing in games than in gymnastics. However, this may be accounted for by the fact that the pupils spend more time engaged in motor activity in games lessons and there is therefore proportionately more time available to observe performance. To ascertain the quality and effect of the teachers' observations it would be necessary to use different and more sophisticated video techniques, identify the focus of the observation and make subjective assessments of the improvements in pupil performance. This is probably beyond the scope of the present study. Nevertheless, in the future it would be possible to concentrate on this category and ask the teacher to 'think aloud' while observing and this could be recorded by means of a radio microphone and subsequently used for detailed analysis.

Other Interacting (Motor)

This category was used significantly more by females and in gymnastic lessons. Its main purpose was to record the putting away of the gymnastic apparatus and the extra time allocation in this subject is to be expected. The content of this category is different from the preceding areas and an examination of the differences between males and females is warranted and this could be done through an examination of the length and content of these episodes. If significant differences still emerge from a larger sample, then suggestions could be made to reduce the time spent on a mainly organizational function.

Other Interacting

This category included personal or general comments not related to the main motor activity of the lesson. Although used significantly more by female teachers in gymnastics it was only used infrequently (an average of 2 per cent) in the pilot sample. Because of the 'fringe' nature of the comments and the more central and fundamental character of the preceding categories to teaching, it is proposed not to include this category for further analysis.

Thus the following seven categories emerge for further analysis:

Category   1 Organizing
Category   2 Preparatory instructing
Category   3 Providing equipment
Category   4 Concurrent instructing
Category   8 Intervening instruction
Category   9 Observing performance
Category 11 Other interacting (Motor)

Subscript

There was significantly more 'sharing' taking place within gymnastic lessons and by female teachers, whereas male teachers were more likely to carry out the function themselves in games lessons. Two areas that were pinpointed for further analysis were the use of question and answer techniques and teacher/pupil demonstration. Both these teaching strategies involved 'sharing' procedures.

No significant differences were revealed for teaching behaviours of males and females and for individual or team activities. It would therefore seem reasonable to discard this as a major area for further focus and consider the direction as a subsidiary aspect of teacher function.

Mode

Overall, there were no significant differences between the male and female teachers, or between the games and gymnastic lessons, in the number of codings in the talk category. However, as the major method of communication, this aspect cannot be ignored.

Although teachers spend significantly more time observing the motor performance of pupils in games, the reverse trend for all forms of observation was revealed in gymnastics but this was due to observing pupils putting the apparatus away in gymnastics.

An area which does warrant inspection is that of demonstration. Males were more likely to give a personal demonstration whereas female teachers involved students more in giving demonstrations. In addition, it was five times more likely in games that a teacher would give a personal demonstration and twice as probable that teachers would use a student demonstration of some kind. Thus the frequency, type and composition of demonstrations in lessons needs further scrutiny.

With the exception of three categories, the levels of intra-observer reliability were acceptable. Further practice is necessary analyzing the reasons for this discrepancy prior to the main study. The method for calculating reliability levels must be by categories and not global totals. The formula to be used is the one recommended by Hawkins and Dotson (1975).

Pupil Behaviour

The learner involvement section of ALT-PE was felt to give a reasonably accurate account of pupil behaviour in spite of some limitations in interpretation and is recommended for continuation. It may well be that not all ALT-PE rates are the same for all activities. A soccer technique for example needs plenty of pressure practice in conditioned games, whereas pole-vaulting would require long intervals between each practice. In 1983, Metzler posed the question, 'Are my students getting as much ALT-PE as can be expected in my situation?' and this is a much more sensitive question and closer to reality. Thus the amount of involvement needs to be considered in relation to the nature of the activity and its relevance to the task that has been set.

6
Pupils' Perceptions of Their Learning in Physical Education

Every subject on the school curriculum should be accountable to the department in the school, the headteacher, the local education authority and ultimately to society. In most subjects this is mainly achieved through the normal internal and external examination system and schools place great emphasis on their academic achievements in public examinations. The evaluation of the physical education curriculum falls outside this context and is much more subjective in nature. Some schools cite the number of pupils who have achieved representative honours in different sports and use this as a major measure of the quality of teaching in their departments. Of course this is an elitist approach and is more closely linked to the coaching of teams rather than the teaching of all the pupils in a school. Certainly it has a valid place in the overall evaluation of a department but it should be considered as a minor aspect. In the past, comparatively few schools participated in the Certificate in Secondary Education (CSE) examinations in physical education although the advent of the General Certificate in Secondary Education (GCSE) has heralded a larger number of schools entering pupils for this particular examination. Thus more widely accepted criteria may be available in the not too distant future. At present, there is no generally accepted method for judging the worth of physical education in a school. Each school or authority will have its own criteria which will vary from place to place.

One possible source of evaluation which is rarely used is to question the pupils, i.e. the consumers. The pilot studies in this research have already demonstrated that the teaching strategies do affect the type of pupil involvement which in turn influences the nature of the subsequent learning. For example, excessive amounts of time spent in organizing, providing equipment and giving instructions will give rise to feelings of frustration. Similarly, if the amount of pupil time-on-task is low (the lowest ALT-PE of learner involvement in the pilot study was 11 per cent in a games lesson), then there is little opportunity to develop motor skills. In contrast, efficient and effective use of lesson time will make optimal levels of learning possible. Inevitably, these processes must play a major part in the pupils' perceptions of, and attitudes towards, physical education.

Physical Education 'Learner Report' Questionnaire

Recently, Crum (1984) formulated a questionnaire based on the supposition that pupils were able to indicate what they had learned from the physical education programme. The questionnaire consisted of twenty-four items and each item was prefaced by the following statement: 'The physical education lessons and sports activities in my secondary school have contributed to my learning the following: ....'. (The full questionnaire is set out in appendix 3). Pupils were asked to indicate on a five-point scale which ranged from 'certainly true' through 'I don't know' to 'certainly not true' their opinion about each question. Responses were subsequently scored '1' for 'certainly true' through to '5' for 'certainly not true'. Factor analysis had revealed four factors and these are briefly defined together with the questions that comprise the factor.

1 TECHNOMOTOR (Q 1,6,8,9,13,22): solve technical and tactical aspects of movement problems.
2 SOCIOMOTOR (Q 4,10,12,14,16,18,19,20): solve the interpersonal problems which are inherent to physical education and sport.
3 COGNITIVE-REFLECTIVE (Q 2,11,15,17,20,21): reflect on the character of these problems and their solutions and their relationship to practical areas.
4 AFFECTIVE (Q 3,5,7,24): enjoy participation in physical education programmes and enjoy exercise.

Within this framework, Crum conducted a pilot study in the Netherlands with a sample of students from secondary schools and first year undergraduates (N = 491). Of particular relevance to the present study were two of Crum's (1986a) comments in his discussion of his pilot survey. The first was that, 'The results of this pilot investigation give some support to the proposition that the learner report can serve as an instrument to obtain an indication of the extent and nature of learning in physical education programmes.' And the second was more far reaching and proposed that 'Further research directed to the relationship between the professional theory of physical education teachers, their daily practices and the learning results of their students' was recommended. On the basis of these observations, the questionnaire appeared to be particularly relevant for use in this study as it was necessary to identify schools with different levels of effectiveness in their physical education programmes.

Crum's questionnaire appeared to fulfil a need in that it attempted to identify the pupils' perceptions of the subject in an objective way and might possibly indicate statistically significant differences between schools as well as between male and female pupils. There was also the additional advantage that it might throw some light onto the relationship between teaching and learning. As a result, a pilot study was carried out in three mixed secondary schools (A,B, and C) and the male and female pupils in year 5 were asked to complete the questionnaire. A total of 207 were returned; 117 had been completed by male and ninety by female pupils. The main scores for the questionnaire in schools A,B, and C were 2.35, 2.17 and 2.19 respectively. Thus, they all showed a tendency towards a positive perception of the subject. However, no significant differences were revealed between the schools. The breakdown into the four factors did indicate some statistically significant differences between schools in the sociomotor and affective areas. In addition, there were also significant differences between males and females on the technomotor, sociomotor and affective factors.

The pilot study had proved to be successful and was able to discriminate on a number of the variables. The administration and the data coding process of the questionnaire had not posed any problems and, apart from two minor changes to the wording, was considered to be suitable for use in this study.

With these amendments, it was considered appropriate to widen the sample to a larger number of mixed secondary schools. The headteachers of twenty-five mixed secondary schools were approached to ask if they would be prepared to participate in the research study. No replies were received from five schools and another five schools declined the invitation to participate — some because they had no fifth form and at least one because the possible videotaping of lessons had been mentioned. Fifteen schools did indicate a willingness to contribute to the project. The response was slightly disappointing but had to be accepted in the context of the educational climate at that time. A teachers' dispute over pay and conditions of service had been in operation for over a year and many physical education teachers were not conducting any extra-curricular activities. Whether or not participation in a research project is considered to be extra-curricular is debatable but the timing of the request was inopportune and undoubtedly contributed to a slightly lower number of participants in the main sample. From the fifteen schools, satisfactory replies were received from fourteen, but one school withdrew due to unforseen circumstances.

The questionnaire was targeted at the fourth year pupils who were starting their twelfth consecutive term of physical education in their secondary school and this was considered to be an adequate period of time for them to have formed firm perceptions of the subject. The required number of questionnaires was sent by post to the heads of department together with instructions for administration.

From the fourteen schools, completed questionnaires were received from 1780 pupils. Of these, 871 (49 per cent) were males, 710 (40 per cent) were females and 199 (11 per cent) were unknown as they had not circled M/F on the questionnaire. (This problem had not arisen in the pilot study but it is recommended that any future questionnaires should ask for the sex of the respondent as a separate question.) Three hundred and sixty-one of the replies (20.3 per cent) did not complete one or more questions and were therefore omitted from the calculation of the overall average. Missing cases in the four factors ranged between 5.6 and 9.7 per cent.

Results and Discussion

The data was subjected to computer analysis using Norusis' (1986) SPSSX package. Descriptive statistics were obtained on the questionnaire responses to give the counts, means, standard deviations, percentages and distributions of the data. The means, standard deviations and rank order for the fourteen schools are set out in table 15.

The mean for all the schools was 2.233 with a standard deviation of 0.583. The means in the sample ranged from 2.053 to 2.590 and indicated

Table 15. Physical Education 'Learner Report' Questionnaire: mean, standard deviation and rankings for main sample

School	Mean	S.D.	Rank
A	2.053	0.560	1
B	2.240	0.632	8
C	2.333	0.560	9
D	2.101	0.560	3
E	2.590	0.898	14
F	2.187	0.632	7
G	2.340	0.526	10
H	2.353	0.445	11
I	2.104	0.523	4
J	2.381	0.699	13
K	2.159	0.470	6
L	2.068	0.390	2
M	2.151	0.558	5
N	2.354	0.590	12

that all schools had a positive score. A score of '1' implied a very positive outcome, a score of '3' suggested pupils were unsure whether or not learning had taken place, and a score of '5' that learning had certainly not occurred. With one exception, the results appeared to fall into two main categories. One grouping contained those schools which scored higher than the sample mean and were ranked 1 to 7 in table 15. The highest mean was 2.053 and the lowest 2.187 with a range of 0.134.

A second group fell below the sample mean and were ranked 8 to 13 with a range between the means of 0.141. The one exception was the fourteenth ranked school where the mean was 0.209 below the mean of the school above. Overall, these results can be regarded as satisfactory, especially when compared with the mean of 2.9 reported by Crum (1984) from a sample of undergraduate students and pupils at two schools (N = 491). All the mean scores in the present sample were much higher than this and it is important to recognize that all the schools in this survey could well be regarded as high-scoring schools. As always, group mean scores do tend to hide individual differences and the spread of the results, as shown by the standard deviations, indicated some uncertainty about learning outcomes. This was especially true with the two last ranked schools (E and J) where the standard deviations extended the range beyond '3'. In approximate terms this meant that one in every five pupils in these schools were unsure about their learning in physical education.

Apart from giving insight into the pupils' perceptions of the subject, the other main purpose was to establish if there were any significant differences between schools. A one-way ANOVA of the mean scores in the sample did indicate a highly significant difference ($p < 0.0001$) between schools. In order to ascertain the level and content of these differences, Snedecor and Cochran (1978) recommend using a test of 'least significant difference'. They caution that this test can only be used when the factor is shown to be significant in the ANOVA table. As this criterion had been met, the test was considered to be appropriate. The calculations indicated that differences between the means in excess of 0.31 were statistically significant at the 5 per cent level, and a difference in excess of 0.41 was significant at the 1 per cent level.

A summary of the significantly different results between schools is presented as follows:

1 per cent level
School A and School E
School D and School E
School F and School E
School I and School E

School K and School E
School L and School E
School M and School E

5 per cent level
School B and School E
School A and School J
School L and School J

There were seven significant differences at the 1 per cent level and all involved one school (E) which had a rather extreme score at the lower end of the scale. The same school also appeared once in the table denoting differences at the 5 per cent level. Thus the first eight schools in the rank order all showed a statistically significant difference from the fourteenth ranked school. Only the first two ranked schools revealed a significant difference ($p < 0.05$) from the thirteenth ranked school. As a result, four schools were deemed to be different on the basis of the attitudes of fourth year pupils (as measured by the Physical Education 'Learners Report' questionnaire) and were considered to be suitable for further analysis. These were:

School A and School E ($p < 0.01$)
School L and School E ($p < 0.01$)
School A and School J ($p < 0.05$)
School L and School J ($p < 0.05$)

Accordingly, schools A and L were designated 'higher scoring' schools and schools J and E 'lower scoring' schools. In order to establish a control, school C was selected as it was clearly placed between the above two groups and was ninth in the rank order. Most importantly, it was the first school in the rank order which did not show a statistically significant difference between the higher or lower scoring pairs. In summary, schools A, L, C, J and E were selected for further detailed analysis.

As well as identifying differences between schools on the total questionnaire, a two-way ANOVA was run on the questionnaire average by sex by school and significance was apparent ($p < 0.05$).

Thus there were differences in the manner in which male and female pupils perceived physical education. A visual inspection of the results in this area showed that the highest score was achieved by male pupils in nine schools and by female pupils in four. The male average score was 2.21 and the female average was 2.27. Thus it appeared that male pupils had a significantly more favourable outlook on the subject but there were clearly some exceptions to this trend. At one time this may possibly have been

attributed to cultural influences in society which reinforced skilled performance and participation in sport for boys to a greater extent than for
girls. Nowadays this emphasis may have changed when one considers that
women's sport is gradually achieving equal status with men and the greatly
increased participation by women in many different kinds of exercise at
health and fitness classes, in the home and in the natural environment. Thus
it has become fashionable to take part in exercise and is regarded as a means
to achieving and maintaining a measure of physical health throughout life.
The reasons for differences between male and female pupils are not
immediately apparent but the way in which the subject is presented in the
school is an important variable. Thus further detailed analysis is warranted.

Descriptive statistics for the four factors are tabulated in table 16.

*Table 16 Technomotor, sociomotor,
cognitive-reflective and affective factors:
mean and standard deviation scores*

Factor	Mean	S.D.
Technomotor	2.01	0.65
Sociomotor	2.24	0.70
Cognitive-reflective	2.67	0.72
Affective	1.96	0.78

It was somewhat surprising that the highest scoring factor was related
to enjoyment and participation in the programme. Nevertheless this was
consistent with Underwood's (1983) finding that most heads of department
regarded the affective areas of attitude and enjoyment to be the most
important indicators for judging the success of their curriculum planning.
Although there was a greater spread of scores for this factor, it did show
that 90 per cent of the pupils had a positive feeling for the subject and
indicated some congruence with teachers' attitudes. The larger standard
deviation pointed to more extreme scores about the mean and suggested
greater polarization of pupils' attitudes for the affective factor. The
development of motor skills which most of the literature supports as being
one of the paramount aims of physical education was a close second with
the smallest spread about the mean. Just over 90 per cent appeared to be
positive about the solving of technical and tactical aspects of movement
problems. As the solving of movement problems through the physical
medium is one of the main functions of physical education, it appeared that
some measure of achievement was being reached for the majority of
children. The social benefits relating to the solving of interpersonal
problems in physical education such as group cohesion, cooperating and
working effectively with team members was again positive for 86 per cent
of the sample. The last ranked factor, cognitive-reflective, was concerned

with the practical aspects of the subject and its related theory. This area was clearly ranked fourth and almost a third of the sample had a negative attitude. The reasons for this are not immediately apparent but may be because teachers are nearly always concerned with the practical aspects of the subject and do not make links with some of the underlying theoretical issues. Topical and controversial issues such as apartheid in sport or the Olympic Games are rarely contained within any physical education syllabus and any discussions with pupils would be incidental rather than planned. It was not surprising that this factor had the least positive outcomes.

A two-way ANOVA of the four factors by sex by all the schools in the sample produced the following results. Firstly, there were highly significant differences ($p < 0.001$) between the schools on each of the factors. However, the same trend was not apparent for the sex variable. A summary table of the significance levels is set out in table 17.

Table 17.   Main sample: ANOVA by sex (male, female and 'unknown' pupils) by the four factors: significance levels

Factor	p
Technomotor	< 0.05
Sociomotor	N.S.
Cognitive-reflective	< 0.0001
Affective	N.S.

Only the technomotor and cognitive-reflective factors indicated any sex differences and both these showed male pupils to have the higher score. Visual inspection of the technomotor means for the schools showed that male pupils had a higher score than female pupils in nine schools. An even greater number (eleven schools) exhibited the same trend for the cognitive-reflective factor. No significant differences were revealed for the sociomotor and affective factors, although the sociomotor factor was approaching significance. Some caution must be exercised in the above interpretations because the results included the 'unknown' category of pupils who had not indicated their sex on the questionnaire. The 'unknown' category will be excluded from the analysis of the target schools.

For both the factors that were significantly different (technomotor and cognitive-reflective), the males had a higher mean score than the female pupils. This may suggest that male physical education programmes place a greater emphasis on the acquisition of motor skills but there was no suggestion in the literature review that this was the case. Perhaps more time is devoted to physical activity both during lessons and within the curriculum and these suggestions need probing further. The higher score for male pupils on the cognitive-reflective factor was highly significant and perhaps could be attributed to a greater emphasis being placed on issues such as health-related fitness programmes for boys. This suggested separate planning for the boys' and girls' physical education and is one of the issues to be probed in the main study. Another aspect of this factor not directly association with the work in schools is that there is much more media coverage for male sport. Thus the links sport makes with the commercial world of business and politics are frequently discussed on television and written about in the press. For example, the money paid to top class athletes in team games and track and field athletics, or sponsorship of teams and important sporting events, is mainly orientated towards male sport. There are events such as the Wimbledon tennis championships where the prize money and media coverage for males and females are approximately equal but this is the exception rather than the rule. It does appear that there may be issues both within and outside the educational context which may have a bearing on pupils' attitudes to the four factors identified in the questionnaire.

One of the problems with breaking down the learning of physical skills into four distinct factors is to create the impression that each one is separate and self-contained. This is far from the reality of the situation. To learn a physical skill involves much more than the motor aspect. Many skills are often learnt in association with other people. Thus interaction is an essential part of the experience. To play a team game against another team will involve striving to do one's best in collaboration with team mates. The ultimate pleasure that can be derived from winning the contest is therefore an integration of the affective, technomotor and social aspects. Similar examples can also be linked to cognitive areas. Although it is valid to examine each of the four factors in turn, the importance of the interrelationships is noted.

Selected Schools

The physical education departments in five schools had been selected for detailed analysis on the basis of the fourth year pupils' responsess to the Physical Education 'Learner Report' questionnaire. To simplify identification, the two high-scoring schools will be numbered S1 and S2 (formerly A and L), the control school S3 (formerly C) and the low-scoring schools S4 and S5 (formerly J and E).

A summary of the descriptive and analytical statistics for the five schools is now presented in order to identify more precisely the similarities

Table 18. *Selected schools: PE 'Learner Report' questionnaire means and standard deviations*

School	S1	S2	S3	S4	S5
Mean	2.05	2.07	2.33	2.38	2.59
S.D.	0.56	0.39	0.56	0.70	0.90

and differences between the schools. Firstly, the mean scores and standard deviations are presented in table 18.

Statistically significant differences ($p < 0.05$ and $p < 0.01$) have already been revealed between the high and low-scoring schools. There was also a closer spread about the mean for S1 and S2. The S2 standard deviation was markedly low and indicated a fairly consistent attitude amongst the pupils. For S4 and S5, the standard deviations were larger and this indicated a larger range of attitudes about an overall lower mean score. Thus it appeared that as attitudes towards physical education in a school became more positive, there was also a contraction in the range. (A positive rank order correlation of 0.49 for the means and standard deviations of the full sample gave some tentative support for this suggestion.)

The mean scores for the four factors are set out in table 19.

Table 19. *Selected schools: PE 'Learner Report' questionnaire mean scores for the four factors*

Factor	S1	S2	S3	S4	S5
Technomotor	1.98	1.83	1.98	2.16	2.33
Sociomotor	1.98	2.13	2.44	2.33	2.55
Cognitive-reflective	2.65	2.48	2.84	2.70	2.86
Affective	1.62	1.68	1.91	2.16	2.36

Analysis of variance of each of the factors for the high (S1 and S2) and low-scoring schools (S4 and S5) revealed significant differences ($p < 0.0001$) for the technomotor, sociomotor and affective factors and a $p < 0.01$ level for the cognitive-reflective factor. Thus there were differences on all four factors between the high and low-scoring schools. In each of the four factors, S1 and S2 had recorded higher scores than S4 and S5, and there was a clear division between the mean scores.

A further statistical analysis of each of the factors by sex (male and female pupils) is presented in table 20.

Table 20. *Selected schools: ANOVA by sex by the four factors: significance levels*

Factor	p
Technomotor	<0.01
Sociomotor	<0.05
Cognitive-reflective	<0.0001
Affective	N.S.

Three of the four factors were significantly different with the sociomotor factor bordering on the 5 per cent level. Apart from the affective area, all the factors indicated differences in the ways in which male and female pupils perceived physical education — with male pupils showing the more positive attitude.

In the technomotor factor, the male pupils in the high and low-scoring

Table 21. *Physical Education 'Learner Report' Questionnaire: mean scores for component questions for each factor in selected schools*

TECHNOMOTOR

Question	S1	S2	S3	S4	S5
1	1.34	1.18	1.42	1.55	1.67
6	2.16	1.62	1.73	2.24	2.21
8	2.02	1.56	2.11	1.94	2.19
9	2.66	3.38	3.11	3.38	3.73
13	1.57	1.50	1.61	1.80	1.88
22	1.82	1.73	1.85	2.08	2.23

SOCIOMOTOR

Question	S1	S2	S3	S4	S5
4	1.82	2.02	2.06	2.19	2.41
10	2.04	1.98	2.02	2.31	2.38
12	1.83	2.82	3.85	2.24	2.88
14	2.41	2.11	2.18	2.26	2.43
16	2.05	1.98	2.30	2.46	2.67
18	1.93	2.28	2.50	2.46	2.57
19	2.15	1.99	2.61	2.49	2.47
23	1.73	1.81	2.08	2.24	2.42

COGNITIVE-REFLECTIVE

Question	S1	S2	S3	S4	S5
2	2.22	2.11	2.22	2.42	2.29
11	2.85	2.35	2.65	2.53	2.85
15	1.89	1.66	2.07	1.89	2.18
17	2.86	2.55	3.37	3.04	2.99
20	1.93	2.42	2.74	2.63	2.90
21	4.19	3.79	4.05	3.62	3.83

AFFECTIVE

Question	S1	S2	S3	S4	S5
3	1.84	1.80	2.07	2.38	2.50
5	1.50	1.55	1.82	2.11	2.34
7	1.78	2.06	2.07	2.28	2.54
24	1.59	1.40	1.68	1.77	2.12

schools all showed a more favourable perception than female pupils. This may be linked with the earlier evidence on pupil behaviour which showed male pupils to be 'motor appropriately' engaged for 28 per cent of the lesson in contrast to the female pupils' involvement of 19 per cent. Thus male pupils appeared to be given much more time in which to develop their technique and apply it into movement situations. As argued earlier, one cannot isolate the motor component, it has to be linked with the other three factors. If male teachers are giving more time to the motor component, then it logically follows there is more time available in which to develop attitudes in other areas. The weakness in this argument is that there were no differences in the affective factor which appeared to be one of the key areas. There were also exceptions to this main trend in individual schools. These differences warrant further analysis in the case studies and may show an important relationship in the teaching-learning process.

A final analysis of the mean scores for the component questions for the four factors in the selected schools was considered to be important in an attempt to reveal differences between the schools on particular questions. The results are set out in table 21.

Technomotor

This factor was concerned with the solving of technical and tactical aspects in physical education and statistical significance ($p < 0.0001$) had been reported between the high and low-scoring schools. Question 1, 'to play well-known ball games' was the most highly rated question in the questionnaire and all schools showed a very positive attitude. This may reflect the strong emphasis that is given to the playing of games in secondary schools. Often, the major portion of the curriculum time is allocated to team games and it would appear that the ability to play games was being achieved. The ability to apply the right technique (Q 13) in games was also scored highly in all schools and supported this contention. The proportion of time allocated to each of the practical areas in physical education is worthy of further examination, and a 'time analysis' based on this suggestion would give some indication of the emphasis given to particular activities. Similarly, all schools showed a positive attitude towards achieving in athletic activities (Q 6) and this was particularly noticeable in S2. The reasons for this are not clear at this stage but may be linked to the time allocation and/or the expertise of the staff. Most pupils appeared to understand the official competition rules of well-known sports (Q 8) particularly in S2. Whether time is specifically devoted to this aspect through CSE Mode III studies in year 4 or whether it is incorporated into the general teaching throughout the school may become apparent during the visits. Both the high and low-scoring schools exhibited a positive trend with regard to why a certain technique or tactic was more appropriate in a particular sport situation (Q 22) and in its application (Q 13). However, the two high-scoring schools scored higher on these questions. It appeared that pupils felt they were able to apply and understand the principles of games playing but were slightly more confident in their application. The only question in this factor which revealed a negative attitude was Q 9 which asked about pupils' learning to perform on gymnastic apparatus. Only S1 showed a slightly positive approach. Again the reasons for this need to be sought. It is a salutary thought that almost all schools include some form of gymnastics in their physical education curriculum and it appeared that the teaching was having a negative effect. The pupils were not achieving sufficiently high standards of personal skill on the apparatus to feel positive about their levels of attainment.

Sociomotor

This factor related to the interpersonal aspects of physical education and there were highly statistically significant differences ($p < 0.001$) between the two categories of schools. The pupils in the higher-scoring schools appeared to be more able to adapt their ways of playing and moving to the level of others (Q 4) as well as being able to cooperate with stronger or weaker performers (Q 10). Whether this is a particular teaching strategy or whether it is related to organizational factors such as mixed ability or elitist grouping will be examined. Whilst there were differences between the schools, it is important to note that they all exhibited a positive attitude.

Mixed physical education has been a contentious issue for a number of years and in many schools, after children have experienced a common core of activity for the first three years, some mixed teaching through the optional activities programme is offered. In answer to Q 12 'how to play and engage in sports with members of the opposite sex.' There was a large spread of opinion. S2 and S5 were approaching a neutral position whereas S1 and S4 were positive. Of particular interest was the score of 3.85 reported for the control school. The reasons for these variations may be due to the amount and timing of any mixed physical education and information concerning this will be gleaned from the syllabuses, schemes of work and visits to the schools. The adaptation of game rules to group needs (Q 14) was scored positively by all five schools although there was no consistent trend. Much of the teaching in games involves small groups working in a restricted space in small-sided team situations. The rules and conditions of play are often adjusted to the needs and possibilities of the group. It will be possible to ascertain if this teaching method is adopted in the schools.

There was a marked variation for Q 16 when S1 and S2 scored higher in their ability to understand and accept others in sport situations. Attempting to make pupils realize that each individual's potential varies and that people react differently to different situations may be part of the underlying philosophy in the department. Most teachers would probably admit to this being an important objective of their work but it is the way it manifests itself in everyday contact and teaching with pupils that will ensure its achievement. Organizational factors and interrelationships between the teacher and the pupils and the pupils themselves should give some clues as to its implementation in the schools. In order to develop an appreciation of another person's role in physical education (Q 18) it can sometimes be helpful to experience, for example, playing in different positions in games or changing roles in a dance duo. Experiences such as these can lead to a more perceptive understanding of the total situation and S1 and S2 scored appreciably higher on this question. The involvement of players of different abilities in purposeful activity (Q 19 and Q 23) appeared to be achieved more readily by the high-scoring schools. Again this may be related to groupings based on the same or mixed ability levels. This may not only apply within the normal timetabled curriculum but also to the extra-curricular programme. Until comparatively recently, extra-curricular activities were mainly training grounds for school teams and the elite performer. The situation has changed in recent years and membership of clubs is now usually open to children of all levels of ability. In an attempt to indicate the reasons for the differences between schools on the sociomotor factor a number of areas have been identified above for further investigation which will act as a starting point.

Cognitive-Reflective

The two questions which received the highest scores were both related to the contribution physical education can make to health and fitness (Q 2 and Q 15). One was concerned with the basic principles of endurance training and the other related to the ways sport can promote health. Slightly better scores were achieved by the high-scoring schools. S2 scored particularly highly on both questions. Consideration will be given to the content of the fitness element in the programmes of the selected schools and in particular whether specific schemes of work are allocated to health related fitness or incorporated within the normal programme of activities. It is relevant to point out that the average score for Q 2 was 2.26. Although positive, it suggested that there was some element of doubt in the pupils' minds about the principles involved in fitness training. The responses to 'how deviations in posture occur and can be correct ' (Q 11) was answered slightly positively in all schools but did not distinguish between the two types of schools. This contrasted with Q 20 where the high-scoring schools appeared to give greater guidance to their pupils in the organization of sporting activities. Recently within the profession there has been considerable emphasis on a 'teaching games for understanding' approach which requires pupils to become proficient in 'how' a skill is performed and in addition 'when' and 'why'. Thus there is a shift in emphasis to tactical awareness. Implicit within this approach is the provision of time for pupils to be allowed to create their own games in broad areas such as invasion, net/racket or striking/fielding games and establish principles of play which may be transferred to similar types of games. This may be a reason which could partly account for the differences. Alternatively, there may be greater encouragement in some schools to allow pupils to be involved in organizing sporting activities.

Two questions revealed a neutral or negative attitude and these were Q 17 appraising media reports (where S1 and S2 scored higher) and Q 21 relating sport to commerce and politics which were all negative with no consistent trend between the two sets of schools. Unless there was a CSE topic-based programme within the school it was unlikely that these areas would be part of the normal physical education programme. The large majority of pupils in this sample felt unsure about making an independent assessment of TV and newspaper reports or relating sport to commercial and political interests. These aspects will be probed further through an examination of the physical education curriculum and pupil interviews.

Affective

The high-scoring schools achieved higher scores for all the questions which comprised this factor. All the responses for all the schools were positive and this was especially true for the question concerning the pleasure pupils had obtained from participation in sport (Q 24). Not only did they enjoy taking part but they also enjoyed the physical exercise (Q 7). This was particularly noticeable for S1 with a mean score of 1.78 as opposed to S5 which had a mean score of 2.54. The reasons for this may be reflected in the aims of the department through the importance attached to the physical element. Discussion with pupils would also be valid. Most pupils indicated that they had a clear idea about their favourite sport (Q 5) and this was particularly apparent in S1 and S2. Almost all schools have a common core curriculum in physical education for the first three years and this is followed with varying degrees of choice. In this way pupils would have a solid base from which to choose their options and know their sporting likes and dislikes. This may be linked to Q 3 which showed that most pupils considered themselves able to cope with their sporting potential, great or small, and this suggested that programmes had accommodated the different levels of pupils' ability.

7
Strategies for Observation in Schools

To date, the study has highlighted a number of differences and similarities in the ways in which male and female teachers approach the teaching of educational gymnastics and netball or basketball. In addition, the behaviour of pupils in these lessons was recorded through ALT-PE and some tentative relationships with teacher behaviour were apparent. In an attempt to identify schools with differing attitudes to physical education, the Crum (1984) questionnaire was administered to 1780 boys and girls in the fourth form in fourteen secondary schools in south-east England. The resulting analyses revealed some statistically significant differences between schools.

In relation to teacher behaviour some important teaching patterns were identified which warranted further study together with differences between male and female teachers. Briefly, these were:

(a) in the Interactive Function categories of Organizing, Preparatory Instructing, Providing Equipment, Concurrent Instruction, Intervening Instruction, Observing Performance and Other Interacting (Motor),

(b) in the Subscript categories of Question and Answer techniques and teacher and/or pupil demonstration.

(c) In the Mode categories of Demonstrations which were either given by the teacher alone or involving pupils.

As far as pupil behaviour was concerned, the ALT-PE gave a clear indication of learner involvement with a time-on-task average of 24 per cent in educational gymnastics and netball/basketball lessons.

The Physical Education 'Learner Report' Questionnaire analyses enabled five schools to be chosen for further examination in the main study on the basis of the pupils' scores. The two highest scoring, two lowest scoring and one in the middle were chosen.

The task now was to spend an extended period of time in each school and make a detailed examination of as many of the above aspects as possible. There can be no doubt that one of the most important phases of the physical education process is the actual teaching of the lessons and the major part of the main study will focus on teaching and learning strategies. The pilot study had concentrated on an individual and a team activity, but it now seemed logical to extend these to all the activities that comprise physical education. This wider spectrum would give a truer perspective of the subject and also facilitate the observation of lessons in the schools. It is also relevant to point out that the schools had been chosen on the basis of the pupils' perceptions of the whole of the physical education curriculum and not selected aspects. Thus an analysis which incorporated a variety of activities in a variety of settings seemed justified. Whilst accepting the central importance of the lesson, the ethos and efficiency of any department is influenced by a number of other factors. For example, the construction of a subject curriculum which incorporates aims and objectives, content, teaching method and evaluation is essential to effective learning and planning and gives a sense of purpose and direction to staff. It should also ensure logical progression throughout the several years of secondary education and is especially important when the subject is being taught by more than one member of staff. Concentration on the teaching process would result in an incomplete picture of the work of a subject department and the main study needs to incorporate an assessment of departmental planning.

The pupil questionnaire identified some statistically significant differences in the four factors (viz. technomotor, sociomotor, cognitive-reflective and affective) between males and females and between schools, and these differences need to be probed.

Nearly all the data that had been obtained in the pilot study and that proposed so far in the main study would be quantitative in nature. The validity of this singular approach was recently questioned by Jewett and Bain (1985) who stated,

> Modern curriculum evaluation acknowledges two major approaches: (i) quantitative studies that emphasise numerical analysis of the most easily observed and empirically verifiable characteristics of the environment; and (ii) qualitative studies that are directed towards broader consideration of observed characteristics and the perception and description of specific qualities identified as personal forms of meaning.

Thus in qualitative evaluation, the observer has greater freedom of observation and interpretation and is more easily able to identify 'significant' incidents which may have particular relevance to an individual or group. However, there can sometimes be an 'expectancy effect' once schools have been labelled high or low scoring which can influence qualitative observations. This must be guarded against and a combination of both approaches would seem justified in the context of the present research.

In order to obtain a wider perspective on the issues that emerged, the following main research strategies were adopted:

1   Teacher behaviour: quantitative recording using pre-determined categories and qualitative recording that attempted to give insight into some of the qualities of the teaching and learning environment.
2   Pupil behaviour: quantitative recording using a group time sampling procedure and qualitative recording of learning situations.
3   Cognitive and motor engagement: a more detailed analysis of the breakdown of these categories would be revealing and should be incorporated. This can best be examined through some form of quantitative assessment.
4   Discussions with teachers: discussion with members of the department which would reflect their planning procedures as well as their aims for the subject.
5   Analysis of syllabuses: an analysis of the syllabuses should indicate the emphasis given to the main components of planning and provide a written statement of planning procedures.
6   Four questionnaire factors: the specific questions which comprised each factor were further analyzed through talking to the teachers, interviewing pupils and lesson observations. Sex differences were examined through statements made by the male and female teachers and through the lessons they taught.

Sample, Data Collection and Analysis

The sample consisted of five schools selected on the basis of the pupils' responses to the Physical Education 'Learner Report' Questionnaire. The two highest and the two lowest scoring schools were chosen because there were statistically significant differences between their average questionnaire scores. In addition, one school was chosen from the middle of the range. One week was spent in each school observing lessons and talking to staff and pupils. This enabled approximately fifteen lessons to be observed in each school. In total this gave a sample size of approximately seventy-five lessons. Additionally, the author was involved in teaching a small number of lessons in each school.

Quantitative Recording

In the pilot study, Anderson's Descriptive Category System had identified a number of differences in the ways in which male and female teachers conducted their lessons and also gave an indication of the nature of the teaching strategies adopted by physical education teachers in a narrow range of practical subjects. The data had been collected through videotape analysis and consideration was given to using this methodology again. However, in view of the reduced number of categories to be examined and the wider nature of the main study, it was decided to use a system that did not require the use of such sophisticated apparatus. In practical terms it would also eliminate the problems of moving apparatus from one setting to the next in a school — especially when the settings were either off-site or on playing fields some distance away from the power supply. Another reason for moving away from camera recording was that the equipment required the constant attention of the author as operator and any analysis would have to take place some time after the lesson was taught. This would therefore make it difficult to make accurate qualitative judgements about a lesson in the actual setting and context in which it took place.

There was obviously a close link between the teaching pattern and the cognitive and motor engaged time and it was considered advantageous if this could be included in the observation procedure. An integration of the teacher behaviour and pupil engagement categories would lead to a clearer understanding of the teaching-learning process.

A methodology was available which had been extensively used in research during the last four years. With minor modifications it incorporated most of the requirements in relation to teacher behaviour and to

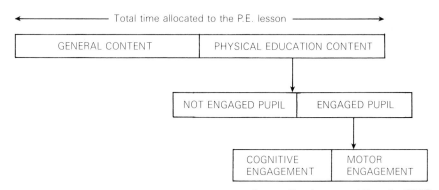

Source: Tousignant and Brunelle (1982).

Figure 1: The major components of the learning time variables.

87

pupils' cognitive and motor engagement. The proposed analysis system was based on Siedentop, Tousignant and Parker's (1982) ALT-PE system (First Level) which required decisions relating to the context of the lesson to be made while the lesson was in progress. Diagrammatically, the major component of the learning time variables are shown in Figure 1.

The system takes into account all the time that is allocated to the physical education activity in the actual setting (for example, gymnasium or swimming pool). Time devoted to changing and showering is not included. Thus the observations start when the teacher begins the lesson in the practical area. Decisions concerning the categorization of the class activity were based on the 'dominant behaviour' or the majority of the class participation.

During the period of observation, the coder has first to make decisions whether the pupils were in the general or physical education content. General content 'refers to class time when pupils are not intended to be involved in physical education activities'. Time devoted to organization, management or physical warm up would be examples in this broad area. Physical education content 'refers to the class time when the primary focus is on knowledge or motor involvement in physical education activities'. During any lesson there are times when pupils are not engaged when, for example, some pupils are waiting or not performing in the lesson. The vast majority however will be involved in either cognitive engagement (where the focus is on knowledge of techniques or strategies related to the activity) or motor engagement which incorporates the actual physical practices of motor skills. Siedentop *et al* (1982) suggest that all the above major components sub-divide into smaller categories as follows:

General content: transition, management, break, warm up.
Knowledge: technique, strategy, rules, social behaviour, background.
Motor: skill practice, scrimmage (applied practices), game, fitness.

Each of the above categories is defined in appendix 4.

The sub-category 'transition' closely paralleled the organizing category definition in Anderson's system. The only discrepancy was 'changing equipment' and as this was a particular area requiring further analysis, it was decided to add providing equipment to the general content list. The original definition was retained, viz. 'interacting to provide equipment or getting the environment ready'.

The amount of time spent on preparatory instruction had been identified as a major teaching behaviour in need of further analysis. The five sub-divisions of knowledge related to physical education content comprised the kind of behaviour that was associated with the teacher giving preparatory instruction and it was considered reasonable to make this inference.

The one major teaching behaviour which did not appear was the important area of feedback. In the pilot study, 27 per cent of the teachers' time was spent in either concurrent or intervening instruction and was of sufficient importance to attempt a separate analysis. The provision of appropriate feedback is essential to all teaching and learning situations. The original recordings merely provided a quantitative record of the instances of feedback. A feedback record which indicated its character (positive, negative or neutral), form (auditory, auditory-tactile or auditory-visual); direction (one pupil, group of pupils or whole class); timing (concurrent or intervening) and social reinforcement (positive or negative motivational comments containing no informational detail about the performance) were considered to be of greater value.

A system which included all these factors would incorporate 72 per cent of the interactive functions of teacher behaviour observed in the pilot study. Admittedly, the categories were not identical but were similar enough to warrant comparison, would give additional insights into the class behaviour and would go some way to make links between the teaching-learning process. In addition, further information would be gleaned concerning the proportion of time allocated to cognitive and motor engagement.

The videotapes had enabled a study to be made of the pupils' as well as the teachers' behaviour. This had been done through ALT-PE at the second level which focused on the individual pupil through the two main sub-divisions of not motor engaged and motor engaged. The results had proved informative and it was considered important to retain this method of analysis. Without the videotape recording this would now have to be done in a 'live' situation through scanning the class at prescribed intervals. This would probably be slightly less accurate than when using VTR procedures, especially when the class was involved in motor activities. However, a measure of reliability could be established by coding the pilot study videotapes without stopping the tape and then comparing the results with the original ALT-PE recordings.

There are a number of ways in which ALT-PE can be measured and a combination of these methods needed to be amalgamated into the present system. Because of the complex nature of all the information required from the analyses, these methods had to complement each other, otherwise it would have been impossible for the recorder to cope with the on-site recording.

It was considered that the context of the lesson needed to be continuous in order that an accurate account could be made of the amount of time a class was involved in a particular category. Thus, duration recording was thought to be the most appropriate. With regard to teachers' feedback, individual time sampling was considered to be appropriate. Using this method, details were recorded every third minute concerning the specific nature of any teacher feedback. To record the pupils' behaviour through ALT-PE, group time sampling at pre-determined intervals was chosen. This allowed the observer to scan the whole class every third minute and record the number of pupils involved in the not motor engaged and motor engaged categories.

A coding sheet similar to that suggested by Siedentop *et al* (1982) was devised and is set out in appendix 5. The central column headed 'context' is marked into minutes and further sub-divided every fifteen seconds. A line is drawn across the column which denotes the beginning of a particular context category and the code initial written under that line. When the context changes, another horizontal line is drawn across the column to denote the end of that particular category. The second space is marked with the new code. At the end of a lesson, the time in each category can be added and then presented as a percentage of the total lesson time.

On the left hand side of the central column between the first and second minute and thereafter every third minute, detailed recordings are made of every instance of feedback behaviour by the teacher.

Group time sampling of the pupils' behaviour is carried out every third minute and is recorded in the box on the right hand side of the central column. To code the behaviour of every pupil it will be necessary to scan the whole of the class in a pre-determined way — usually from left to right. When the class is moving it will be difficult to ensure that every pupil is included in the scan but the large majority should be included using this method.

Siedentop (1983) stated, 'ALT-PE is probably the best single criterion variable now available for making on-site judgements about teaching effectiveness.' The system has been extensively used over the past four years in student teaching practice situations and research studies. Once familiarity with the system has been mastered, the coding process will not take up all the observer's time and this will allow him the opportunity to make qualitative judgements about other aspects of the teaching and learning process which is a requirement of this particular study.

Establishing Reliability

There are three ways in which it was proposed to establish an acceptable level of reliability prior to visiting schools. Firstly, Siedentop *et al* (1982) have produced a sequential set of written tasks in their coding manual to help the observer become familiar with the system. These tasks involve learning the definitions and the symbol system, assigning behaviours to descriptions of actual class and/or teacher behaviours and then familiarity with the use of the coding sheet. These tasks were answered on several different occasions until complete agreement was achieved with the coding manual. Few difficulties were experienced, but it did help to clarify the meanings and interpretations of some categories.

Secondly, it was possible to use the coding procedure with the original pilot study videotapes. Initially using feedback, context and learner involvement separately and then in combination. A direct comparison of the learner involvement should be possible with the original data and give a measure of intra-observer reliability. Some problems were encountered at this second stage. The separate recording of the context level, learner involvement and feedback did not pose too many problems. However, once combinations were attempted, the process became more difficult. A combination of the three became all-consuming and did not allow time to form impressions or concentrate on critical incidents. The observer felt continuously pressurised to record. As a result, the recording became very intense and required a lot of concentration. Of even more concern was the realization that errors began to occur. With the possibility of five hours recording each day it was felt that the reliability might seriously be affected.

It was not possible to match the recordings with the original pilot study codings. For example, pupil behaviour had been 'stopped' on the videotape at a precise second, whereas with the continuous recording the observer had scanned the class from left to right which could have taken anything between ten and fifteen seconds. Thus there was a different time sample and in some cases a different grouping of pupils if the camera had moved during the time span.

The biggest problems were experienced with the feedback which was recorded every third minute. It proved to be difficult to record the five different aspects of feedback when there were changes taking place within the context of the lesson. This was especially true when the teacher gave several instances of feedback to pupils in rapid succession.

Some amendments were considered to be necessary and the details included in the feedback recordings were reduced and placed outside the context of the lesson. Accordingly, three columns were drawn to the side of the main sheet to indicate the nature of the feedback as either positive, positive with information about the performance, or negative. The number of times each form of feedback was used was recorded. It was recognized that some interesting data would be excluded from the analysis but perhaps detail of this nature warrants a separate study. The amended ALT-PE Coding Sheet 2 (appendix 6) proved to be entirely satisfactory and at the end of seven different videotaped lessons, intra–observer reliability levels of the major categories were all in excess of 85 per cent.

Again, the only slight problem was the placing of pupil behaviour in the motor appropriate or inappropriate category. With the scanning procedures in operation, it was difficult to decide if pupils were practising at an 'easy level of difficulty.' Without prior knowledge of a pupil's ability and the lack of time to observe each individual, nearly all the codings were placed in the motor appropriate category.

Finally, once an acceptable level of reliability was achieved, coding then took place in actual physical education lessons. A volleyball and a gymnastic lesson were coded using the amended system. Occasionally, it was not possible to hear the teacher giving feedback to pupils if the noise in the gymnasium was too high or the teacher was speaking to individuals or a group some distance from the observer. These instances were not recorded. Apart from this, the system appeared to be functioning properly and the observer felt confident and comfortable to do the recording in schools and at the same time form qualitative impressions of teaching and learning.

The successful completion of these stages had now placed the observer in a position to collect reliable data in the schools.

Qualitative Recording

The study has generated a lot of quantitative data related to learning and teaching effectiveness — all of which can be objectively evaluated. However, it is important to emphasize the quality of any educational experience and this needs to be taken into account in the evaluation procedure. There is no suggestion that one method is better than the other. They are merely different and when combined can give greater insight into the teaching and learning process in physical education.

In making qualitative judgements about lessons, it is valid to have a number of prepared questions to act as guidelines. However, this does allow other significant incidents to be included as and when they occur. One of the advantages of having some form of framework is that it assists in making comparisons if a similar framework is used in each school. Wherever possible, the responses to questions will be illuminated by teachers' and pupils' comments. The comments of the pupils are seen as being particularly important and these will be elicited during and at the end of lessons.

During the observation of lessons, qualitative judgements were made to the following questions:

1 Is the teacher able to communicate effectively?
2 Is there a good working atmosphere in the class?
3 Does the teacher have a sound subject knowledge?
4 Does mutual respect and confidence exist between the teacher and the pupils?
5 Is the class organization effective?
6 What is the quality of the question and answer techniques used?
7 Does the teacher involve the pupils in demonstrations?
8 Is there logical and related progression in the lesson?
9 Do the practices cater for individual differences?
10 Is the teacher consistently fair in his/her dealings with pupils?
11 Does the teacher value each pupil's contribution?
12 Are the pupils interested and motivated in the lesson?
13 Are the pupils cognitively, motorically and affectively involved in their work?

This is by no means an exhaustive list but it does provide a basis on which to begin qualitative evaluation.

There were statistically significant differences between the two high-scoring and two low-scoring schools in each of the four factors identified in the Physical Education 'Learner Report' Questionnaire. In addition there were significant differences between the responses of the males and females in factors technomotor, sociomotor and cognitive reflective. No differences were found in the affective factor. The factors were based on a number of questions which contributed to the naming of a particular factor. As differences had been highlighted through the pupils' answers to these questions, it seemed logical to examine the causes of these differences by attempting to obtain answers to the same questions through observations in the schools.

Discussions with Teachers

The planning of the physical education curriculum in any school is the sole prerogative of the staff who teach the subject and is the ultimate responsibility of the head of department. Consideration was given to using a similar questionnaire to the one administered by Underwood (1983) to a large national sample of departmental heads on *The Planning and Implementation of the Physical Education Curriculum.* However, it did not seem entirely appropriate to do so for a number of reasons. One of the main concerns was that the generated data would only provide a limited insight into the answers to some of the questions. Such is the nature of this type of questionnaire which only allows a limited and often pre-specified choice of response. Another reason was that the questionnaire would only have been directed to the head of department and whilst he or she is in charge of the department, the views of all the staff were considered to be important. The questionnaire could have been given to all the staff which would have provided some insight into their planning procedures, but it would not have overcome the rather 'barren' nature of the information. Lastly, more quantitative data would have been generated. All the research strategies in a study should link together and complement each other. In this case it was felt that a more wide-ranging approach which included interviewing members of the department would be more appropriate and enable the author to probe particular issues that had arisen during the visits to the schools.

Accordingly, it was decided to conduct an interview towards the end of the visit to the school. Kerlinger (1973) identified three main formats for conducting interviews and these were structured, unstructured and partly structured. The questions in structured interviews were pre-specified, rather formal in nature and allowed no deviation from the prepared order. However, comparisons between schools would be comparatively straightforward. At the other end of the scale, unstructured interviews encouraged a very flexible and open-ended approach. Whilst the information generated would have been interesting, it would have been almost impossible to have made comparisons between schools because the discussions may well have revolved round different issues. As neither of these methods appeared to be particularly suitable to the requirements of this research, consideration was given to the partly-structured interview. This method allowed topic areas to be pre-specified together with a number of prepared questions in each area. The order in which the questions were asked was flexible and it did not preclude the discussion of issues which were particularly relevant to one school. This allowed for a more fluid type of discussion and enabled comparisons to be made between schools. As all the schools in the sample were mixed schools, this was reflected in the staffing and it was decided to invite all members of the department to take part in the discussion. This was especially important in view of the sex differences that had been identified in the teaching of physical education, the pupils' involvement in lessons and their attitudes to the subject.

In order to obtain an accurate account of the discussions, it was decided to tape record the interviews. Objections to this form of recording are raised because of the inhibitory effect it may have on the interviewees. Whilst accepting that this will vary with the individual, any such inhibitions did not mar previous interviews with physical education teachers about their planning procedures conducted by the author in 1983. One important difference in this case was that there were a number of staff present which would result in a group discussion and lessen individual concerns about having their views tape recorded.

Having established the procedure, it was now necessary to select the appropriate questions to probe some of the issues that had been identified. Based on Underwood's (1983) study, these were categorized under the following headings:

1 Planning Procedures
How is the physical education curriculum planned?
Are the male and female departments separate or integrated?
Is there a written syllabus available?
Do you have regular department meetings?

2 Aims and Objectives
What are the main aims of physical education in this school?
Are the aims and objectives communicated to the children?
Do you cater specifically for health and fitness?

3 Content
Is there any mixed physical education in the curriculum?
Is there a 'balance' in the amount of time devoted to different activities?
Has a 'time analysis' been made for each activity?
Are there any principles or guidelines for selecting content?
Is there a common core followed by options?

4 Learning Experiences
Is there horizontal planning throughout the year?
Is there vertical planning and progression between years?
Are all extra-curricular activities open to all children?
Is an attempt made to ensure that each pupil experiences a range of activities for example individual, team, mixed, aquatic, expressive?
Is attendance at physical education lessons in the senior school optional or compulsory?

5 Evaluation
How do you judge the success of the physical education curriculum?
Do you try to evaluate your original aims?
How is the school report on each pupil's progress formulated?

6 Additional Factors
Are there any aspects of planning that you consider to be important which have not been included?

Answers to the above questions should give an insight into the planning procedures adopted in the schools and copies of any physical education syllabuses will be obtained and analyzed wherever possible. The resulting information should go some way towards indicating differences both between and within schools.

There will inevitably be other areas which will warrant discussion but these will emerge during the course of the visits to schools and cannot be pre-specified. Indeed the spontaneous nature of any additional areas gives reality and increased 'ecological validity' to the investigation.

Pupils' Opinions

The opinions of pupils about their attitudes to physical education was sought in two different ways.

Informal Discussion or Comments

Whenever the opportunity presented itself, the author talked to pupils and encouraged them to talk about their perceptions of physical education. This happened through comments made during the lesson, talking to pupils in the changing room before and after a lesson and talking to pupils who were unable to take part in a particular period. The author also taught some classes and was able to elicit pupils' opinions in a different setting.

Interviews With Pupils

A number of discussion questions were formulated which were based on the Physical Education 'Learner Report' Questionnaire. The inventory of questions was given to four pupils from year 4 or year 5. Pupils from the upper school were chosen as they had already experienced the greater part of the physical education curriculum planned for the school. The staff in the department were asked to select pupils who could be classified as either of high or low ability — one male and one female in each category.

The discussion began with two general questions about their feelings towards, and experiences in, physical education and the remaining questions were categorized under the factor headings from the questionnaire. The schedule was as follows:

Introduction
What do you think of physical education?
What has happened in physical education that makes you feel like this?

Technomotor
Do you have enough time in lessons to practise your physical skills?
Do you think you have learnt to perform on the gymnastic apparatus?
Do you know most of the rules of well-known sports?
(How have they been taught to you?)
Have you been taught any principles of games–playing which can be applied to all sports (for example in attack or defence)?

Sociomotor
If you are playing with others who are either better or not as good as you, do you find you can still join in and cooperate with them?
Is there any opportunity to play sports with members of the opposite sex?
What is your reaction if there is someone in a group activity who is not good enough and cannot cope? (Adapt rules? Accept or reject?)
Do you belong to any physical education clubs or teams? (Why?)

Cognitive-reflective
Can you give me any examples of sponsorship in sport?
What do you think about sponsorship?
Which English city recently made a bid for the 1992 Olympics? (Why?)
How is it possible to develop strength or endurance?
Do you know how deviations in posture can occur?
Are you ever involved in organizing any sport?

Affective
Do you get any pleasure from taking part in physical education?
Do you enjoy the physical exercise? (Is it challenging enough?)
What is your favourite practical activity in physical education?
Do you consider physical education has enabled you to make the most of your physical talents?

Thus a variety of methods incorporating quantitative and qualitative evaluation, together with discussions with the teachers and pupils, were used to gain insight into the teaching and learning of physical education in a school setting.

Chapter 8
Evaluating the Effectiveness of a Physical Education Department: Five Case Studies

Having established the procedures for the quantitative and qualitative analysis in the schools, the author approached the five schools that had been identified as significantly different from each other. Permission was sought to spend one week in each school observing the teaching of physical education and talking to the staff and pupils. The headteachers and heads of department readily agreed to the request and a preliminary visit was made to each school explaining the purposes of the observation and meeting all members of the departments.

During each observation week, the author acted as a member of the department and was appropriately dressed for teaching the subject. As well as observing and talking to the teachers and pupils, the author was also involved in the teaching of small groups and, on a few occasions, a class of children. Through these different approaches it was hoped to gain a thorough insight into the work of each department.

The main hypothesis to be tested was that, based on the results of the Physical Education 'Learner Report' Questionnaire, S1 and S2 would be more efficient and effective in their teaching of physical education than S4 and S5. (S3 was a 'control' school which was not significantly different from either pairing.) In addition, the investigation probed the similarities and differences in teaching styles between the male and female staff as well as between different activities. With this background the author spent one week in each school collecting data with which to test the hypotheses.

Case Study: School 1 (S1) — Amos Secondary School

This school was a large secondary modern school in a semi-rural setting. There were four double periods each day on the timetable and each period was of 1 hour and 10 minutes duration with a break of at least fifteen minutes after each lesson to cover any necessary travelling time between two buildings. Each class had two periods of physical education each week. During the observation week thirteen lessons were observed and coded according to the ALT-PE format. Of these seven were taught by the male and six by the female staff. The average length of these lessons was forty-seven-and-a-half minutes of practical working time and this excluded the time needed for changing and showering at the beginning and end of every lesson. In addition three other lessons were either taught or observed by the author.

Staffing

There were four full-time physical education staff (two male and two female), all of whom had received specialist training in the subject. In addition, two other staff contributed one-half and one-quarter of their timetable to physical education — both of these staff were well qualified in the subject.

Since the administration of the questionnaire one important change had occurred in that the head of department had left the school and been replaced on a temporary basis. The headteacher was in the process of interviewing for a new head of department but at the time of the visit no appointment had been made. As a result, the department was working without the clear direction of a leader. In spite of this it is important to record that the group of teachers were working together cooperatively during this interim period.

Facilities

As already mentioned, the school was on two sites. One site had a well-equipped hall/gymnasium and a playground area, but the majority of the facilities were on the other site and comprised a large indoor heated sports hall and a particularly large and well-equipped gymnasium. Staff also had their own spacious changing rooms in this area. There was a large playground marked for netball and tennis, and extensive playing fields adjoining the sports complex. There was no shortage of equipment and there were adequate storage rooms in all the practical areas.

As well as the very good facilities available at the school, the pupils in the fourth and fifth years used the nearby community sports centre for one period each week. The facilities at the centre were excellent and included a larger indoor heated swimming pool and a learner pool, a huge indoor area for badminton, basketball and trampolining, squash courts, a weight training room, a golf driving range and a dry ski slope. With the addition of these facilities, the school had excellent accommodation in which to conduct its physical education programme.

Dress

Wearing the appropriate dress for the activity was stressed for both staff and pupils. There was a school uniform for physical education and this was worn by most pupils. Some relaxation of these rules was allowed for senior pupils. In gymnastics all the pupils had to perform in bare feet and the staff also followed this ruling. Many of the girls wore leotards for gymnastics and dance. Overall, the pupils were well dressed for physical education. At the end of every lesson there was an insistence that pupils showered and this was rigorously enforced. Invariably, the staff were appropriately and smartly dressed for the activity they were teaching and set a good example.

Structure and Content

A varied programme was observed which included gymnastics, basketball, volleyball, hockey, swimming and over-the-net activities. Several of these lessons were taught with boys and girls in the same class. Indeed, mixed physical education classes were to be found in every year except the third. True integration was observed on a number of occasions. For example, in a first year gymnastics lesson, the children worked in mixed groups and helped and supported each other on the floor and on the apparatus. This was done quite naturally and appeared to be an extension of the class organization they had experienced in the primary school. Basketball in the fourth year was also mixed and was accepted by the pupils. Certainly some of the girls were equally as skilful as the boys and took a full part in the playing of the game. During discussion with pupils who were waiting to substitute in the game, they all expressed the opinion that they were 'happy to play mixed basketball'. In contrast to this true integration there were times when the 'mixed' was in name only. Second year boys and girls were reluctant to play badminton with each other and in gymnastics all the groupings separated out according to sex. Thus in some classes mixed physical education was being implemented in the true sense of the word, whereas in others the implementation was only being partially fulfilled.

The teaching of gymnastics provided a number of contrasts. One first year lesson was probably the best taught lesson of any activity in any of the schools. There were many reasons for this. The lesson was well planned with the warm-up related to the floor sequences which in turn related to the large apparatus work. Thus the progression was logical and clear. The tasks set were challenging and the children worked hard. The teacher was a knowledgeable and creative gymnast and often suggested ideas verbally as well as through her own personal performance. The important point was that the suggested movements were within the upper ability range of the pupils. The teacher was often smiling and had established an excellent class-teacher relationship with the group. Consequently everyone was working purposefully in a creative and busy atmosphere. The fact that the teacher stressed the importance of hard work and informed practice ensured the pupils had specific goals to aim for. The large apparatus was handled correctly and was placed into position quickly and efficiently. This resulted in a high 'time-on-task' and the motor appropriate recording of 47 per cent was particularly high for a gymnastics lesson. The children cooperated and helped each other and produced high quality work. There was evidence of real learning and improvement taking place within the lesson. This contrasted with a second year group who spent the whole of a lesson lasting fifty-three minutes on floor work without using the large apparatus. An inordinately long time was spent on a sequence of work on a mat which resulted in some boredom and mediocre work. Much more stimulus and challenge was necessary — especially for the able gymnasts in the group.

A rather more formal type of gymnastics was taught to two different classes in the third year. Both the classes needed firm handling and the teacher had good control. There was a lot of technical detail involved in the execution of particular movements and this comprised almost one-third of the lesson time. The responses of the two classes to similarly taught lessons were strikingly different. In one the pupils responded positively, asked questions and were generally cooperative. There were over fifty instances of positive feedback and this appeared to foster a supportive climate which led to even more success. Overall, this was a very satisfactory lesson. The other class responded quite differently and produced little work of any quality. Seventeen positive feedback statements were made by the teacher but these were mainly at the beginning of the lesson and tailed off dramatically as uncooperative and unruly behaviour developed. The reasons for this development were not clearly apparent but the class obviously did not react positively to the large amount of technical detail (32 per cent) associated with the gymnastic routine. Also, fifteen minutes was spent jumping on and off a bench. Although the lesson structure was similar to the other third year class, this group experienced difficulty in creating movement ideas. As a result, some pupils started to opt out whenever they could and become 'bystanders'. The low motor appropriate recording of 11 per cent was the lowest recording of any lesson in any school.

The games teaching also provided a series of contrasts. One first year netball lesson taken on the playground area on a cold day was a typical example of positive teaching of a directed games lesson. Because of the inclement weather the teacher sensibly began with and long and active warm up. This was followed with some dodging and passing activities under competitive conditions which were replicas of situations that would be met within a game. The second half of the lesson was devoted to games playing in two six-a-side games which were alternately coached by the teacher. The pupils responded well to this lesson. Because it was very cold the teacher kept the instructions down to a minimum and the explanations clear and precise. Effective class organization resulted in no waiting and a high motor involvement with 72 per cent being recorded in the motor appropriate category. A similar lesson format was followed in a hockey lesson to third year boys but with less success. The problem here was that some pupils would not commit themselves to cooperate within the lesson and this manifested itself by pupils not feeding the ball to the correct side in the technique practices, deliberately hitting the ball too hard for their partner to control and stopping the ball with the foot. This kind of behaviour undermined the effectiveness of the practices and impaired the learning. One volleyball lesson with a mixed group from the fourth year had the least educational content of any lesson observed in any school. The lesson began badly in that it took seven minutes to assemble the necessary equipment while the pupils sat down on the benches and did nothing. The introductory practice, for which twenty-one pupils were divided into three groups, involved keeping a ball in the air using the hands. Little or no teaching took place and the practice degenerated into a noisy free-for-all which bore little resemblance to the original task. Two-thirds of the lesson was spent playing a game during which time the teacher sat on a bench and gave no help or feedback to the pupils. This was reflected in an overall subject knowledge input of 1 per cent and a 0 per cent recording in the cognitive category of learner involvement. The teacher only intervened when it was necessary to change teams. Even with a high games playing element to the lesson, 48 per cent of the pupils' time was spent waiting. There was no feedback, no demonstration and no challenge. Needless to say it was highly unlikely that any positive learning took place. It was almost certainly a negative experience for most of the group. The fact that the class laughed at pupils who failed to keep the ball in play because of a lack of skill could only have had a detrimental effect in the long term. This was an experience the pupils could well have done without.

Sometimes the warm-up practices in volleyball and basketball did not appear to have much relationship to the game that was eventually to be played. Typically, relays were used to start the lesson either with or without the ball. There would appear to be two main functions of a warm up. One is to condition the body physiologically in order that no muscle strains occur and the other is to familiarize the performer with already established ball skills. Lessons which begin with competitive relays fail on both these counts. To engage in a flat-out run over a short distance from a stationary start without a preliminary warm up is conducive to injury. It also means that only one member of the team is participating while the remainder are waiting and watching. In these situations, ball skills can only be practised by a relatively small proportion of the class and it would be better to consider using activities which involve more pupils with more apparatus. In this way the intensity of the physical workload can be increased gradually and there is greater opportunity to practice ball handling skills. As there was no shortage of equipment or space in the working area, the warm-up practices in some lessons were not effective for the reasons outlined above. One final comment about this form of introduction is that it is not related to the main part of the lesson and therefore does not provide a consistent theme.

Most games lessons incorporated several small-sided team games which were miniature versions of the full game. The teachers spent their time coaching these games and mostly displayed a competent knowledge in the activity, although, there were one or two exceptions to this. In the main, the pupils reacted well to these situations and played with a great deal of enthusiasm and commitment.

During the past year the games course in the first two years had been taught through a 'games for understanding' approach which involved the children learning skills and knowledge of a game through playing the game or an adapted version. Thus, an understanding of the principles of play such as creating and denying space is experienced early in the course and can be applied to many situations. The department had identified five main concepts which replicated Bunker and Thorpe's (1982) ideas and which they considered to be vital to this method of teaching. These were that (i) the game should closely parallel the adult version bearing in mind the children's abilities; (ii) the development of an appreciation of the rules of the game; (iii) the development of an understanding of tactical awareness and the principles of play common to all games; (iv) through a problem-solving approach pupils would be able to make decisions based on the environmental circumstances and a recognition of the relevant cues; and (v) techniques and skills should be taught as required in a particular game. Four lessons were observed which attempted to incorporate this approach in 'over-the-net' activities. Three of these lessons were devoted to the development of skills and techniques in badminton or volleyball and the content reflected the traditional format of games lessons. Only passing reference was made to tactical aspects or the reasons for decision-making as outlined above. Indeed, one group was taught the techniques of the dig and underarm serve in their first volleyball lesson. Next week the lesson content was to be allocated to badminton. Both these activities had a rightful place in any 'over-the-net' programme but to change the activity after only one lesson did not allow for the consolidation of any skills that may have been learnt. It may have been possible that there was some misunderstanding about the principles behind this approach. Only one lesson attempted to use the 'games for understanding' principles of teaching. In this instance, the teacher was asking the pupils such questions as 'How could you stop an opponent getting the ball?' or 'How can you move your opponent about the court?' Answers to these types of question were elicited from the pupils and then attempts were made to solve them in movement situations. Thus, the concepts identified above as being essential to this approach were being followed in this instance, but this was not the case with some staff. It was probably not coincidence that the correct approach was being followed by the member of staff who had attended a course on this subject. Some staff needed greater knowledge and under-standing of the concepts involved. Until this consensus is achieved, it will be difficult to develop the games programme logically.

The department had recently instituted a separate health and fitness course which was part of the physical education programme for the first three years. The purpose in starting in the first year was to encourage pupils to develop a positive attitude to their personal health and fitness from the start. The practical elements of the course included circuit training, interval and cross-country running, aerobics and fitness tests, while associated topics such as hygiene, diet, smoking, and drugs were also discussed. Many of the results from the practical activities were scored on record cards which enabled each pupil to monitor his or her own fitness level. During the second year, outside speakers and videos were scheduled to enhance and impress the importance of a healthy lifestyle and comp-lemented the practical work. A continuation of this programme was available in the third year but the details were not specified. Unfortunately, none of this work was time-tabled during the observation week apart from one class which ran a cross-country route. Because of this it was not possible to observe any of the lessons at first hand.

As mentioned earlier, the local sports centre was used by the senior pupils on one occasion each week. Every pupil had to pay a small fee on entry and this was not subsidized by the school. Presumably they welcomed the opportunity to use the excellent facilities available to them and, so far, no pupil had refused to pay the entrance fee. The visits also served another purpose in that they introduced and familiarized the pupils with the centre. Hopefully, they would continue to use these facilities in their leisure time once they had left school. Having made these arrangements at the sports centre, it was necessary to examine the quality of the experiences encountered by the pupils. In a fourth year basketball group, most of the time was spent playing a five-a-side game. This meant that several were on the side lines and a percentage score of 34 was recorded in the waiting category. The lesson was mainly recreative with little teaching taking place. The teacher did not appear to be particularly knowledgeable in the activity and the coaching was at a very basic level. A 4 per cent knowledge input tended to support this contention. With unlimited space available it seemed a pity not to involve all the pupils all the time. In another area of the sports hall a trampoline group was under instruction but ten pupils to one piece of apparatus resulted in a lot of waiting for a turn. Several badminton courts were being used but none of the pupils was under instruction. In fact, some pupils were playing a game with members of the public who were using the courts at the same time.

Weight training has become a popular activity over the last few years and a dozen pupils (mainly girls) were using a multi-gym in the weight training area. Some initial instruction had been given on the use of the apparatus and all appeared to be familiar with the activities at the different exercise stations. All the pupils were busy and active and only using light weights. A discussion with the pupils revealed that they had no understanding of the concepts behind weight training or how to develop the different fitness areas of strength and endurance. They were just doing what they had been told to do. No attempt had been made to assess maximum performance on an exercise and then take a percentage for training purposes dependent on which component of fitness was to be developed. Thus it appeared that maximum benefit was not being derived from the activity.

Another option allowed pupils to use the swimming pool and this was supervised by the staff at the centre who acted as life guards and gave no instruction. Again the session was recreative. The eleven pupils in the group thoroughly enjoyed the time doing exactly what they wanted to do. About half was spent diving and jumping from the 1 metre board and the other half playing a 'no rules' games of water polo. There was a great deal of noise and laughter throughout. The work load of one pupil, Sarah, was monitored over a period of thirty-eight minutes. During that time she swam a total of approximately 160 metres, made eight dives from the diving board and five entries from the poolside, and made two passes in the water polo game. Sarah would have been classed as an average swimmer and her physical involvement was typical of the girls within the group. The boys would probably have had a slightly higher work rate. The physical commitment was markedly low and contained little of any educational worth.

One of the reasons for this lack of instruction was that not enough staff were available to supervise every activity. Although it was admirable to offer the pupils a choice of activity, this was at the expense of having a teacher present who could teach the group. As a result, staff were often acting in a supervisory role for two or three activities. This meant that the programme of work for each group was not being planned to ensure the development of skills in a logical and related order. On educational grounds the quality of experience encountered by many of the pupils left much to be desired because of the lack of teaching.

Extra-Curricular Activities

As in most schools there had been little extra-curricular activity over the last year because of industrial action. The situation was gradually returning to normal with the advent of after-school practices and weekend fixtures. Over the years the school had achieved a satisfactory record in competitive games and many of the teams had been successful. The headteacher gave support to a number of ventures in term-time and these included residential outdoor activities courses as well as ski trips to Europe. The physical education staff were keen to re-establish extra-curricular activities and regarded them as an important part of the contribution they made to the life of the school.

Questionnaire Factors

The Physical Education 'Learner Report' Questionnaire had revealed four main factors and the mean scores for the male and female pupils on each factor were subjected to a t-test for independent samples (separate variance). The results are set out in table 22.

Table 22: S1: T-test on PE 'Learner Report' Questionnaire factors for male and female pupils

Factor	Male		Female		
	Mean	*SD*	*Mean*	*SD*	*p*
Technomotor	1.85	0.65	1.99	0.66	N.S.
Sociomotor	1.81	0.74	2.13	0.49	<0.01
Cognitive-reflective	2.27	0.54	2.99	0.88	<0.01
Affective	1.64	0.69	1.60	0.66	N.S.

The above results indicated that male pupils were significantly different from female pupils in their scores on the sociomotor and cognitive-reflective factors. In both instances the male pupils had a higher score. A subjective analysis of the lessons could not account for these differences — especially in the sociomotor factor which was concerned with interpersonal relationships as most of the classes contained a mixture of boys and girls. One important variable that was not possible to take into account was the effect and influence of the head of department who had left the previous term. His attitude and teaching style may have had an influence on these results but this is speculative.

Both groups scored the affective factor highest and having observed the physical education programme in the senior school this was not surprising. The generally recreative nature of the work in conducive surroundings would inevitably lead to high enjoyment by the pupils. In turn this may have influenced the second ranked mean score for male pupils on the sociomotor factor which was concerned with the relationships between pupils. It was rather surprising to find the technomotor factor ranked third for male pupils as the development of motor skills is generally regarded as one of the major aims of physical education. The same trend was not apparent for the female pupils and as many of the senior classes were mixed it is difficult to suggest the reason for this difference.

Academic Learning Time — Physical Education

ALT-PE data for the content level for the thirteen lessons taught by the male and female teachers in S1 are presented in appendix 7 and summary data in table 23.

In this school male teachers spent proportionately more time on general content and in particular on transition behaviour related to managerial and organizational activities related to instruction.

No differences were noted in the overall amount of PE knowledge content but the distributions within this overall category were different. Male staff spent almost twice as much time than their female colleagues on

Table 23: S1: Average percentage time spent by male and female teachers on general content, PE knowledge content and PE motor content

	Male %	Female %
General content	29.3	20.2
PE knowledge content	18.0	17.5
PE motor content	52.7	62.0

Table 24: S1: Average percentage of pupil time spent in ALT-PE learner involvement categories when taught by male and female staff

Not motor engaged	Male %	Female %
Interim	0.1	0.7
Waiting	19.0	17.0
Off-task	0.4	0.1
On-task	23.3	15.7
Cognitive	20.9	19.5
Motor engaged		
Motor appropriate	36.1	46.2
Motor inappropriate	0.3	0.0
Supporting	0.0	1.0

the technical aspects of motor skills whereas the reverse trend was true for the strategical aspects of skill acquisition. The emphasis on the techniques of a particular skill inevitably led to a greater proportion of time (24.4 per cent to 12.5 per cent) being spent on skill practices outside the applied context by male teachers. Conversely, female teachers spent more time on strategies and plans for action and game playing. Well over half the lessons were devoted to the motor content but almost 10 per cent more of the lesson was apportioned to this by female teachers.

The average percentage of time pupils spent in the learner involvement categories is set out in table 24.

The above data revealed that pupils spent over one-sixth of every lesson waiting for a turn which was a high proportion. Male teachers encouraged more on–task behaviour from their pupils and this was directly linked to their greater use of transitional and organizational factors. Conversely, female teachers engaged their pupils in more motor appropriate behaviour (46.2 per cent to 36.1 per cent).

Because many of the lessons in S1 were mixed, it is important to note that the learner involvement percentages do not reflect the sex of the teachers.

Planning Procedures

As stated earlier, it was not possible to talk to the head of department because he had recently left the school. Pending a new appointment, the discussion about planning procedures was therefore carried out with staff who did not have overall responsibility for the subject but who had been on the staff for at least three years.

It soon became apparent that prior to the current academic year there had been no physical education syllabus in the school. Indeed one member of staff said, 'When I came three years ago, nothing was ever presented to me to say what was going on.' It appeared that the curriculum evolved from the timetable. Once the school timetable was published it was then decided which activity would be taught in a particular block of lessons. 'Basically that was the syllabus ... work was done in isolated units' was the reaction of one teacher. The lack of a coherently presented programme of work indicated rather haphazard planning. This was substantiated when it transpired that the department rarely held a meeting in spite of the fact that it was school policy to meet once a week. Physical education staff usually had extra-curricular practices at this time which took priority. Occasional meetings had taken place at lunch times but these were nearly always concerned with administrative and organizational matters. Full-time staff had usually been kept well informed but part-time staff were sometimes unaware of decisions that had been taken. Thus the school had experienced some management and communication problems.

Staff were quite clear about the main aims of physical education. One stated, that his aim was 'To see every child participating and enjoying the subject and getting something from it.' The hope was also expressed that pupils would 'continue to do something that is physical'. Other aims expressed were the development of positive attitudes and an 'improvement in performance standards'. Short-term objectives for a half-term block of work were rarely stated to the pupils at the beginning of the course. Indeed it was questioned whether the practice of informing pupils about what they were to learn over an extended period would be beneficial. There was a greater likelihood that this might be done at the outset of a lesson and there were occasions during the period of observation when this was done. The one exception appeared to be the explanation of the similarities and relationships of the different games to the first year pupils in the 'games for understanding' course.

For the past year staff had catered specifically for health and fitness as one of their aims. This course had been introduced in an attempt to promote a positive attitude to the body in all pupils at the start of their secondary education. Statements such as 'physical exercise is beneficial in a variety of ways' and 'improving training techniques and methods' were given as justification for this course. This component had also been introduced as part of a body management concept and included in its content such aspects as diet and nutrition, stress and relaxation, smoking and drinking, and the components of fitness.

The content of the curriculum consisted of a common core of activities for the first three years followed by a progressively increasing range of options. To some extent this was a guided choice based upon the availability of staff and facilities but the use of the local sports centre had a big influence on the range of options offered to pupils. The use of these additional facilities also influenced the selection of content and this resulted in activities like squash, golf and swimming being included. The staff were also aware of current trends in the subject and had attended a number of in-service courses and had read a number of key articles in innovatory areas. This had resulted in new curriculum components being introduced during the last academic year. A 'time analysis' had recently been carried out for each activity which revealed the number of hours devoted to each activity in each year and over the whole curriculum. As a result they were able to state that in the first two years slightly more than 50 per cent was allocated to games and slightly less to body management activities. The proportion for games increased slightly in the third year.

After a successful pilot study, most of the physical education was taught in mixed classes which meant that the girls played soccer and the boys netball in the games for understanding course. Approximately half of the second and fourth year work and nearly all the fifth year programmes were mixed. The one exception was in the third year where pupils were segregated. This was unlikely to continue next year as the new policy worked its way through the school. Regardless of sex, all pupils were required to participate in physical education and this applied to all years.

The progressive planning of work during the academic year (horizontal) and between years (vertical) is essential if there is to be continuity in the work presented. This was not being done in S1. Notes on the work covered were occasionally made but not in any systematic way and they were not available for other staff to consult. Any vertical planning was carried out 'by word of mouth and a quick five minutes discussion'.

The group were asked how they would judge the success of their curriculum and the replies indicated that this was done mainly through their own subjective observations and pupils' comments. One teacher stated that he often questioned the children at the end of a block of work about their understanding while another administered a written test at the end of the health and fitness course. The success of school teams in inter-school competition was also cited. No attempt was made to evaluate any aims as these had not been identified at the outset. A record of each pupil's progress was made through the school report but some dissatisfaction was expressed about its appropriateness for physical education. It was hoped to establish a more relevant method in the future. Certainly there was no central record kept within the department.

Overall, the planning left much to be desired. The absence of a written syllabus and regular department meetings for full and part-time staff, together with a lack of progressive planning and adequate methods of recording, were all evidence of poor management procedures. However, the signs for the future were more optimistic as current staff had produced a written syllabus which would go some way towards alleviating some of the problems identified above. It was very much to their credit that this had been done voluntarily and as a result they had established a sound basis for the development of a clear concept of the overall physical education programme.

Case Study: School 2 (S2) — Crinson Secondary School

S2 was a large secondary school situated in extensive grounds. The school timetable was based on a daily allocation of four lessons of 1 hour 15 minutes. Two periods a week were allocated to every class for physical education throughout the school. During the period of observation thirteen lessons were coded. Of these six were taught by male staff and seven by female staff. In addition two other lessons were taught or observed by the author. The average length of each lesson was forty-two minutes which gave a total involvement during the week of eighty-four minutes. For a variety of reasons, the actual teaching time in each lesson varied from twenty-five to fifty-three minutes.

Staffing

Two male and two female full-time physical education staff had received a specialist training in the subject. All the staff made a minor contribution to other subjects on the curriculum and in return, other staff gave some assistance with the more recreative activities in the senior school. Four or five who had a particular expertise were making this kind of contribution.

The boys' and girls' departments were considered to be separate and autonomous within the school organization. There did not appear to be any problems caused by this arrangement and there was an excellent working relationship between the staff. Obviously there had to be meetings to discuss the allocation of money and the use of facilities at the start of the academic year, but these appeared to be fairly and amicably distributed according to the needs of the pupils and the curriculum.

Facilities

The school was very fortunate in the number of facilities at its disposal.

There were two indoor spaces, one of which was a large, fully-equipped gymnasium and the other a large hall which was normally only used for assemblies. The playing fields were extensive and in good condition, and were marked for hockey, soccer and rugby. A number of grid areas were also permanently marked for the playing of small-sided games.

The school was fortunate to have a swimming pool on the site. A large playground area was situated just outside the gymnasium but had not been used for some time because of the uneven surface. This was in the process of being resurfaced and would provide a useful additional working area. Because of the dangerous condition of the playground, netball had to be played on another area outside the school boundary which was five minutes walk away. This obviously shortened the teaching time available within the lesson.

As well as the on-site facilities, a number of sports areas were used in the locality and this enabled senior pupils to participate in golf, squash, weight training, and water sports. A small charge was made to each pupil for the use of these off-site facilities.

The boys' and girls' changing rooms were large and spacious. One of the boys' rooms had been converted into a classroom/assembly area with tables and benches. Originally it was intended to accommodate the fourth and fifth form pupils who were studying for a Mode 3 CSE in physical education. This provided an environment for related theory to take place near to the practical facilities. Subsequently it was developed to show film and videotapes for theory work with all classes. Every pupil in the school had a physical education notebook which was kept in the department. Whenever it was felt necessary to include some theory work, the written aspects were set out in the notebook. On arrival for physical education, all classes sat down in the classroom area where their attendance was registered and note taken of any pupil not participating or without kit. Many posters adorned the walls in the physical education area and gave a pleasing visual display. The staff had separate and spacious changing rooms which were also large enough to be used as work areas.

The department had more than enough equipment for use in lessons and there was never any shortage. Most of the equipment was in good condition and well looked after. A good stock of videotapes on sporting events and health-related areas formed part of the library.

Dress and Showers

The staff insisted on the pupils showering after every lesson. The school had a uniform for physical education and pupils were required to wear it for every lesson. They were immaculately dressed for physical education and mirrored the high standards of personal appearance set by the staff.

Structure and Content

Overall, all members of the department appeared to be confident and well-organized and this impression was also apparent in many of the lessons. The games lessons mainly comprised the teaching of techniques and strategies in particular games, and many of these showed logical and related progression with a consistent theme. The teachers had clear objectives in mind and set about the task of achieving them. This was particularly apparent in a first year rugby class where tackling was being taught for the first time. Because of the potential danger of minor injury, the practices were carefully structured to minimize any physical risk and the pupils were placed in a safe learning environment. Tackling in rugby is a particularly difficult activity to teach but through graded progression and a sympathetic and encouraging attitude by the teacher, the pupils made good progress.

Usually, the initial practices were closely related to the full game. In outdoor lessons the small grid areas (approximately 10 m × 8 m) were frequently used for small groups, and simulated the kind of situations that would be met in a game. Thus 2v1 or 3v1 with the larger number attempting to keep possession of the ball were commonplace examples. In this way there was a greater and more realistic probability of achieving positive transfer from the practice to the games playing situation. Occasionally, some of the passing practices were static and did not seem to mirror their eventual performance within a dynamic game and some concern must be expressed about their relevance.

Because the playground surfaces were unsafe to use, courts five minutes walk away from the school were used for netball. This was an unsatisfactory arrangement as the seventy-five minutes lesson was reduced to less than half-an-hour of teaching time. Two fourth year netball classes were observed working under this arrangement. As the weather was cold most of the lessons were devoted to practical work. One initial practice was based on a half court four-a-side attack v defence practice which was particularly appropriate for this age range and immediately involved everyone in active participation. Class organization was effective with clear explanations. The teacher was particularly knowledgeable and provided some pertinent coaching within the game. The greater proportion of lesson time was spent in playing a full game of netball with pupils involved in the officiating. The only problem appeared to be that one of the teams in both lessons was better than the other team which meant that the goal keeper in the dominant and the goal attack in the non-dominant team were rarely involved in the game and by their own admission were 'too cold to enjoy the lesson'. These pupils were peripheral to the main activity of the lesson and became rather isolated. This emphasizes the need to choose teams of approximately equal levels of ability in order that pupils have a fair chance of winning a competitive game. Unfortunately, the play was rather one-sided on these two occasions. Usually the teachers placed pupils into teams and, apart from the problems noted above, this resulted in equal ability grouping. This produced games in which pupils felt they had a reasonable chance of succeeding. The only departure from this practice was by one teacher who selected four pupils to choose teams in rotation. It was not surprising that the least able pupil who was left until last to be chosen stated that he would have preferred the teacher to have chosen the team because 'I don't like to be left to last'. Such practices are a strong source of negative feedback and should be avoided wherever possible.

Bringing out principles of play in attack and defence were noted on a few occasions in a variety of games. There were obviously sound reasons for doing this as it provided a framework for performance in several different games. For example, knowing how to deny an opponent space in an attacking position could equally be applied to netball, basketball, hockey and soccer. Occasionally teachers were attempting to draw parallels between different games and this was sound practice. However, these were isolated examples. No attempt had been made to adopt a 'games for understanding' approach as a core foundation for the games course. The staff were aware of this approach and were keen to attend an in-service course in this teaching method in order to assess its potential.

Reference has already been made to the pleasant teacher-pupil relationship which existed within the school. This was a two-way process in that the teachers showed a genuine interest and concern for the pupils and they, in turn, had respect for the staff. All the staff were readily approachable and children often engaged them in conversation in the changing rooms and at the end of lessons. Staff were firm yet fair in all their dealings with pupils and often explained why certain decisions were being made. They were also sympathetic to the pupils' needs and one example typified this approach. One slightly overweight third year pupil called Peter had recently joined the school and had changed rather self-consciously for a basketball lesson. During the initial skill practices he dropped the first three passes and became so apprehensive about the ball that he collided with other boys on several occasions. The teacher put him at his ease by explaining that he could not be expected to be as skilful as the other boys as he had missed several lessons. Two boys were assigned to help Peter and this was very helpful to him. Later in the week he was again encouraged in a hockey lesson and took part in a teacher-pupil demonstration. These were the actions of an experienced and sympathetic teacher who recognized the needs of a less able pupil. This kind of genuine concern for pupils' welfare was often in evidence.

The physical education notebook was used on two occasions prior to practical work on the field. Once pupils were required to write down information related to positions in the game of rugby and again when they copied down the hockey rule relating to the hit-in. This process lasted for several minutes and reduced the practical part of the lesson to just over half-an-hour. Thus almost three-quarters-of-an-hour was taken up with changing, showering and related theory. Time spent copying down a rule from the laws of a game into a book does need some justification and in this instance it was difficult to understand its relevance, especially as it was not followed up or included in the practical work. There was remarkably little skills technique or strategy input (2 per cent) in this lesson and the teacher's knowledge appeared to be rather limited.

Because of inclement weather, two games lessons were taken in the gymnasium. The group consisted of two classes, each of twenty girls. Another reason for the combined grouping was that the hall was not available. The indoor game of hockey called unihoc was played and consisted entirely of a succession of four-a-side games lasting three minutes. Two teachers were involved in the coaching and gave helpful advice concerning personal skills and positional play. There was a full commitment and involvement from the girls who were playing the game. The only problem with this kind of organization was that while eight were playing, thirty-two girls were watching which resulted in the highest 'waiting' recorded of 71 per cent. The lack of facilities and unusual class size were obviously extenuating circumstances but activities which would have provided greater involvement perhaps need to be considered in the future. The other indoor lesson related to netball and again most of the lesson was spent playing five-a-side games with sixteen pupils sitting on the side-lines. Again there was a high 'waiting' time of 50 per cent.

In the first two years gymnastics was an important part of the curriculum and a problem-solving approach was mainly used. This involved pupils finding their own solutions to movement tasks set by the teacher. However, some direct teaching of specific skills, especially for the boys, was not precluded. Three girls' educational gymnastic lessons taught to first and second year classes were observed. The teachers used question and answer techniques effectively to identify differences in, for example, symmetrical and asymmetrical movements. Often this was done in conjunction with pupils' demonstrations. Although attempts were made to follow a theme throughout a lesson this was not always adhered to. The first lesson in a unit of work for one class had a theme of 'locomotion' and began with the pupils exploring a variety of pathways using different body parts. This included finding different ways into and out of forward and backward rolls. All of these movements were logically related to the locomotion theme. The incongruous part of the lesson came when a head stand, which is a static balance, was taught as a specific skill. If a thematic approach is to be used then it is necessary to set tasks consistent with the theme. This does not preclude the teaching of specific skills but it is essential that they are incorporated into the work of the main theme. In this instance, this did not appear to be the case. On another occasion a double foot take-off to hand stand was taught as a class activity during a lesson on symmetry. Although related to the theme, this was far too difficult for the majority and led to a lot of ungainly movements. Overall, the teachers did attempt to encourage the pupils to develop their movement ideas and at the same time improve qualitative aspects such as timing and control.

Demonstration was invariably used in all thirteen lessons. Only rarely did a teacher demonstrate a skill by him or herself. Wherever possible pupils were involved and this was sound practice as it gave an indication of peer group levels of performance. Usually the demonstrations were relevant and effective, and were accompanied by pertinent comments from the teacher which tended to underlie their knowledgeable approach. There was, however, one form of demonstration which needed to be questioned. In one gymnastics lesson this involved the showing of partner work on mats at the end of the session. There were probably two main reasons for doing this. One was to give the pupils an opportunity to show to the remainder of the class what they had learned, and the second was to suggest ideas which other pupils might incorporate into their own sequences of movement. The problem with this demonstration was that it was time-consuming and in this lesson lasted for twelve minutes out of a total of fifty-two minutes contact time. It also assumed that every pair had reached a level of performance suitable to show others. This was certainly not the case in this instance and resulted in some rather poor work being shown. So many ideas were presented that it was impossible to remember them all let alone incorporate them into any personal movements. Finally, because the demonstrations took place at the end of the lesson there was no opportunity for further practice. As little would be remembered to the next lesson, their effectiveness must be seriously questioned.

The programme in the fifth year presented a series of options from which pupils could choose. Because of the extensive facilities available at the school, most of the activities took place on-site and were all under instruction from the staff. In order to increase the range of options, a number of off-site venues enabled golf, squash and outdoor activities to be added to the list. All of these were staffed by qualified coaches. Wherever possible it was hoped that the activities would be mixed and there were a few instances when this did occur.

There was a health education component within the physical education programme which was taught as it 'arises naturally' during the course of a lesson. Thus the importance of showers and personal hygiene was stressed. A number of other topics such as exercise, diet, drugs and smoking were also introduced to pupils within the 'wet weather' programme. Videotapes, films and information sheets were available on all the topics. This component was therefore taught incidentally as and when the opportunity arose rather than as a self-contained course in its own right. Staff had expressed an interest and a desire to obtain more information about health-related-fitness courses and was an aspect which they wished to develop in the near future.

For several years the boys in the fourth and fifth years had been offered a CSE Mode 1 course in physical education and this had proved to be a popular and successful option. The course consisted of four main options namely: health and hygiene; anatomy and physiology; first aid; and practical performance in four selected activities. The staff were keen to develop this into a GCSE course for boys and girls and this seemed to be a logical development. However, no more curriculum time was available over and above the normal allocation and this was a limitation. In addition, senior staff in the school had expressed reservations about the quality of some of the specimen questions which had been circulated with the syllabuses. One example asked for the weight of a hockey stick and the factual remembering of trivial information such as this had not enhanced the worth of the subject at GCSE level. It transpired that the CSE course had originally started because another subject in the boys' curriculum had been withdrawn and it had been administratively convenient to allocate this time to physical education. Thus it appeared that the subject had been introduced to satisfy a timetable requirement rather than on its own educational merit.

Feedback

It proved impossible to record accurately the number and types of feedback given by the teachers and this observation applied to all schools. Sometimes this was because of poor acoustics and noise in the working area and on other occasions it was because the recorder was not close enough to hear the comments. The instances of feedback that were noted were all recorded as positive, and on a few occasions positive with information. No negative feedback was heard. Thus supportive statements such as 'Well done' or 'Good effort' were commonplace. This type of feedback was usually a reward for good performance but rarely identified which particular aspect of the performance was being reinforced. Effort was also rewarded in this way regardless of ability. Two of the staff were excessive in their use of feedback to the extent that one always said 'Good girl' after every successful pass in a game, whilst the other used words such as 'Superb' and 'Excellent' for the execution of quite ordinary performance. If this continues for any length of time the statements eventually become meaningless.

Extra-Curricular Activities

After almost a year in which there had been little extra-curricular activity, there were signs that some of the clubs were being revived. There was considerable support for the team games and as many as three or four teams from each year group were playing competitively against other schools. Staff and pupils had taken part in ski-ing trips during the vacations. Several male non-physical education teachers with expertise in a particular activity assisted with the clubs. As in most schools, few female staff outside the physical education department are prepared to assist with extra-curricular activities.

Questionnaire Factors

The four sub-factors from the Physical Education 'Learner Report' Questionnaire were analyzed by means of a t-test for independent samples (separate variance) to determine whether there were any differences between the responses of the male and female pupils. The results are set out in table 25.

No statistically significant differences were recorded between the male

Table 25:   S2: T test on PE 'Learner Report' Questionnaire factors for male and female pupils

	Male		Female		
Factor	Mean		Mean	SD	p
Technomotor	1.82	0.37	1.84	0.47	N.S.
Sociomotor	2.16	0.43	2.10	0.56	N.S.
Cognitive-reflective	2.52	0.52	2.43	0.68	N.S.
Affective	1.61	0.55	1.78	0.62	N.S.

and female pupils on any of the four sub-factors. The rank order of affective, technomotor, sociomotor and cognitive-reflective was the same for both groups and all indicated a positive attitude. The standard deviations about the mean were all smaller for the boys than for the girls and suggested there was less variance in the boys' attitudes.

Academic Learning Time — Physical Education

The content level of ALT-PE data for male and female teachers is summarized in table 26 from the complete data in appendix 7.

Marginally more time was spent by male teachers on the general content of the lesson with the bulk of this time being devoted to transitional and organizational aspects. Although there was again slightly more time spent by male teachers (25.5 per cent to 21.6 per cent) on knowledge content, the sub-categories of information which dealt with techniques and strategies were distributed differently. Male teachers spent almost twice as much time transmitting information concerning the physical form of a motor skill whereas female teachers spent a similar proportion of time giving information concerning plans of action for individuals or groups. This tended to suggest that the male staff had a slightly more skill-orientated approach which was reflected during the period of the visit.

With lower percentages in the above categories, this inevitably meant the female teachers spent a greater proportion of time in the motor content. Again the distribution was markedly different with male teachers devoting much more time (28.8 per cent to 8.7 per cent) to the practice of skills outside the applied context whereas female staff spent a similar imbalance of time (43.7 per cent to 15.2 per cent) on the refinement and extension of skills in an applied setting. In theory, provided pupils have a reasonable technical standard to play some form of conditioned game, there would be a greater likelihood of more positive transfer within this kind of applied context.

With the learner involvement, there were a number of differences in

Table 26: S2: Average percentage time spent by male and female teachers on General content, PE knowledge content and PE motor content

	Male %	Female %
General content	29.7	26.7
PE knowledge content	25.5	21.6
PE motor content	44.8	52.4

Table 27: S2: Average percentage of pupil time spent in ALT-PE learner involvement categories when taught by male and female staff

Not motor engaged	Male %	female %
Interim	0	0
Waiting	19.5	25.9
Off-task	0	0.1
On-task	20.3	12.1
Cognitive	31.5	25.1
Motor engaged		
Motor appropriate	28.5	36.6
Motor inappropriate	0	0
Supporting	0.5	0

pupil behaviour dependent on the sex of the teacher and these are summarized in table 27.

Approximately two-thirds of every lesson was spent in a not motor engaged category, and within this time pupils spent almost one-third waiting – hardly conducive to high time-on-task, which averaged one-third of the lesson – 28 per cent for male and 36 per cent for female teachers. One interesting comparison showed that in spite of female pupils spending greater amounts of time appropriately engaged in motor activities, no significant differences were apparent in the pupils' attitudes in the technomotor sub-factor. Perhaps the most surprising result in lessons associated with physical activity was that male teachers involved their pupils in a greater proportion of time in cognitive than in motor behaviour (31.5 per cent to 28.5 per cent). The same trend was not apparent for female staff.

Planning Procedures

A written syllabus was available and had originally been prepared several years ago by a previous head of department. This consisted of a brief statement of the general aims and evaluation procedures, the organization of the activities in each year and a very detailed scheme of work for each practical area. Each scheme had been prepared by a member of staff who had a particular expertise in the area. Other colleagues were given the opportunity to comment and amend any proposals before they were incorporated into the syllabus. These discussions usually took place at the half-termly department meeting. Although there was no longer a head of department with overall responsibility for physical education, the boys' and girls' departments had compiled a joint syllabus with shared aims and objectives. The general aims were wide-ranging and incorporated the development of positive attitudes to the subject and health and fitness, enjoyment, body management, aesthetic appreciation, leisure, self-realization, social relationships and understanding. With such a comprehensive list it was somewhat surprising that in response to the question, 'What are your main aims of physical education?' the staff only mentioned enjoyment and involvement. The aims certainly did not appear to be consciously underpinning their philosophy of physical education and there was never any attempt made to tell the children either the long-term aims of the subject or the short-term objectives of a course.

The staff expressed a desire to develop health and fitness as a separate course from its present position as an incidental aspect of all their work. Some aspects were being taught in other subjects in the school and there was a desire to coordinate all the work into the physical education department. A start had been made but it was only in the early stages of planning.

A prescribed common core content of activity was in operation for all pupils during the first four years and this was followed by a range of options in the fifth year. Attendance at physical education lessons was compulsory for all pupils in all years. For girls there was an equal balance in the amount of time devoted to gymnastics, dance, netball and hockey in the first three years and then a complete shift in emphasis to games in year 4. Apart from some gymnastics in the first year, all the boys' activities were games-orientated. The justification for this was made on the grounds that games reflected the expertise and ability of the staff. All lessons were segregated apart from some fifth form options in golf and swimming. Some consideration was being given to encourage more mixed activities in the senior school but the staff were waiting for a suitable year group with a positive attitude to the subject before implementing this idea. The head-teacher had suggested there should be some mixed dance in the first year programme but the response of the department was that this was 'something we are thinking about'.

All staff kept a complete written record of their work in a record book which was based on the schemes of work as outlined in the syllabus. Thus an accurate check-list was available during an academic year and between years for staff to consult. In this way it was relatively easy to check the work a class had experienced in previous lessons.

Extra-curricular activities formed an important part of the physical education programme. For the girls, any pupil who wanted to attend was welcome and in the team games was assured of playing in the team at some stage in the season. The female staff indicated that they did 'not have much success in picking up trophies' but believed that encouraging a wider participation was more important. Until comparatively recently the male staff had insisted on an elitist approach which only allowed those boys of proven ability to belong to the club. After a period of almost two years, when there had been no extra-curricular work in the school, the men were now 'concentrating on more teams and spending less time with the first team'. They were prepared to accept some possible slight diminution in standards in exchange for wider participation. Their philosophy was summed up when they all agreed that 'anybody and everybody can come regardless of ability'. Attendance did not even have to be on a regular basis which gave an indication of the lengths staff were prepared to go in order to encourage participation.

The initial response to the question 'How do you judge the success of your physical education curriculum?' was a long period of silence. Eventually, female staff referred to some 'negative things' such as a low drop-out rate, few excuse notes and small numbers not enjoying the subject. On the positive side, the men mentioned enjoyment as well as 'remembering kit, punctuality, organizing themselves and being in the right frame of mind for a lesson'. Staff appeared to be unsure whether or not they had achieved their aims. One teacher stated that occasionally there was an attempt to evaluate aims, 'but not as much as I should do'.

Staff commented generally on each pupil's performance at the end of a block of work on the school report. At the time of the interview the staff had been asked for five criteria by which they could evaluate a pupil's performance in physical education and these had been identified under the headings of physical ability, personal organization, attitude, skill acquisition and effort. In this way it was hoped to provide a more detailed and accurate assessment for every child.

Overall the department was quite well organized and the detailed schemes of work for the different activities were particularly impressive. They provided a good reference point for staff to plan their work but were not regarded as prescriptive. The fact that all staff kept a permanent record of their work ensured some degree of continuity. Although the aims were clearly stated in the syllabus, they had been written by a former member of staff and appeared to have been accepted without a great deal of thought or discussion. There were a number of important areas which were being considered for development, viz. mixed physical education, health-related fitness, games for understanding and assessment procedures. From a sound base the department planning appeared to be going through a transition stage. If all these new developments were implemented, they would go some way to achieving what one member of staff hoped would become a 'well-structured, well-planned and related curriculum'.

Case Study: School 3 (S3) — King Secondary School

This school was situated near the centre of a large town on two adjoining sites. The timetable consisted of four double periods each day and every class was allocated two periods of physical education each week. There were a number of department projects in operation during the visits which affected the normal programme. As a result, it was only possible to observe four lessons taught by male staff and seven by the female staff. In addition, two lessons were taught by the author. The average length of each lesson was forty-seven minutes which resulted in a weekly contact time of ninety-four minutes for each pupil.

Staffing

There were six full-time members of staff (three male and three female) all of whom had received a specialist training in physical education. One male staff member had recently been appointed to the school, but apart from this, the staffing had remained stable for a number of years. Two separate and autonomous departments operated within the school — one for boys' and one for girls' physical education. There was shared use of facilities and this was agreed between the two heads of department at the planning stage at the beginning of each term. Although the departments were separate, there was a great deal of interaction and cooperation between the two groups of staff.

Facilities

On the larger site, the most used facility was a large multi-purpose sports hall which accommodated the playing of most games and had a good range of fixed gymnastic apparatus. In addition, a climbing wall had been built at one end. A tarmac playground area marked for tennis and netball adjoined the hall and could be used for a variety of activities. The department also had the use of an assembly hall. This was mainly used when inclement weather made it impossible to work outside.

Extensive playing fields surrounded the school. There were several pitches for hockey, soccer, rugby and lacrosse, and all were in excellent condition. Grid practice areas were permanently marked in three different positions to provide training grounds for the various team sports.

On the other site there were playground areas available as well as two indoor facilities, a fully equipped gymnasium and an all-purpose hall which, after morning assembly, was used for gymnastics, dance, trampolining and indoor training.

An impressive amount of equipment was available for all the activities and there did not appear to be a shortage of money for the purchase of new equipment.

Spacious changing and showering facilities for the pupils existed on both sites. Showering after each practical period was encouraged and invariably insisted upon. Staff accommodation was adequate, if rather crowded at times.

The foyer of the sports hall had a variety of coaching posters on the wall as well as the results of pupils' fitness tests. The school also awarded sporting 'colours' to their outstanding pupils and their names were inscribed on 'colours boards'. These records extended over several years.

Dress

A smart school uniform for physical education ensured that the pupils were well and appropriately dressed at all times. The personal appearance of pupils was certainly a credit to the school.

Structure and Content

Four lessons of educational gymnastics were observed — three taught by female staff and the other by a male member of staff. None of the lessons used any of the large groupings of apparatus. Most of the work was carried out on mats with the occasional use of benches. It is relevant to mention that the observation period coincided with the first week of changeover to a new block of work and that apparatus may have been used in the later development of the work.

Only one male member of staff appeared a little unsure about teaching gymnastics through a problem-solving approach and stated that he found the teaching 'difficult' and was much happier teaching specific skills in a directed manner. In spite of his personal feelings about using an open-ended approach, his communication was clear and effective and he had a pleasant manner in his dealings with the children. However, there was serious imbalance in the class organization in that 80 per cent of the lesson was devoted to general content and subject knowledge. Naturally this reduced the pupils' practical involvement and resulted in a very low motor appropriate recording of 13 per cent. At the end of the lesson a short relay-type game was played which bore no relationship to the theme of the lesson and was quite incongruous. Such a practice was advocated many years ago but has long since disappeared from lesson planning in gymnastics.

Well over one-third of every gymnastic lesson was devoted to subject knowledge and the majority of this was linked to strategies that could be useful to pupils to find solutions to tasks. There was one exception when a teacher spent a long time teaching a specific skill which required a lot of technical input. Whenever a gymnastic skill was to be taught, the teachers in this school tended to demonstrate it themselves and used pupil demonstrations as examples of movement solutions to a task.

Occasionally the teachers referred to mechanical principles associated with balance and the movement of body parts. These were usually taught with the liberal use of question and answer which elicited information such as the different kinds and types of base which can be used in balancing activities.

All the staff had a pleasant manner with the children and good class-teacher relationships were evident. Staff were firm, fair and polite at all times and often displayed a sense of humour. Pupils of all ages readily approached and spoke to the staff. Building this kind of relationship takes time and is founded on trust and understanding. One small example typified a sympathetic approach when a teacher was approached by two overweight girls who stated they did not wish to change and participate in a gymnastic lesson. With persuasion, the teacher encouraged them to take part with the assurance that they would not be asked to do anything beyond their capabilities. The two pupils were motivated to participate throughout the lesson and received a lot of positive support. At the end of the period they said how much they had enjoyed the lesson and were looking forward to using the apparatus. An insensitive approach by the teacher could have had a disastrous effect and this incident was regarded as important in the development of these pupils' future attitudes.

The girls' physical education department was particularly strong in the teaching of gymnastics and dance and produced public concerts and demonstrations every year. To a large extent this reflected the wide range of knowledge and expertise of the staff. Their commitment and obvious enthusiasm in teaching these activities had resulted in the girls achieving good standards of creative work.

The teaching of outdoor games was generally well-prepared and well-executed. The style of teaching was mainly directed and the lesson format usually consisted of a warm-up, applied techniques and a conditioned game. The warm-ups were relevant and incorporated activities which were part of the pupils' repertoire of skills. This meant that the initial part of the lesson served the dual purpose of a physiological warm-up and a familiarization with the skills that were to be used later in the lesson. Grid areas were used intelligently and occasional reference was made to common features in related skills. The principles of catching a ball in lacrosse and its application to other catching games was one example. The small-sided games were appropriate and contained the essential elements of the full game. Thus three–a–side in a restricted area was commonplace. Approximately the last third of the lesson was devoted to some form of game which was coached by the teachers. Through their comments, they all showed that they had a sound knowledge of the games they were teaching and had the ability to communicate this to the pupils.

The teaching of indoor games was less impressive. In two basketball lessons the introductory practices were far too static and the relay activities only involved a few pupils at a time. Logical progression throughout the lesson was not always clearly apparent and there was certainly no consistent theme mentioned. Some enthusiastic games playing was observed but there was little coaching from the teacher in this context. In one lesson the teacher spent far too long on one practice without feeding in additional information and this inevitably led to boredom and some poor behaviour. As a result of these lesson formats there were many times when the pupils were 'bystanders' and over one-third of the contact time was spent waiting. It was interesting that in both these lessons only 10 per cent was allocated to subject knowledge. This was a low amount of input and perhaps reflected a need to impart into the lessons more knowledge, ideas and feedback based on observation.

Although not officially part of the physical education syllabus, the department did teach a theory module on health–related fitness in one senior school course, timetabled for one period each week for five terms. Wherever possible, the theoretical work was supplemented with practical experience. One lesson on diet also involved measuring the percentage of body fat. The pupils had given a mixed reception to the project and most were not particularly enthusiastic or positive about its content. One boy said he found the work 'boring' and another whose body fat level was well above the norm said, 'I don't care, I won't change what I eat'. Indeed it appeared that none had changed their dietry habits as a result of the course. However, in spite of these rather adverse reports, the concept of the course was sound. There was also an opportunity to measure and evaluate personal development over an extended period as well as gaining an understanding of the different aspects of physical fitness. First aid was also introduced by a visiting lecturer. The choice of orienteering, climbing or trampolining as practical activities was slightly incongruous. It would have been possible to have linked the work with the extensive JCR (jumps, chins and run) fitness testing that was carried out in the junior school. Stronger links with circuit training, keep fit and cross-country might have given more meaning to the course. From this creditable beginning further development was necessary. The fact that one member of staff had recently attended a course on health-related fitness and was keen to contribute some ideas augered well for the future. The department deserved to be encouraged in this worthwhile project.

The department did not incorporate a 'games for understanding' approach in the teaching of games in the first and second years. Its relevance was seriously questioned by one senior member of staff who felt it was essential for skills and understanding to be developed in a specific context.

Some choice of activity based on the activities which had been offered in the earlier part of the syllabus was offered to pupils in the fourth and fifth year. Only orienteering appeared as a new activity. Some pupils in the fifth year were allowed to choose a different activity each week. The justification for this was that it catered for all choices which meant that pupils would at least participate in their first choice fairly frequently. As a result, they were more willing to take part in other activities which were less popular to them. Whilst this may be true, the optional programme became very recreative in nature and it would be almost impossible to plan a developmental course for an activity with a different group of pupils each week.

Extra-curricular Activities

Over the past two years there had been a complete division of opinion between the male and female staff about the provision of extra-curricular activities. Because of the industrial action, the men had decided not to run any clubs and as a result there had been no clubs or competitive fixtures with other schools. This contrasted with the attitude of the female staff who had continued with their clubs and teams during the lunch break, after school and at weekends (including Sundays). Consequently there were two or three clubs in progress on all these occasions. They proved to be very popular and the trampoline club had as many as fifty or sixty pupils attending three times a week. Pupils of all levels of ability were welcomed and there was no elitist selection.

Questionnaire Factors

The four sub-factors from the Physical Education 'Learner Report' Questionnaire were analyzed according to the mean scores obtained by male and

Table 28: S3: T-test on PE 'Learner Report' Questionnaire factors for male and female pupils

	Male		Female		
Factor	*Mean*	*SD*	*Mean*	*Sd*	*p*
Technomotor	2.00	0.50	1.94	0.64	N.S.
Sociomotor	2.46	0.73	2.40	0.67	N.S.
Cognitive-reflective	2.82	0.75	2.87	0.81	N.S.
Affective	2.06	0.69	1.69	0.77	<0.05

female pupils. A t-test for independent samples with a separate variance was used and the results are presented in table 28.

No significant difference were revealed in the technomotor, sociomotor and cognitive-reflective factors but a significant difference at the 5 per cent level was apparent for the affective factor with the girls recording a more positive score. The reasons for this are not completely clear as all the staff had a good relationship with the pupils and most children appeared to be enjoying their participation in physical education. One possible explanation may have been that the female staff had continued with club activities and team practices. The vast majority of pupils who participated in these extra-curricular activities were girls, although a few boys attended some of the individual clubs such as trampolining. The clubs were popular as was evident by the large attendances and there is no doubt that they do tend to foster positive attitudes to the subject. However, the only significant difference was in the affective factor. A similar difference might also have been expected in the other factors but this was not the case.

Academic Learning Time — Physical Education

ALT-PE data for the content level of the eleven lessons observed during the observation week is set out in table 29 (fuller details appear in appendix 7).

Approximately one-third of each lesson was spent on general content and there were no differences between male and female staff. More

Table 29: S3: Average percentage time spent by male and female teachers on general content, PE knowledge content and PE motor content

	Male %	Female %
General content	31.3	31.3
PE knowledge content	21.0	32.0
PE motor content	47.5	37.0

Table 30: S3:Average percentage of pupil time spent in ALT-PE learner involvement categories when taught by male and female staff

Not motor engaged	Male %	Female %
Interim	0.5	0.7
Waiting	20.8	18.1
Off-task	1.5	2.3
On-task	4.0	10.6
Cognitive	41.0	44.1
Motor engaged		
Motor appropriate	32.3	24.3
Motor inappropriate	0	0
Supporting	0	0

knowledge content was fed into lessons by female teachers (32 per cent versus 21.1 per cent) and they spent a greater proportion of this time on techniques and strategies related to the practical work. Inevitably, there was a corresponding reduction in time for the motor content (37 per cent to 47.8 per cent).

An examination of the learner involvement was possible from the datas presented in table 30. It was clear that both groups spent the majority of their time (67.8 per cent and 75.8 per cent) not engaged in motor activities, with over 40% recorded in the cognitive category. This figure was higher than the knowledge content input (see Table 29) and implied that an appreciable amount related to general content. For example, organizational features of a lesson which involved pupils making decisions about the placing of gymnastic apparatus, or listening to instructions about the organization of a small-sided game would all require a cognitive involvement. Finally, there was a substantially higher motor appropriate recording for the male teachers (32.3 per cent to 24.3 per cent), but this higher time-on-task did not result in any significant differences in pupils' attitudes to the technomotor aspects of skill acquisition in the analysis of the sub-factors.

Planning Procedures

The boys' and the girls' departments had autonomy over the presentation of their physical education curriculum and each had produced their own syllabus. There was some common agreement about the aims of the subject which incorporated the development of personal skills, fitness, social and moral skills, leisure participation and enjoyment. The only addition was the development of expression and creativity through dance and gymnastics for the girls. The boys' syllabus indicated those activities which contributed to particular aims, whilst the girls' syllabus comprised a very brief scheme of work for each activity. There was also a diagrammatic representation of the contribution each activity made throughout the five years for both departments. The presentation was clear without going into great detail.

As in many schools, the curriculum was evolving and developing and the female staff were 'in the process of discussing the curriculum' and were reviewing some areas. Clear initial emphasis had been given to the content of physical education with 'little concern for the objectives'. Naturally, account had also been taken of the facilities, resources, staffing and time allocation.

All the staff strongly believed that their subject had an important contribution to make to the development of each pupil. At the beginning of a block of work the female staff would indicate to the pupils what they would be doing for the next several weeks without setting specific goals to be achieved. This procedure had not been adopted by the male staff as they felt there was a danger of setting an expectation that was either too high or too low. They felt it was better to work at a developmental level for each individual.

The content of the programme differed slightly in that the female staff devoted half of the curriculum time in the first two years to imaginative and creative movement in gymnastics and dance, and the other half to games. This contrasted with the male staff allocation of three-quarters of the time to games and the remainder to gymnastics and cross-country. Regardless of sex, there was an increase in the time allocated to games from year 3 onwards. Thus, there was a clear bias towards a range of competitive games. However, both departments stated that they attempted to cater for the different needs of each pupil and to 'allow a child to work individually and not competitively, and ... compose his or her own work and enjoy it'. This was coupled with the need to satisfy 'the child who is competitive and loves team games'. An examination of the two syllabuses suggested there would be a greater likelihood of achieving both these needs through the girls' programme because of the more equal distribution of time between games and the creative activities.

During the first three years there was a gradual increase in the number of activities on offer which culminated in nine sports in the third year programme for boys. There was a reduction in the practical time in the fourth and fifth years and the choices were limited. In addition, the pupils were directed by staff to particular activities. The choice of activities was governed by their potential as a leisure-time activity for pupils once they had left school. On this basis, 'tennis and cricket were included for social reasons' whereas athletics was excluded because of its limitations for future personal involvement. Boys and girls were not allowed to participate in the same activity and this seemed to be a lost opportunity, especially as many of the post school activities, for which the school was keen to prepare their pupils, were played by both sexes.

Each member of the female staff kept a written record of their work and this was readily available to their colleagues. This served as a record of work that had been completed and if used properly would ensure logical progression. The male staff adopted a different policy, referring staff to the syllabus for an activity (which incidentally was not set out for each year group). No recording system was in operation as it was stated they had 'all failed in the past' and at present there was 'nothing remotely concerned with official record keeping'. With three staff in the department it was difficult to envisage how a teacher could make an accurate assessment of prior teaching by another member of staff.

A flourishing extra-curricular programme was in existence for the girls and all pupils were welcome. Some clubs could not cater for the larger numbers and had been split into two groups — one catering for team members and the other for the non-team members. Senior pupils were often used to coach the younger pupils on these occasions. The boys' department had adopted a different policy and limited attendance at the team sports to members of that particular squad. Other clubs such as five-a-side soccer, weight training and fitness clubs were open to all the boys but had received a mixed reception. Often they had 'been closed down because of the lack of response'. Indeed, the staff indicated they had 'never had a completely successful extra-curricular programme'. This was difficult to understand in view of the good facilities and range of expertise available on the staff. One reason advanced for this non-participation was that the pupils preferred to spend more of their time at the on-site youth club which offered social clubs, a bar for soft drinks, discos, pool and table tennis. Also, a number of competitive games had been arranged with similar organizations and these clashed with the physical education department's extra-curricular programme.

Evaluating the success of the curriculum was monitored through the 'customer response and whether pupils enjoyed the lessons'. The number of pupils who participated in extra-curricular activities was also an important indicator for the female staff. None of the staff attempted to evaluate their original aims but the female staff said they were 'attempting to do this shortly'. The senior male teacher said that he consciously did not attempt this. He went on to remark that 'what appears before you is reality. To transpose this to aims and objectives seems to be an unrealistic situation — just manufacturing something that isn't real. I think in concrete terms that are practical and definable, and how children react. I am happy not to follow the theoreticians path.' This clear and forthright statement does not support the claims made by many curriculum theorists about planning procedures.

A brief summary of the planning in S3 would suggest that although a syllabus was in existence for both departments, this needed amplifying in relation to the specified aims. Both departments appeared keen to preserve their autonomy and because of this they have missed an opportunity to allow boys and girls to participate in the same activity. The records of work by the male teachers were very limited and inhibited progressive planning. The rather indifferent extra-curricular programme for the boys contrasted sharply with the flourishing work for the girls. Evaluation procedures were rather vague and subjective, and were not linked to the overall aims of the subject.

Case Study: School 4 (S4) — Simpson Secondary School

S4 was a large secondary school in a rural setting. During the period of observation nineteen lessons were observed during which the ALT-PE coding system was used. Ten of the lessons were taught by male members of staff and the remaining nine by the female staff. The average length of each lesson was forty-two-and-a-half minutes and because a ten-day timetable was in operation, each class had two periods one week and three the next.

Staffing

There were three male and two female full-time staff, and one female part-time teacher, in the department. All had received a specialist physical education training. They were all knowledgeable about the subject and every teacher taught most activities. There was never any feeling that staff were struggling because of a lack of knowledge or understanding. Obviously they had their strengths and weaknesses and teaching preferences. One male teacher felt that his teaching of educational gymnastics could be improved and this may also have applied to the other male staff. There was a firm but pleasant working climate due partly to the fact that the staff were confident in what they were doing. The teachers were genuine in their interaction with pupils. They were always encouraging and could laugh and smile with them. Thus a warm atmosphere was usually present in the working area. This staff-pupil relationship continued into the changing rooms where the pupils chatted freely with the staff. There was a genuine respect in both directions.

Facilities

The facilities in the school were classed as very good. There was a large indoor heated sports hall which could be used for many different activities, as well as a fully equipped gymnasium. An assembly hall area was also available and used for dance. Apart from these three indoor facilities, there were large playground areas frequently in use, and extensive playing fields nearby marked for the normal range of games activities. As well as these on-site facilities, the pupils in the fifth and sixth form were allowed to used other facilities in the area such as the swimming pool and badminton and squash courts.

There was no shortage of equipment and apparatus. Three large rooms were all full of large and small apparatus, mostly in good condition. This meant there was never any problem in the provision of equipment in the lessons.

The boys' and girls' changing rooms were spacious and adjoined both the sports hall and the gymnasium. This ensured that all pupils had adequate changing facilities when they took part in physical education.

Dress

Without exception, the staff were smartly and appropriately dressed for the different physical activities. These high standards were also reflected in the pupils' attire when an all-white uniform was required for indoor work and an all purpose shirt for outdoor activities. Some deviation from these standards was permitted for senior pupils but the criterion of 'appropriate dress' was still applied. This relaxation from the school physical education uniform was appreciated by senior pupils and one boy remarked that he preferred wearing his own kit because it was smarter and he felt a greater sense of personal identity. For pupils in the lower school the wearing of the correct kit was compulsory and in gymnastics, for example, all sweaters and footwear had to be removed and the practical work was carried out in bare feet. Regardless of the activity, all pupils in the first three years had to take a shower after every physical education lesson and pupils in other years were encouraged to do so. This early training had made the taking of a shower part of the lesson and most senior pupils availed themselves of the opportunity.

Structure and Content

All the lessons had a structure and in most instances the objectives were clear although they were rarely stated to the children. The continuity in some lessons was apparent in a number of ways. In gymnastics the mastery of balance activities on the floor and their application to the larger pieces of apparatus was a good example. So too was the netball lesson in which the initial warm-up was carried out with a ball, then linked to the skill practices and finally related to the playing of the game. These types of pre-determined structures provided frameworks on which lessons were built and had a self-evident continuity. This contrasted slightly with those lessons where the links were still there but the continuity was less obvious. A common example was in hockey where the initial practice was carried out with no opposition, for example a relay dribble, and this was followed by an expectancy that this would transfer into the full game situation. Other examples of this type of initial practice occurred in passing in soccer and shooting in basketball. Such unopposed techniques can be justified if they are being practised in the initial stages of skill acquisition. Different types of competition were often introduced which required pupils to perform within a time limit or against other pupils, and this placed the technique under some kind of pressure that might be met later in the playing of the game.

There were rarely any instances of unclear instructions. The tasks were nearly always set in a clear and unambiguous manner. As a result, there was never any need to repeat instructions and this gave the pupils a clear framework in which to work and they usually knew what was required of them. Not only did this apply to the learning and performance of motor skills but also to those organizational phases of the lesson which related to the movement of equipment, collection of apparatus, or the location and grouping of pupils. However, just because a teacher gives clear instructions it does not necessarily follow that they will be carried out, and there were instances where some pupils worked within the organizational framework but did not carry out the specifics of the task. Incorrect technique in basketball shooting and failure to play within the framework set by the teacher in fielding/striking games were examples of this type of behaviour.

In a few games lessons almost all the time was spent in the playing of a game with the teacher usually playing and coaching within that context. On these occasions there were no or few introductory practices. In an indoor hockey lesson it was impossible for all the pupils to play at the same time and this resulted in ten pupils playing and fifteen watching and waiting. Consequently, the majority of pupils were on the sidelines for most of the time. In another lesson conducted in the same facility, exactly the same number of pupils were accommodated playing basketball and badminton. Ten boys played basketball at one end of the hall while the rest of the class were involved in badminton. Nearly all the author's observation focused on the basketball game where there was a high physical commitment and total involvement. As a result, 92 per cent was recorded in the motor appropriate category. The standard of play was sound and because of the nature of the activity, there was a high fitness component. This contrasted markedly with the motor appropriate behaviour of 27 per cent of the hockey lesson. Inevitably, this raises questions about the effect that long periods of inactivity in a lesson can have on the learning of physical skills and the development of attitudes towards the subject. Both the lessons described above were with pupils in the fourth year and there is no doubt that pupils of this age do like to apply the skills they have learnt into the full game situation. Nevertheless, the issue being raised is whether pupils ought to sit out and watch for long periods of time. To some extent the problems are linked to the types of game being played and the amount of space available in which to play them. When hockey was played outside on the fields, all the pupils were involved in a full game. This meant there was no waiting on the sidelines. In two such lessons, the teachers made many valid coaching points which arose during the course of play and related to specific situations. In one of the lessons the contribution of one girl was monitored for eighteen minutes. The account of this period of time ran as follows:

00.00   Game restarted with a pass back from the centre. Samantha had taken up a defensive position in the goal area.

00.55   First physical movement from her original position.

01.15   Hit the ball

02.15   Stopped the ball, followed by a mishit and then another hit to clear.

03.10   Hit the ball.

04.00   Goal scored and Samantha retrieved the ball from the goal.

04.15   Took a sixteen yard hit. (For the next two minutes the ball was in the opposition half and Samantha used the hockey stick like a drum major and talked to friends.)

06.45   Hit the ball to an opponent who scored.
        Retrieved the ball from the goal and then propelled it with the stick to the half-way line. Walked back very slowly to the defending area. Took no part in play for the next few minutes.

11.00   Retrieved the ball from the goal after the opposition had scored.

13.45   Again took the ball out of the net.

16.03   Stopped the ball followed by a hit.
17.30   Hit the ball twice.
18.02   Hit the ball.
18.20   End of episode.

Thus in eighteen minutes and twenty seconds, Samanatha successfully hit the ball eight times, mishit once and misdirected a hit to the opposition once. All other activity was incidental to the game and occurred when the ball was out of play. There was little or no movement off the ball in relation to marking the opposition. This descriptive account suggests that Samantha's low skill level is unlikely to improve because of her minimal involvement in the game. Surprisingly enough the goalkeeper at the other end of the pitch only hit the ball once in a fifteen minute period but said that she 'enjoyed the lesson, am keen on hockey and play for the school team'. It is only fair to report that the teacher changed the goalkeeper to a forward position because of her lack of involvement.

The alternative to playing a full game is to have two smaller sided games on a smaller area and this was invariably done by all the teachers. This ensured greater and more frequent participation by the pupils with a higher time-on-task profile. Teachers coached within the context of these games and there were no problems relating to unsupervised groups. The pupils were used to this organizational arrangement and received clear instructions about the conditions under which they were to practice and could be relied upon to carry them out. Relevant information and teaching concerning skills and strategies can then be taught in the games setting. The rules and laws of the various games were also incidentally taught in this way. Some problems were encountered in one lesson with fourth year boys playing hockey on a hard surface. The group was divided into two four-a-side games and the teacher spent most of his time with one group. As a result, the other group played unsupervised for thirteen minutes. This proved to be too long a period and their attention and commitment to the game waned. Some positive feedback and motivation was necessary which could only be done by the teacher. This was an exception to the normal teaching in the department.

Staff were doing their best to teach in all the observed lessons. When they were not teaching on a class basis they were always involved with individuals or small groups. In gymnastics this could be seen through the teachers encouraging new and creative ideas or challenging the pupils to improve their levels of skill in a variety of games. The teachers often used the pupils to demonstrate good performance and apart from acting as a visual stimulus, this had the additional merit of showing what could be achieved by other pupils. A common feature in their gymnastic teaching was for each group to demonstrate what they had achieved at the end of a lesson. Whilst this may be valid at the end of a series of lessons to show good work, there are a number of reservations about spending at least five minutes of precious working time showing rather mediocre work. The mediocrity was inevitable because of the short time that was available for practice. One justification for this methodology was to stimulate new ideas and incorporate them into their own sequences. As the demonstration was at the end of the lesson, there was no time to put any of the ideas into practice and by the time the next lesson arrived the ideas would have been long forgotten.

All the feedback that was recorded was positive and usually commented on pupils' performance. The usual phrases of 'Good' and 'Well done' were commonplace but rarely contained any additional information about the activity. Positive comments of this nature were used sparingly to applaud good work or effort and were considered to be meaningful to the pupils. No instances of negative feedback were detected during the week's observation.

During the past two years there had been two recent innovations within the physical education curriculum. The first had been to teach games through a method that has become known as the 'games for understanding' approach. This emphasizes the tactical considerations and an appreciation of principles of play (for example, depth and penetration) which can be applied to all games. One member of staff had attended an in-service course on this topic and had become convinced of its validity. As a result he had persuaded his colleagues to teach games in this manner to mixed classes in the lower school. All the staff were responding positively although one or two expressed some uncertainty about the direction in which their work was taking them. Five lessons were observed involving striking and fielding, invasion games and over-the-net activities. In all instances, the teachers were trying to make the pupils think about the tactics of the game and bring out the underlying principles. This was reflected in the type of questioning. Questions related to passing in invasion games incorporated 'when and why' a pass should be given and received rather than merely concentrating on its execution. The pupils' responses were used to further understanding in relation to ways of marking an opponent and creating space. Other principles such as depth and width were emphasized in the net games. Children were often required to make up their own rules within a framework designated by the teacher, and in some cases given a limited amount of equipment and space and asked to invent a game within set guidelines. With one exception this was completed successfully by all the groups. There was usually a great deal of discussion within the groups and some pupils obviously contributed more than others. Sometimes a clear leader emerged who took control, but usually agreement was arrived at through mutual consent. The groups were keen to begin a game and were quite prepared to alter the rules and modify the game during the course of play. Many ideas were forthcoming and a great deal of purposeful activity resulted. The one exception was a group of five first year girls who could not agree about the format for a game. The teacher spent a long time with this group trying to get consensus. Once some framework had been established he left them to their own devices and went to help other groups. It soon became apparent that the group was unable to cope with the situation and there was a great deal of disagreement. This manifested itself in one girl falling over when batting, several screaming and one girl jumping up and down in anger when she could not persuade the others to her way of thinking. There was a great deal of loud behaviour and shouting. When a high ball (about head height) was bowled, the striker shouted 'That was in my ear 'ole.' One girl refused to be 'out' and continually shouted 'shurrup' at the other girls. Eventually they appealed to the teacher. Some calm was restored to the situation but they had achieved nothing worthwhile in the lesson. At the end the teacher brought out the qualities of cooperation, sportsmanship and the importance of clear rules. In spite of this, the arguments continued after the lesson and were still going on as the pupils disappeared into the changing rooms. Although this was one isolated incident, it is worthy of report. When a problem-solving approach is used, a task is set and pupils have to find a solution, it does presuppose a degree of cooperation from the pupils. Clearly this group would require particular help and attention in the future.

Although this method of teaching games was in an experimental stage, it had the hallmarks of eventual success. Nearly all the pupils were achieving during the lessons and were being made to think about the strategies and tactics of the game. The staff were constantly asking pupils the kinds of questions which encouraged this train of thought and the pupils were responding in a manner which suggested that the principles of play were being understood.

The second innovation area had been the introduction of a course in the fourth and fifth year specifically allocated to 'health-related fitness'. Again this had been suggested by the head of department, discussed and agreed by the staff and been included into the programme for two years. Prior to this, health and fitness was incidental to the teaching of the practical activities. The course was extremely well documented and the schemes of work in the syllabus provided many practical suggestions and information that were invaluable to the staff in their lesson preparation. Only one lesson was observed in this area and this was to a group of fourth year girls. The lesson was a mixture of practical and related theory. It began with a brief introduction to the importance of fitness and its relationship to a person's life style. The teacher even quoted from recent newspaper articles which were relevant and topical. The theme of the lesson was on endurance which inevitably involved exercises that could be repeated many times. The principle behind endurance training of 'many repetitions with light loads' was clearly stated and experienced through the practical work. Popular music was used as a rhythmic aid for the introductory exercises led by the teacher. During the course of the lesson she produced handouts which referred to the benefits of different types of activity such as aerobics, badminton and yoga. These were then discussed with the children. This resulted in a high cognitive component of 50 per cent, but as 46 per cent of this time was spent on background knowledge related to fitness this was not surprising. The practical was not neglected as the children worked hard and a motor appropriate score of 33 per cent was recorded. During this third of the lesson the practical work was intense and the author's subjective opinion was that it would have had a beneficial effect on an individual's level of fitness. One successful motivational technique informed the class of norms achieved by similar age groups for various exercises (for example, trunk curls and ski jumps) and asked them to compare their own standards with these norms. Incidental comments were made on the value of healthy diets and the hazards of smoking and their effects on a person's fitness. This was an impressive lesson which captured the attention and interest of these adolescent girls. The purpose of the two-year scheme of work was incorporated within the department's stated overall aim 'to promote a desire for good health and physical and mental fitness'. If this lesson was a representative sample of the teaching in this area then there was every prospect of achieving this aim with many pupils.

Questionnaire Factors

The Physical Education 'Learner Report' Questionnaire had identified four sub-factors and a t-test for independent samples (separate variance) was carried out between the male and female pupils scores. The results are set out in table 31.

Thus it appeared that there were no significant differences between the male and female pupils in any of the four sub-factors. This was not surprising because of the consistent level of teaching by the male and female staff and the fact that many of the classes were mixed. The only point of departure between the results in table 31 was the rank order of the mean scores. The technomotor factor was ranked first by male and third by

Table 31: S4: T-test on PE 'Learner Report' Questionnaire factors for male and female pupils

	Male		Female		
Factor	*Mean*	*SD*	*Mean*	*SD*	*p*
Technomotor	2.10	0.74	2.43	0.90	N.S.
Sociomotor	2.38	0.82	2.13	0.70	N.S.
Cognitive-reflective	2.66	0.70	2.79	0.76	N.S.
Affective	2.22	0.95	2.25	1.11	N.S.

female pupils and the reverse order applied to the sociomotor factor. Thus there is a tendency for the boys to score higher ratings in the skill area, whereas girls rated the social aspects higher.

Academic Learning Time — Physical Education

In relation to the context level which described the context within which the pupil behaviour occurred and the learner involvement level which described the specific nature of the learner's involvement, summary data is presented in appendix 7. A summary of the three major sub-divisions of the context level for the nineteen lessons taught by the male and female teachers is presented in table 32.

There was virtually no difference in the amount of time devoted to general content relating to organization, providing equipment and warm-up activities. With regard to subject content related to knowledge it appeared that female staff spent a greater proportion of the lesson time (29.1 per cent to 17.7 per cent) on techniques and strategies associated with practical activity. Inevitably this showed up at the learner involvement level where classes taught by female staff spent 33 per cent of their time on cognitive activity compared to 19.2 per cent for the males. As a result of the differences in the PE knowledge content there were corresponding differences in the motor content with male teachers showing the higher recording (64 per cent to 51.3 per cent).

The differences in the content level manifested themselves at the pupil

Table 32: S4: Average percentage time spent by male and female teachers on General content, PE knowledge content and PE motor content

	Male %	Female %
General content	18.9	19.7
PE knowledge content	17.7	29.1
PE motor content	64.0	51.3

Table 33: S4: Average percentage of pupil time spent in ALT-PE learner involvement categories when taught by male and female staff

Not Motor Engaged	Male %	Female %
Interim	0.2	0.4
Waiting	9.1	12.4
Off-task	0.6	0.2
On-task	13.2	13.4
Cognitive	19.2	33.0
Motor engaged		
Motor appropriate	57.8	40.3
Motor inappropriate	0	0
Supporting	0	0.3

level with motor appropriate engaged percentages of 57.8 for the males and 40.3 for the female staff. These were especially high periods of time-on-task and the male percentage was the highest recorded in any of the schools. In spite of these differences, there were no significant differences in the mean scores of the pupils in the four sub-factors of the questionnaire.

The average percentages of time pupils spent in the learner involvement categories is set out in table 33.

Female staff appeared to engage pupils almost twice as much in cognitive behaviour (33 per cent to 19.2 per cent) and three of the nine lessons devoted at least half of the lesson to this behaviour. None of the lessons taught by male staff ever exceeded 38 per cent. It appeared therefore that female staff in this school spent more time involving pupils in cognitive tasks related to the subject than to the organization of the lesson. The 'waiting' time of approximately 10 per cent is quite a substantial part of the lesson and might be an area where more profitable activity could take place.

Planning Procedures

A very detailed and comprehensive written syllabus had been produced by the staff. This 'Faculty Document' was in two sections. The first section provided information about the faculty, its aims and objectives, basic philosophy and structure, and the second section itemized detailed schemes of work for all the practical activities. The document was well presented, well written and gave a full and clear account of the physical education in S4. It was an impressive syllabus and an invaluable source of reference. Each scheme of work had been written by one member of staff and had subsequently been discussed and amended by all the staff at one of the monthly department meetings. Thus all the staff felt they had made a worthwhile contribution. There was one person who had overall responsibility for the subject and, within this framework, another staff member who was responsible for girls' physical education.

One of the major aims of the department was to increase the skill levels of their pupils and to help every child to achieve his or her highest potential. Concern was expressed that all pupils should have the opportunity to succeed and this included the less able.

Social relationships and cooperation were also mentioned together with the hope that children would 'learn to enjoy sport and physical education'. The desire to promote good health and fitness and inculcate methods of maintaining fitness were important aims of the programme. The syllabus not only specified the general aims and objectives but also the possible means of achieving them. Thus there was a direct link between theory and practice. This was especially true of the recently instituted course on health-related fitness which was to form an important part of a coordinated health education programme in the school, already in an advanced stage of planning. When the department had introduced the HRF course, the children had been told the reasons for its inclusion and the objectives they hoped to achieve. Usually the short-term objectives of a course were not stated, but this was an exception.

Games formed a high proportion of the content of the programme. This was acknowledged by the staff who felt that the course reflected their strengths. A recent examination of the types of games had revealed a preponderance of invasion-type games and as a result more over-the-net and striking/fielding games had been included. The lack of expressive activities was acknowledged by the staff but a part-time teacher had recently been appointed to teach dance and it was hoped to expand this area if staffing levels permitted. A common core of activities was followed during the first three years with some slight choice in the fourth year. In the senior school one afternoon each week was allocated to physical education. This was an optional programme as, alternatively, pupils could choose to become involved in a community project. As a result, many opted out of physical education. During the autumn term eleven activities were on offer, some of which took place on off-site facilities. A few of the activities were merely supervised with no teaching taking place and this was causing some concern within the department. In one or two activities, the groups had received some basic information and provided there were no safety problems, the pupils were allowed to work with minimum supervision. It is important to record that most of the groups were taught by staff competent in the activity and some non-physical education staff were timetabled for this purpose. Staff would liked to have offered pupils a greater range of options to prepare them for their leisure in the post-school period, but some facilities were not available and others, such as golf, were prohibitive because of cost.

There was a strong commitment to the teaching of mixed physical education and all the first and fourth year groups were taught in these groupings, apart from some games in the fourth year. The intervening years were taught in single sex groupings because of the timetable arrangements, but there was strong support for boys and girls being taught in the same group wherever possible and this policy had been implemented in the senior school options.

The schemes of work indicated which skills should be taught in each year and they all showed clear progression. As staff did not keep a written record these appeared to be the main source of reference showing what had been covered in each unit of work. A thriving extra-curricular programme had recently restarted and all clubs were open to all children in a particular year group. The statement 'anyone, regardless of ability can go to a practice and is incorporated into the practice' seemed to sum up the situation. Having said that, it appeared children in this school chose the activities they were good at and as a result instituted their own streaming system.

The head of department did review and up-date the syllabus at the beginning of each academic year. In response to the question 'Do you ever evaluate the original aims?', he stated, 'Yes I do, because I need to change an aim if I haven't fulfilled it'. The staff had met on many occasions to discuss their philosophy behind the curriculum and this had resulted in some changes each year. Their assessment of the success of the physical education curriculum was subjectively based on the pupils' commitment and enjoyment of the range of activities during the lessons and in extra-curricular activities. Another indicator was the number of pupils who joined local clubs once they had left school.

The staff were adamant about not giving attainment grades on the report form. 'It doesn't do pupils any good to tell them they are no good at physical education' remarked one teacher. 'In a subject that is non-examinable it is not necessary to tell them they are failures' said another. In the main, an effort grade was recorded but obviously they did comment on the high achievers and on representative honours where it was appropriate to do so.

In summary, the department was well-organized and planned effec-tively. The written syllabus was impressive by any standards and contained a wealth of information for teaching as well as setting out a clear philosophy. The staff were keen to keep up-to-date with new ideas and all were encouraged to attend in-service courses and report back to their colleagues. This was only one of the ways in which the curriculum was being constantly monitored. The department had equal status with all the other departments in the school and the head teacher took a keen interest in physical education. The head of department met with the head teacher once a term to discuss the work and the department appreciated his supportive attitude. All members of the department had other responsibilities outside the department and played an active part in the life of the school. Overall, the staff were a cohesive, hard-working and effective group.

Case Study: School 5 (S5) — Webb Secondary School

S5 was a secondary modern school accommodated on a large site in an urban setting. The visits to this school took place immediately after half-term break. Eighteen lessons were observed which were ALT-PE coded, thirteen of which were taught by male staff and five by female staff. The reasons for this imbalance were recent staff changes and absences. The teaching time in each lesson was an average of thirty-two-and-a-quarter minutes and all classes were timetabled for three lessons each week. In addition to the observed lessons, the author taught or was involved in some group teaching with five other classes.

Staffing

The male staff comprised two full-time and one half-time teacher, all specialists trained in physical education. During the observation period the female department consisted of one specialist trained teacher and four different part-time staff making up one full-time equivalent. Additionally, a few non-physical education staff were also timetabled to assist in the work of the department.

Without exception, the specialist physical education staff were knowledgeable in their subject and confident in their control of classes. Usually there was a good working atmosphere and the teachers were fair in their dealings with pupils. The same level of knowledge was not so apparent with the part-time staff and in one case this was leading to some discipline problems. Most of the staff had an easy and pleasant relationship with the pupils. The proximity of the staff and pupils' changing rooms gave pupils ample opportunity for interaction and most pupils freely engaged staff in conversation.

Since the administration of the questionnaire in the summer, there had been two significant changes within the school. The first was that the head of the girls' physical education department had left unexpectedly at the end of the summer term and it had not been possible to make a new appointment. The school had been unable to employ any one person on a full-time basis and it had been necessary to employ four teachers in a part-time capacity to cover the work. Thus the school was having to cope with some difficult problems. The second change related to some reorganization within the school which had necessitated changing the timetable from four double periods to six single periods in a day. The physical education staff were not happy with this new arrangement and felt that they were always rushed to complete their work during a lesson. As a result of this, a conscious decision had been made to work to the end of each period, thus omitting showering time. Even when pupils have been involved in heavy physical work output and were perspiring heavily, or were muddy after playing games on the field, there was never an opportunity to shower.

Facilities

The school had good outdoor facilities with two large games fields and a playground area large enough to accommodate four tennis courts. The indoor facilities were not as good and consisted of one narrow traditionally equipped gymnasium and the use of a hall. In addition some facilities were used in the local community, for example, a water sports centre and golf course.

Storage for the indoor equipment was poor and some of the larger gymnastic apparatus had to be kept in an adjoining corridor. The equipment room leading from the gymnasium was narrow and inadequate and led to some congestion when apparatus was needed during a lesson. Some of the outdoor equipment such as hockey sticks, flags and cones, was kept in a locked hut adjacent to the fields and the opening and closing of this storage space proved to be rather inconvenient at times.

Changing facilities for the male staff were very restricted and completely inadequate. The physical education staff room adjoined the boys' changing room and allowed very little privacy.

The changing rooms for the boys and the girls adjoined the gymnasium and were adequate in size. A few posters on soccer, gymnastics and netball were displayed on the walls together with some team sheets for school teams. Showers adjoined these areas but, as previously explained, were never used.

Dress

The department insisted that all pupils changed for physical education and there was a school uniform for lower school pupils. Some freedom for the type of dress was allowed for children in the upper school but there was an insistence on 'appropriate clothing for the activity' being worn. All the pupils appeared to accept this situation and complied with these standards. Because of the shortness of the lesson, some pupils used the break period to change. These pupils were obviously keen on the subject and because they were ready when staff arrived, they were sometimes given equipment and allowed to practice on their own. However, this was not always the case and there were several occasions when everyone had to wait until the last person was ready. This may have been because of organizational factors such as choosing teams. In these instances, the waiting seemed a poor reward for those pupils who had given up part of their break-time.

Structure and Content

All the observed lessons were associated with the major games and the majority of these took place on the games fields. The overall impression was that there was a great deal of 'games playing' and very little practice of techniques and individual skills. This led to a lot of coaching within the game situation which was generally of a good standard. There were several occasions when the principles involved in the playing of all games were mentioned. For example, 'just like moving into space in football' was a comment made by one teacher in a hockey lesson and 'give and go' in basketball was also linked to soccer. Two lessons were completely devoted to full-sided eleven-a-side games in soccer. Defending players in the dominant team were rarely called into play and although they were part of the game, they had little opportunity to improve their skill levels. This form of organization was the exception rather than the rule as classes were invariably broken down into smaller units and conditioned games played in restricted areas. This ensured greater involvement for all pupils and there was generally a high work rate but obviously the teacher had to spread his attention between the groups and sometimes this was not done very effectively. In one soccer class of fourth year boys this was particularly noticeable. The class had been divided into six groups of six, and three games of six-a-side were being played. There was a high work rate (a motor appropriate score of 69 per cent was recorded) and the teacher coached two of the games. The third group received no attention. This may have been partly due to the pressure of time, but it did mean that one group had been involved in a 'self-learning' situation. Very little knowledge was fed in on a class basis. Throughout the lesson the teacher was busy and coached within the game, but ignored one group.

As mentioned earlier, there were a few lessons in which timetabled help was received from non-physical education staff. The quality of this additional help left something to be desired. In one first year soccer lesson a teacher came outside dressed in his ordinary clothes and an anorak. One third of the lesson was spent in organizational aspects of choosing teams and then the class was divided into three six-a-side games. This teacher was given responsibility for one group while the physical education teacher coached the other two. During this thirty-minute lesson the teacher stood on the touchline and made no comment to any pupil at any time. This was in marked contrast to the physical education teacher who was constantly involved with his two groups. Again, this seemed to be an unsatisfactory arrangement to say the least. More control by the physical education staff, followed by group work within a clearly defined framework, might overcome this problem.

There was some suggestion that one of the lessons each week should be devoted to techniques and the other to the playing of the game. This was only a tentative idea and made in response to the new timetabling arrangements. However, this was not apparent during the observation week and did not appear to be a consistent policy within the department.

The girls' programme of games alternated each week between hockey and netball. This arrangement was preferred to blocking each activity into six-week periods. One teacher made the comment that she 'was seeing no improvement in the first year groups but that fourth year pupils were willing to alternate and were not losing enthusiasm'. It may be that the basic skills of a particular game are best learnt in a series of consecutive lessons rather than being alternated with a different activity. Only when pupils have learnt to discriminate between the skills in the different games is there less chance of interference. At fourth year level it may also be true that some pupils prefer not to play the same game each week.

Where introductory techniques and practices were part of the lesson they were usually taught satisfactorily and the accompanying explanations and demonstrations were clear and relevant. One basketball lesson was particularly noteworthy because the teacher was not satisfied with the initial attempts and made an all-out effort to achieve some quality performance. Because of this insistence by the teacher, the pupils' performance improved markedly. A constant theme of work from the early to the later part of the lesson was not always apparent. Thus techniques practised at the beginning became incidental within the game, and logical and related progressions were not obvious.

The department obviously believed in a high commitment to the playing of the game. In this kind of skill learning situation which Poulton (1957) referred to as an 'open' skill where the temporal and spatial factors are continually changing, it is essential that pupils are placed in situations where they are made to interpret the sensory input from the environment and make the appropriate decision. This assumes adequate levels of personal skill and a sufficient amount of information being provided by the teacher. Certainly pupils were being placed in small-sided team games and encouraged to make perceptual decisions. Within the limited observation period it was difficult to make categorical statements. Some pupils were obviously playing with a full commitment to the game. Others did not have the necessary skill level to compete successfully and although they probably enjoyed the lesson there was little evidence of any learning taking place.

The overall questioning was sound and made pupils think about the reasons for doing the various techniques and strategies. Questions such as 'How can you get more power into the hockey pass?' elicited information related to the mechanical principles involved as well as to the positioning of the hands on the stick. Thus there were numerous occasions when pupils were asked 'why' and 'how' an activity was to be performed rather than merely being shown the skill and told to practice it. Often this questioning procedure was linked to demonstrations which almost invariably involved the pupils.

The fourth year boys' basketball lessons were taught by different teachers and provided a real contrast. In one the teacher constantly challenged the class and introduced a competitive element based on each person's level of ability. Attacking and defending practices introduced in the early part of the lesson were finally transferred to the half-court four-a-side practice with the other pupils officiating. This produced a high motor content of 55 per cent. The pupils responded positively to this challenging, competitive environment and showed a very satisfactory level of skill. The only incongruous note was the attitude and behaviour of one good player who was intolerant of team mates responsible for a breakdown in play. This was a good lesson in which the knowledge and enthusiasm of the teacher inspired the children to work hard and there was no doubt the environment was conducive to effective learning. The other lesson involved basketball shooting practices with four teams. Only four balls were made available which meant that four practised while fourteen waited for a turn. In spite of a clear demonstration of shooting techniques by the teacher, the boys' performance bore little resemblance to the model. This was mainly because the practice involved shooting the ball between two sets of beams which the pupils found difficult. Quite naturally the boys were only interested in getting the ball through the beams rather than performing the skill correctly. Consequently, all manner of techniques were used and none was criticized by the teacher. More important perhaps was the fact that wrong techniques were being reinforced. The skill level was markedly low and there were few signs of improvement. In spite of this the teacher said the class was 'definitely getting better'. This statement was far from the truth but may have been said for motivational purposes. The latter part of the lesson involved a game but because of the size of the gymnasium, half the class was sitting on the side lines. As a result of this lesson organization 42 per cent was recorded in the pupil 'waiting' category. In turn this was mainly responsible for the low motor appropriate recording of 18%. Another criticism was that the lesson theme of shooting used in the introduction was not incorporated into the games playing section. Thus the lesson lacked any progressive skill development and continuity.

Other problems existed within the fourth year girls' programme. The observation of a fitness lesson on aerobics was cancelled because the pupils refused to participate as they considered the music to be too juvenile. No amount of persuasion from the teacher could encourage them to take part. The ensuing discussion revealed that they were quite prepared to participate in aerobic activity as long as the music was more appropriate and modern. In the end it was agreed that the department would purchase new cassettes chosen by the pupils and suggestions were asked for. All the girls in the group stated they would not wish to opt out of physical education even if they were given the chance and the discussion then focused on the kinds of activity they would like to see included in the programme. There was considerable support for mixed activities such as basketball, hockey and badminton. In addition, there was an interest expressed in weight training. A suggestion was made that this could be linked to the health-related fitness programme but the group thought there was overlap and duplication with science lessons. The next day the group took part in a basketball lesson. They wore a mixed range of personal clothing but they had all changed for the lesson. A rather pointless introductory period of aimless shooting and warm-up was followed by a coached game. The decision to play a full game was probably the right one for this group on this occasion and an acceptable level of game playing resulted.

Because of the emphasis placed on competitive games it was nearly always necessary to group pupils into equal teams. Usually this was carried out by the teachers who chose teams of equal strength based on their knowledge of the pupils' ability, by placing several children in the same group at the same time. On two occasions an alternative method was used whereby pupils stood in front of the class and chose teams. Inevitably this resulted in the more able performers in the activity being chosen first with the least able left until last. To be left until last must have a devastating effect on a pupil's self-esteem and reduce his or her personal standing within the peer group. This is an organizational method that is best left out of physical education lessons.

The continuous and accurate monitoring of feedback proved to be impossible — mainly because most of the lessons were outside and groups were spread over quite a large area. Apart from one instance of negative feedback when the teacher remarked 'That was poor' to one quite able pupil, all the rest were positive. The negative comment was possibly used to motivate this pupil to greater effort. Rarely were there any informational properties in the comments. Thus if a pupil had moved into space to receive a pass, the teacher would say 'Well done' or 'Good' without any amplification as to exactly what had been done well. During the course of the coaching of the games, the teachers made many relevant comments but these were mainly of a 'feed forward' nature which helped pupils anticipate future moves. Thus coaching points such as 'moving off the ball' and encouraging numerical superiority were commonplace.

As has already been stated, the curriculum was strongly biased towards games and this was reflected in the sample of lessons observed during the observation period. Some gymnastics and dance was timetabled for first and second year girls but the lessons were not taught because the teacher was absent. No gymnastics was included in the boys' physical education curriculum at any time, but it was hoped that this situation would be changed when new staff were appointed.

With a few exceptions in the fifth year, all the lessons were taught on a single sex basis. Some staff were keen to start teaching mixed physical education, but the idea had not been implemented at this stage. One member of staff had attended a 'games for understanding' course and was attempting to teach through this methodology to the first year pupils. Occasionally other staff were assisting him in this venture and the concepts were being introduced through some team teaching. A first year games lesson exemplified this approach when two staff combined to teach around the theme of creating space using a rugby ball in a small grid area. All the subject knowledge input was based on strategical considerations of when, why and who should move into space and very little emphasis was placed on the techniques of passing. Thus an attempt was being made to teach the underlying principles concerning spatial awareness.

A health-related fitness course had been in operation in the senior school for some time. Considerable concern and interest by a number of physical education teachers in the area had resulted in a group of staff meeting to form an outline syllabus which could be adapted to each school. Extensive notes were available on the main components of fitness and these were supplemented with knowledge tests and individual fitness and physical activity profiles. The course also involved a theoretical element, at the end of which each pupil accumulated a set of notes. HRF appeared to be given greater emphasis in the boys' programme and this may have been partly due to the expertise of the staff. The head of department was so convinced of its value that he had started to introduce the course much earlier. Two second-year lessons were observed in which the author was involved in the teaching. The warm-up activities were led by one of the pupils with the teacher stressing the correct movements. All these were performed satisfactorily and did not violate any of the principles of warming up exercises. Both classes were questioned about the components of fitness viz. strength, flexibility and endurance, and most understood the meanings of the terms and good knowledgeable responses were given. More important, they had sound introductory knowledge about the training and development of these components. The practical part of the lesson related to endurance training and consisted of a circuit of six activities. The boys worked together in pairs and completed the circuit twice. On the first occasion they worked for one minute on each activity and on the second circuit this was reduced to forty-five seconds. At the end of this very strenuous period of activity during which the boys worked extremely hard, there was a time for a 'warm-down' which included some flexibility exercises. The pupils displayed an excellent commitment and there was a good working atmosphere. Thus the practical element was being supported by sound-related theory and this augers well for their future understanding.

One half day each week was allocated to the fifth year programme and was based on four groupings. The first group had one hour outdoors on one of the major games or cross country, and a second hour indoors on basketball, badminton, table tennis or weight training. The second group visited a nearby Outdoor Pursuits Centre which offered a choice of water and outdoor activities. The third and fourth groups were involved in cycling or horse riding. Most of the activities were under supervision and in some cases instruction, but the time was mainly considered to be recreative.

For many years the school had successfully taught a CSE course in physical education and additional time was available on the timetable. Unfortunately none of this work was in progress during the observation week. Consideration was being given to embarking on a GCSE programme but syllabuses from different boards were still being discussed.

Extra-curricular Activities

No regular extra-curricular activity had taken place for almost two years because of industrial action. However, there had been a few inter-school fixtures and it was indicative of the keenness of the pupils that it had been possible to select as many as four teams from within a year group. The extra-curricular programme was just beginning again and a few lunch time and after-school practices were in progress. Nevertheless, it would probably take some time before a full programme was in operation, and some doubt was expressed whether it would ever reach former levels. The lack of commitment of non-physical education staff was considered to be a crucial factor.

Questionnaire Factors

The four factors derived from the Physical Education 'Learner Report' Questionnaire were subjected to statistical analysis by means of a t-test for independent samples (separate variance). The means and standard deviations for the male and female pupils are set out in table 34.

On each of the four factors, the male pupils had a higher score and a lower standard deviation, but none was statistically significant. Apart from this spread of scores, the rank order varied slightly with the female pupils ranking the affective factor first and the technomotor second, whereas the order was reversed for the males. The boys' programme had a strong games bias and this may have accounted for their higher ranking in the motor skills area.

Many of the mean scores for both groups are close to a neutral score of '3' and the spread indicates that there are substantial percentages of pupils with negative perceptions of their learning in physical education. A number of reasons could be advanced for this such as the poor indoor facilities, the excessive games bias in the curriculum, some indifferent teaching and some staffing problems. It is difficult to pinpoint the reasons

Table 34: S5: T-test on PE 'Learner Report' Questionnaire factors for male and female pupils

	Male		Female		
Factor	*Mean*	*SD*	*Mean*	*SD*	*p*
Technomotor	2.25	0.78	2.58	0.83	N.S.
Sociomotor	2.38	0.92	2.91	1.11	N.S.
Cognitive-reflective	2.79	0.77	3.06	1.12	N.S
Affective	2.31	0.97	2.49	1.19	N.S.

for similarities and differences in table 34, especially as it had not been possible to observe the teaching nor to talk to the former head of the girls' physical education as she recently left after eight years on the staff.

Academic Learning Time — Physical Education

The ALT-PE data for the context level for the eighteen lessons taught by the male and female teachers is presented in appendix 7 with summary data in table 35.

Table 35: S5: Average percentage time spent by male and female teachers on General content, PE knowledge content and PE motor content

	Male %	Female %
General content	19.6	31.0
PE knowledge content	18.5	11.0
PE motor content	62.0	58.2

Female teachers spent a greater proportion of the lesson time on general content matters than their male colleagues (31 per cent to 19.6 per cent). Thus longer periods of time were devoted to organizational activities related to instruction, moving from one space to another, changing activities, providing equipment and warm-up activities. Approximately one-third of the time was given to this broad area by the female staff. The reverse trend was apparent in the knowledge content where male teachers spent more time (18.5 per cent to 11 per cent) — especially in the strategical and tactical areas of games playing. When the motor content was examined, both groups devoted nearly 60 per cent of the lesson to practical work. This in turn resulted in a very high motor appropriate recording of learner involvement with an average of 46.5 per cent (see table 36). The overall balance of lessons between the male and the female teachers did appear to be rather uneven and this was particularly true of the female teachers where the knowledge content input to the lessons was the lowest of any group within the main sample. This may be attributed to the fact that the staff in S5 preferred to spend their time coaching within the game. Perhaps a reduction in the general and an increase in the knowledge content might have an effect on learning levels. In spite of the differences in the allocation of time, it was perhaps surprising that there were no significant differences between male and female pupils on any of the four sub-factors.

The average percentage of time pupils spent in the learner involvement categories is set out in table 36.

Table 36: S5: Average percentage of time pupils spent in ALT-PE learner involvement categories when taught by male and female staff

Not motor Engaged	Male %	Female %
Interim	0	2.0
Waiting	17.2	7.6
Off-task	0	0.6
On-task	8.8	33.2
Cognitive	25.3	12.4
Motor engaged		
Motor appropriate	48.7	44.2
Motor inappropriate	0.3	0
Supporting	0	0

The high percentage of waiting time for male pupils was mainly due to boys sitting out waiting to take part in a game of basketball. In one lesson this reached an unacceptably high level of 42 per cent. Excessive periods spent in transition and organizational aspects by female teachers would account for the high on -task recordings. On average more than twice as much time was spent on cognitive behaviour by male pupils and this reflected the input of knowledge content of 18.5 per cent for male and 11 per cent for female teachers.

Planning Procedures

The boys' and girls' departments each had autonomy over the presentation of their work although one male teacher, as head of department, had overall responsibility for administrative matters such as finance and the allocation of facilities. There was a separate written syllabus for each department and each began with similar statements about the aims of the programme. These included the development of health and fitness, skilled performance, leisure time pursuits, an awareness of others and self-realization. The similarity of some of the wording of these aims suggested there had been some measure of cooperation in their formation. During the interviews, the staff emphasized the importance they attached to the pupils achieving and gaining satisfaction in the physical education programme. 'Through this enjoyment we hope they will carry on when they have left school' was a statement which seemed to sum up their main aim of physical education. The written aims were then followed by a dozen or more pages outlining the schemes of work for each of the practical activities in each year. Overall, the syllabus was well presented and had formed part of the submission made by the school for a recent LEA inspection. The teachers who had written the syllabus had been on the staff of the school for several years and the present programme had gradually evolved during that time. The available facilities were the most important factor influencing the programme and concern was expressed about the poor indoor facilities. The departments met separately and informally at the beginning of the academic year to plan the curriculum and to 'have a chat about it'. The staff in both departments never met as a group to discuss curriculum planning.

Participation and membership of local clubs was encouraged and even displayed on posters in the changing rooms. One poster read, 'ARE YOU BORED? WHY? These are things you could be doing ...' This was followed by information concerning courses and clubs in the locality. Apart from this it did not appear that staff communicated the long-term aims of the subject to the pupils. Additionally, there was little likelihood that the short-term aims of a unit of work would be stated, although there was some suggestion this might be done for some of the individual sports such as cross-country.

Not only did the staff operate as separate departments but there was also very little mixing of the sexes in the teaching of physical education. The only place where some integration did occur was in some of the fifth-form option groups. The curriculum was planned with a common core of work for all pupils during the first four years followed by a range of options in the fifth year using some of the facilities available in the local community. There appeared to be no objection in principle to mixed physical education and some tentative consideration was being given to a trial with the first year pupils. However, this was partly dependent on a new staff appointment and the impression was gained that this innovation would not be implemented in the immediate future.

There was a strong games bias in the school, especially for the boys. This was justified on the grounds that the teaching strengths of the staff and the lack of indoor facilities necessitated this approach. In fact, the boys were not taught gymnastics. This had been highlighted by the Inspectorate and the school hoped that a new staff appointment would have some expertise in this area and overcome the problem.

The schemes of work gave a clear indication of the nature of the content to be covered in each unit. As a result, a clear progression was evident throughout the curriculum. Additionally, the staff kept brief lesson notes and records which were available for colleagues to consult. Physical education in the fifth year was truly optional and approximately 25 per cent of the boys and a slightly higher percentage of girls chose not to take part. The subject was timetabled against 'work experience' in the locality which partly accounted for these percentages.

Apart from some limitations within year groupings, all the extra-curricular activities were open to any pupil. Most of the clubs were games biased and ran competitive teams and sometimes as many as four from one year group. No elitist or selection system was operated and all pupils were welcomed and encouraged to attend.

The success of the physical education curriculum was judged by the pupils' level of participation and enjoyment and, consistent with one of the main aims, their continued participation in physical activity once they had left school. There was little attempt to evaluate the stated aims of physical education except at a 'sub-conscious' level. There may have been some informal discussion but this was rather tentative. School reports on the subject were in three parts. There was an A to E grading for effort, a 1 to 5 grading for attainment, and an optional written comment. Examples were given where it was possible for a pupil of low ability to be given a '5' grade for attainment and an 'A' grade for effort.

In summary, there were adequate written statements about the boys' and the girls' physical education syllabuses in the school. Great stress was placed on competitive games — especially for the boys. The main emphasis of the programme appeared to be to encourage pupils to participate in leisure-time activities once they had left the school and links with the local community were encouraged. A number of non-specialists assisted in the teaching but they did not appear to participate in any of the planning procedures and their contribution and commitment was somewhat limited. The clear progressions in the schemes of work and the links with teachers' records gave staff every opportunity to achieve continuity in the different activities. However, it was unlikely that the non-physical education staff consulted these records. The specialist staff were knowledgeable but the quality of the teaching was rather mixed. A cautionary note was expressed by one teacher at the end of the interview who wondered whether 'the specialist teacher would cease to exist ... and that the subject would be made optional'. This seemed to indicate some insecurity about his feelings for the status of physical education in the school.

9
Pupils' Opinions of Physical Education

Apart from the informal comments made by pupils during lessons or in casual conservation with the author, all the information concerned with pupils' perceptions of physical education had so far been anonymous and generated through responses to a questionnaire. Whilst this information was valuable, it was felt that it could be enriched through semi-structured personal interviews with a number of pupils in each school. Interviews of this nature can reveal a great deal of insight about a person's attitudes and opinions of physical education. These glimpses of a pupil's perceptions of the subject will be expressed verbally and often contain a richness of language that is missing from purely quantitative data.

In order to explore a range of opinions it was decided to approach pupils with a high and low range of motor ability in physical education. This would then enable a comparison to be made between pupils at both ends of an ability continuum. By doing this it might be possible to contrast extreme points of view. In addition, the sex of the teacher and the pupil had been under investigation in this study and it was therefore considered appropriate to explore possible sex differences between boys and girls. Thus a range of opinions could be explored through interviews with pupils differentiated on the basis of motor ability and sex.

It would have been interesting to have identified pupils in these two categories who had scored at the extreme ends of the PE 'Learner Report' Questionnaire. However, this was not possible because of the anonymous and confidential nature of the questionnaires.

On the basis of the above guidelines, four pupils from the fifth year, all of whom had completed the Physical Education 'Learner Report' Questionnaire the previous term, were interviewed in each of the five schools. As explained, the pupils were chosen by the physical education staff according to motor ability and sex. Thus one high ability (HA), and one low ability (LA) boy and girl were selected for interview in each school. Every pupil who was approached agreed to take part and none had prior

157

knowledge of the questions other than that they were concerned with their opinions of physical education. The interviews were conducted at school in a quiet environment which was familiar to the pupil and where there were no distractions. The interviewees were told there were no right or wrong answers to any of the questions and that it was important for them to state their own opinion. An assurance was also given concerning the confidentiality of their name and the name of the school.

The schedule of questions closely followed the format of the PE 'Learner Report' Questionnaire and the detailed inventory is set out in appendix 8. Thus, apart from two general introductory questions, the remainder of the questions were related to the technomotor, sociomotor, cognitive-reflective and affective factors. Once the questions had been formulated, a pilot study was undertaken with a fifth form pupil from another school. As a result of this it was considered necessary to begin by thanking the pupils for agreeing to take part and telling them that the purpose of the interview was to discover something about their opinion of physical education. The need to encourage pupils to justify and expand their answers was anticipated and this frequently led to supplementary questions asking them to give reasons for a particular response. There were periods of silence when pupils were thinking about their response to a question and it was important not to interrupt these too soon as their considered views were important. Although the questions were in a set order, they were not always asked in that order when the natural development of the interview dictated otherwise. This helped to preserve some continuity and flow. Each interview lasted approximately half-an-hour during which time notes were taken on a prepared sheet and these were amplified as soon after the interview as was conveniently possible.

An analysis of the twenty interviews was subsequently undertaken. The pupils' responses to the questions were considered under five main headings, viz. opinions and experiences in physical education, technomotor, sociomotor, cognitive-reflective and affective areas. In addition, the two variables of motor ability and sex were highlighted. The results of this analysis now follow.

Opinions and Experiences in Physical Education

The first question simply asked 'What do you think of physical education?' The responses were clearly divided according to ability. All high ability (HA) pupils used phrases such as:

'It's good, keeps you fit.'
'I think its great. I try my hardest in every lesson.'

'I couldn't go to school if there was no physical education. I couldn't bring a note.'
'I think its good, better than any other subject.'

These contrasted markedly with some of the low ability (LA) pupils who remarked:

'Sometimes it is boring.'
'I don't like the activities.'
'I used to like physical education, but not now. I don't enjoy it.'

However, there were two LA pupils who did consider that physical education was helpful in maintaining fitness levels.

Thus at the extremes of ability, pupils with high levels obviously had a more positive opinion of the subject than those at the lower end. The positive reaction is to be expected as high ability and positive feelings are invariably interlinked. Personal feelings of worth can often be enhanced and reinforced through achievement in motor skills. Conversely, LA pupils who have failed, achieve what Dweck (1980) referred to as 'learned helplessness' and it would appear that the low opinion of their ability transfers to their feelings for the subject.

The reasons for these differences of opinion were probed and the pupils asked to identify the kinds of activities or experiences which had contributed to their present attitude. The HA group advanced several reasons. The variety of activities was certainly a factor and the opportunity to compete in those activities in which they had shown aptitude was frequently mentioned. Most of this group had gone on to play representative sport at a higher level outside the school and some had competed at national level. This had obviously given them public recognition. The social aspects of working as a team and the development of team spirit were also influencing factors. Experiences such as these had given them a great deal of enjoyment and contributed to their self-esteem. One girl was particularly appreciative of the help and support given by her parents who frequently watched her play. These experiences contrasted markedly with those pupils in the LA group. Low levels of ability were usually associated with poor opinions of the subject, although there was one LA boy who stated that he liked the subject whilst recognizing his low performance level. Frequent mention was made of the fact that they did not like going outside in the rain and cold. One girl made the positive suggestion that cross country should be a summer rather than a winter activity. A sensible comment, but cross country is usually undertaken in the winter when the playing fields are unfit for use and there is no indoor space available. Thus, the demands of the situation in the school can sometimes determine the activity. One of the current debates in physical education is the diversity of activities being offered to pupils in the secondary school in the optional programme of the curriculum. The danger is that the subject becomes 'a mile wide and an inch deep'. This feeling was confirmed by one boy who felt that the activities were constantly being changed round which 'mucks me about' and did not allow sufficient time to develop his skills. Another adverse feeling had been generated in one girl in dance who felt that the teachers used unsuitable and 'old music'. This coincided with the opinions of a group of fourth-form pupils in another school who had refused to take part in a dance lesson because they considered that dancing to *Thomas the Tank Engine* music was completely unsuitable to their level of maturity. Another concern was expressed about the borrowing of clothing and this was forcefully stated by two of the girls. It is common practice for physical education departments to have a certain amount of 'lost clothing' in the changing rooms. Whenever a pupil has forgotten his or her physical education clothing, then they are allowed to borrow items. These girls obviously resented borrowing 'smelly clothing' and as a result just brought notes signed by a parent to excuse them participating — even though the reason was false. A particularly unfortunate experience had happened to one girl who had been a gifted netball player in the first year and was chosen by the teacher to play in the year 2 team. This had been resented by the other girls in the team who had 'picked on' her and made her unwelcome through verbal comments and by stealing her games clothing. This had resulted in a chain reaction of the parents eventually refusing to buy more clothing, 'more hassle from the teacher', a dislike of borrowing kit and subsequently the bringing of excuse notes. Thus a promising games player had not realized her potential and was now regarded as being of low ability.

Technomotor Area

In the technomotor area, all the HA pupils felt that there was not enough time to practise their physical skills in lessons and would welcome more time being devoted to the subject. Only two pupils from the LA group felt this way. The remainder either considered there was enough or too much time allocation. Comments such as 'Doesn't interest me just hitting a shuttle' and 'Sooner just play and do without the teacher's comments' were not untypical. One pupil remarked on 'a lot of sitting out' which was certainly confirmed by the ALT-PE analyses.

In the practice of skills related to performance on the gymnastic apparatus, the responses of all the pupils were either neutral or negative.

Not one felt any competence in this aspect. The response of one LA boy who said, 'No, not really, the teachers haven't taught us' was not uncommon. Similarly one HA boy said 'I can't remember using them. They are not used to their full potential and are wasted.' These comments also reflected the fact that gymnastics was not part of the physical education curriculum in his school. Again, this reflected limited learning and minimal use of sophisticated and expensive gymnastic equipment.

Knowledge of the rules of well-known sports was answered quite differently by the two ability groups. The HA pupils nearly all felt they were knowledgeable in the area and that the rules had been taught incidentally by the teacher during the lesson. It is perhaps important to remember that this group of pupils would almost certainly have taken part in extra-curricular activities where the rules and tactics of games would be related. As a result, greater periods of time would have been available to assimilate such knowledge. The LA group nearly all responded negatively apart from one boy who said that he knew 'only the basics'. Another boy remarked that he had 'been taught, but it goes in one ear and out the other one'. Such forgetting was not uncommon within this group.

One aspect which is common to all games is that there are a number of principles which can be applied to all situations. Examples would include creating and moving into space to attack or denying space to the opposition in defence. The HA group had only the vaguest idea of the principles even when prompted with examples. The group of LA pupils had even less idea and one boy remarked that 'the teacher says "come out wide" but I don't know why I should'. In response to the suggestion of 'width' as a principle, one girl could only relate it to the width of a swimming pool. It was abundantly clear that this sample of pupils had little or no idea about the principles of games playing and that it was an aspect which was either absent or ineffective in the teaching strategies of most teachers.

Sociomotor Area

The first question in the sociomotor area asked the pupils if they could join in and cooperate when they were playing with others who were either better or not as good as they were. Regardless of sex or ability, the pupils felt that they were able to take part in spite of the differing ability levels. However, the responses were not unqualified and there was often an additional comment made. Almost all the HA pupils felt they could make a contribution in a high level performance situation, would try their hardest and probably learn from the more able players. Where they were involved with less-able performers, most felt they would encourage by telling them what to do. However, some did express a measure of frustration in these circumstances and would not be afraid to 'stick the not-so-good in defence'. There was also a suggestion that the best players would 'more often than not, not pass to the poorer players'. This approach was also confirmed by a boy and a girl in the LA group who commented that 'the best pass to each other'. Even within the same activity which encouraged differing ability levels there was some indication of separatism and elitism in the organization and playing structure. One HA boy even remarked on 'them and us' situations.

In a similar vein, pupils were asked to give their reaction to a situation of someone in a group activity who was not good enough and could not cope. Nearly all the pupils replied that they would still accept a less-able person and make some attempt to help them either through verbal encouragement or by simplifying the performance of the skill. This was exemplified by one girl who said that she would 'take extra care when passing and try to make it easier'. A few in the HA group felt they would experience some frustration in these circumstances and two girls made comments such as 'Reject a little bit and wouldn't pass to them' and 'A bit annoying they are put with me, but they will stay away from us.' This again suggested that the pupils structured their own grouping according to ability. The balance of the comments from the high and low ability groups suggested there was a little more sensitivity to the situation from the LA group. Perhaps this was because they were more likely to have experienced this situation themselves. More able performers usually have a sufficient level of skill to be able to cope in school physical education and occasionally may not be able to distinguish between low ability and lack of effort. Any suggestions that a pupil was 'not trying' in these circumstances would have led to rejection and isolation.

Remarkably few felt that they had experienced any real opportunity to play sports with the opposite sex. Most said they would welcome the chance, a few were non-committal and one LA girl was definitely against the proposal because the boys were 'too rough'. Pupils from one school referred to some mixed hockey that had taken place at their request. They had obviously enjoyed the occasion but this had been an isolated case.

None of the LA group was a member of the physical education clubs or teams in their school. A few had joined in the lower school but had either lost interest or found other hobbies to pursue. One girl felt that the trampoline club had become too elitist with too much concentration on the better performers and had become disillusioned. Without exception, all the HA group were members of a least three or four clubs and gave several reasons for their membership. The development of personal skill levels along with the feelings of satisfaction, enjoyment and achievement which were generated were frequently mentioned. So too were the social aspects of striving to achieve within the framework of a team as well as meeting and mixing with other people.

Cognitive-reflective Area

The questions in the cognitive-reflective area were related more to the theoretical aspects or opinions in physical education. The first question asked the pupils to give examples of sponsorship in sport and then to give their opinions about its value. Answers from the two ability groups were clearly divided. Whereas the HA group gave many examples, the LA group advanced very few. The purpose of sponsorship was generally clear to the HA pupils both in terms of advertising and the financial rewards to the sponsoring organization as well as to the sport. A boy and a girl in this group both disagreed with the advertising of tobacco and cigarette smoking and though it to be hypocritical in the sporting context. In the LA group, hardly any opinions were expressed about its value or purpose. This was not surprising in view of the fact that so few could give any examples of sponsorship. Obviously this was a subject in which they had no interest or understanding even though at that time there had been a great deal of media coverage about the bid the city of Birmingham had made to host the 1992 Olympics. All but one girl in the HA group were able to name the city whereas only four (two boys and two girls) were able to do so from the LA group. The pupils were also asked to suggest reasons why they though Birmingham would wish to stage an Olympic festival. All the HA pupils gave valid reasons for such a bid which included tourism, national pride, industry, profit, employment, prosperity and publicity. Only two from the LA group were able to offer any reasons and these were rather superficial. This would suggest that there was a positive correlation between sporting ability and understanding of this related theoretical issue in this sample of pupils.

The recent upsurge of interest in and emphasis on 'the physical' in physical education has already been emphasized. A question which asked 'How is it possible to develop strength and endurance?' was directly related to the health and fitness programmes and the answer should incorporate the principles underlying the development of two of the essential components of physical fitness. All the boys and two of the girls in the HA group were able to give adequate definitions of strength and endurance, whereas only one boy in the LA group could do so. The remaining pupils either had no idea or were confused. This confusion ranged from one girl who thought endurance was the same as initiative and another who equated strength with 'fighting harder'. (An incorrect interpretation in the present context.) Only four boys (three in the HA and one in the LA group) were able to indicate how it was possible to develop these components of fitness. It was perhaps relevant that three of these pupils came from schools which had a specific health related fitness programme in the curriculum. Misconceptions were commonplace and included beliefs that endurance could be improved by 'not too much alcohol' and that strength was developed through jogging, aerobics and light weights. This left the remainder of the sample (ten girls and six boys) with no clear idea or understanding how to develop these two aspects of personal fitness. This is a sad reflection on the effectiveness of the teaching in one of the core elements of the physical education curriculum.

A quarter of the sample were able to give some indication how deviations in posture can occur and their answers revolved around the importance of sitting, standing and moving correctly. The importance of muscle tone was also mentioned. The remainder of the group just gave a negative reply and felt unable to discuss the question any further. In retrospect, a question which was related to their own posture might have had more relevance.

In response to the question 'Are you ever involved in organizing any sport?' only two boys from the HA group gave a negative reply. The remaining eight pupils all assisted with the organization of school teams either from their own year group or from groups in the lower school. Apart from one boy who was form captain for rugby, none of the LA group was involved in any organizational capacity in the sport of their school. A few had been involved in their first year but their enthusiasm had quickly waned. The link between high ability and organizational responsibility (which frequently took the form of captaincy) was not unexpected as it would be comparatively rare for anyone at school to assume this kind of responsibility unless they had some proven playing ability in the activity.

Affective Area

It will be recalled that the affective factor was either first or second in all the schools which suggested that most pupils, regardless of ability, would have positive perceptions in this area. This was borne out by the replies in the interviews as only two LA girls said they derived no pleasure from taking part in physical education. One girl was particularly averse to the subject and said she felt 'Oh God, I've got PE again' whenever it appeared on the timetable. This may be partly attributed to being hit by a hockey stick and ball in a number of lessons. All the remaining responses expressed enthusiasm and enjoyment for the subject. Typical comments from the HA group were:

'I enjoy physical education more than any other subject.'
'It gives me a sense of fulfilment.'
'It helps me to meet and communicate with people.'
'It makes me feel healthier and fitter.'
'It gives me a boost and I'm glad I do a lot of sport.'

The response from the LA group were not quite so enthusiastic but were nonetheless still positive.

The next question was more specific and asked whether they enjoyed the physical exercise. Again there was a strong positive response from seventeen pupils. A subsidiary question probed whether or not they found the exercise challenging enough. Over half of the HA group stated that they did not consider there was enough challenge and were 'not pushed to the limit' and 'wanted it to be harder'. Only three from the LA group replied in a similar way, as the remainder considered the lessons to be challenging enough for their needs. Thus there appeared to be a much greater demand for physical challenge by the pupils in the HA group. Obviously physical fitness is an essential element in high level motor performance and this group appeared to recognize this.

Apart from one girl in the LA group, all the pupils were able to state the name of their favourite practical activity in physical education. The only differences between high and low ability groups were that the HA pupils often named more than one activity and two of the LA pupils referred to activities outside the normal curriculum, viz. baseball and cycling. If nothing else, it did appear that the experiences the pupils had received during their physical education had enabled the vast majority of pupils in these five schools to know which activities they liked. Not surprisingly, the more physically gifted named a greater range from which they could choose.

One of the main purposes of physical education is to develop the physical talents of every child to the highest possible level. All the HA group thought their school had achieved this aim. Thus such comments as 'I have got better over the years' and 'I've been stretched' were not uncommon. Many also remarked that their physical prowess had enabled them to join outside organizations which would be helpful to them in their leisure time pursuits once they had left school. This trend of response was repeated by four LA pupils, but the majority in this group did not consider that their physical talents had been developed to the full. One remarked that he felt he 'should be better' whilst another considered she had not learnt enough from the teachers. Another boy felt that he wanted the opportunity to develop his strength through weight training and was 'peed off' with the fact that there was no opportunity to use the equipment available in the school.

Summary

Overall, there did appear to be a marked difference in the responses of this sample of twenty pupils concerning their opinions of physical education. Pupils who were classified in the group of high ability had more positive feelings towards the subject. This may have been because their behaviours had been positively reinforced in lessons. As a result, they would have welcomed a longer timetable allocation to physical education. They also knew more about the rules of sport, belonged to a greater number of extra-curricular clubs and were more involved in the organization of school sport than the LA group. In addition, they considered that their talents had been more fully developed. However, all the pupils considered they could cooperate with others, help the less able and derive pleasure and satisfaction in physical education. Remarkably few knew anything about the principles of games playing or of developing strength and endurance. Similarly, not many had experienced the opportunity to play sports with members of the opposite sex, although many stated they would have welcomed this innovation. Thus there were differences of opinion according to ability but there appeared to be few underlying trends according to the sex of the interviewee.

Finally, a comment must be made about the sample of pupils who were chosen by the staff in the schools. There had been no difficulty in choosing the HA pupils as they were well-known and well-liked by the staff. However, there were times when the author considered that some of the pupils in the LA group had been chosen because they had a good attitude to physical education. An alternative sample who had scored negatively on the Physical Education 'Learner Report' Questionnaire might be considered on a future occasion. Nonetheless, the sample was perfectly acceptable as there are many pupils of low ability with a good attitude towards the subject.

10
Comparisons Between Five Schools

The previous chapters have analyzed the physical education curriculum in each of the five schools separately. The purpose of this chapter is to make a comparison between the five schools in the light of the main hypothesis that S1 and S2 (the two highest scoring schools) were significantly different from S4 and S5 (the two lowest scoring schools). S3 was a 'control school' mid-way between these two extremes. These assumptions were made on the basis of the pupils' responses to their own learning in physical education. The analysis will be wide-ranging and incorporate the administrative arrangements within the departments as well as detailed qualitative and quantitative considerations of the teaching in the different schools.

Department Administration

Staffing

All schools in the sample were large secondary schools whose headteachers supported the physical education staff. The qualifications and commitment of the physical education teachers appeared to be on four levels. Firstly, there were the full-time specialists who were on the staff of all the schools. The second level comprised a number of staff (many of whom had also received a specialist training) who also contributed to the teaching of physical education as well as making contributions in other subjects or in the administrative life of the school. Thirdly, there were those teachers who had received a minimal training in the subject but had an interest, and ability, in a particular activity and there were several staff in this category who were teaching lessons and becoming involved in extra-curricular activities. This was done mainly with senior classes and the teachers' knowledge and enthusiasm were clearly evident. Finally, there seemed to be a few staff who taught the occasional lesson and were really filling a gap in the timetable. Teachers in this last group only appeared in S5. The quality of their teaching was not as good as the specialist staff and there were times when they did not even change for a lesson on the games field. In one instance some rather serious discipline problems were beginning to emerge. Obviously staff had strengths and weaknesses in their teaching, partly because of the wide spread of practical activities which comprises physical education. Overall the teachers were knowledgeable about their subject. It was, however, possible to pin-point one area of weakness and that was the teaching of educational gymnastics by the male staff. Whilst most accepted the contribution it could make to the education of their pupils, few taught the activity beyond the second year and in one school (S5) it had not been taught as part of the boys' curriculum for several years.

Apart from some administrative and financial arrangements, the male and female staff were organized into separate departments in S2, S3 and S5. Each department had complete autonomy over their curriculum content and worked as single sex departments. The only occasions when there was any mixed physical education was in the optional programme for senior pupils but this was minimal. A similar type of arrangement had existed in S1 until the term prior to the observation when the head of department had left, apart from a pilot study which had allowed some of the boys and girls in the lower school to be taught together for some of the activities. The experiment had been so successful that the current staff were in the process of implementing this teaching policy throughout the school. Only S4 was considered to be fully integrated. There was mixed teaching in the first, fourth, fifth and sixth forms wherever possible and this was the policy of the department. The reason for the single sex teaching in the second and third years was purely an administrative one beyond their control. The syllabus also reflected this integration with an impressive and well-planned document. S2 also provided a joint syllabus, whereas S3 and S5 provided separate syllabuses for boys' and girls' physical education with some common ground between them. S1 had only recently produced a written syllabus of any sort but was following an integrated approach.

Only two departments met on a regular basis and this was a requirement deemed by the policy of the school. S4 met each month and S2 every half-term and male and female staff came together to discuss issues which were pertinent to their subject. Two of the other schools (S3 and S5) only met occasionally and as separate male and female departments. This was usually done informally at the start of the academic year but did not appear to be a substantial planning exercise. Any meetings in S1 were also informal and occasional, and the school requirement that departments should meet once a week had been quietly ignored for a long time and precedence had been given to extra-curricular activities.

In summary, the physical education staff in all the schools were well qualified and knowledgeable in most practical areas. The main exception to this was in the teaching of educational gymnastics by male teachers who found the subject difficult to teach and did not develop it beyond the second year, apart from S4 who incorporated a block of gymnastics into the third year boys' programme. The same could not be said for the non-physical education staff who were 'filling in' on the timetable. Their teaching ranged from poor to non-existent and only applied to S5.

The best integrated department was in S4 by virtue of the mixed teaching that was taking place, the compilation of one syllabus to explain the philosophy and organization of the department and the regular department meetings. Although its content was not as detailed, S2 also had a similar syllabus presentation which represented the whole department and they also met on a regular basis. However, the work was carried out quite separately according to the sex of the staff and pupil. The syllabuses from S3 and S5 could only be described as 'just adequate'. The staff never met in any formal way and there was little integration of staff or pupils in the work. S1 was in a rather unique position as there was no departmental head and the remaining staff had only recently produced a written syllabus. Nevertheless they had begun to work as one department with mixed groups and it will be interesting to see if this continues.

Facilities

All the schools possessed a fully equipped gymnasium, hall, hard play-ground areas and extensive playing fields on site. In addition, most departments had adequate stocks of large and small apparatus suitable for the variety of activities associated with physical education. Two of the schools had a sports hall on site and another used a nearby sports centre which was run by the local council. Apart from S3, which had a rather isolated geographical position, all schools used facilities which were available to the local community.

The school with the least favourable facilities was S5. The gymnasium and hall were smaller than similar facilities in the other schools and less well kept. The storage space in the gymnasium was hopelessly inadequate and necessitated keeping some of the larger apparatus in the corridor. The hall was some distance from the storage areas which was inconvenient and meant that all the apparatus had to be carried. The netting round the hard-surface area was in need of substantial repair before the start of the tennis season. The pupils' changing rooms were only just adequate and the staff changing room was not only hopelessly inadequate in size but also lacked privacy. It was for these reasons that S5 was considered to have the poorest facilities of the five schools.

Dress

All schools insisted that the pupils in the lower school wore the same style of clothing for all practical activities. Some freedom was allowed for senior pupils and the criteria of 'appropriately dressed for the activity' was acceptable in all schools. The physical education staff always set good standards of personal appearance and these were reflected in the standards adopted by the pupils.

Showering after a period of activity was compulsory for all pupils in S1, S2 and S3, but only compulsory for the first three years in S4. Thereafter they were encouraged to shower and most pupils did so. Only in S5 was there a deliberate policy not to shower and this was a direct result of a recent timetable decision to change the weekly time allocation in physical education from two double to three single periods. Staff did not consider the single period long enough for their teaching and were not prepared to shorten their lessons even more by allowing time for pupils to shower.

Overall the standards of pupils' dress was high. The only problem area was in S5 which considered it did not have sufficient time allocated to physical education lessons to allow pupils to shower.

Teaching Time

Excluding changing, travelling and showering, the amount of time given to actual teaching was timed for seventy-four lessons in the five schools. The average time for each lesson was multiplied by the number of lessons in a week to give a weekly average for each school. Table 37 shows the data for each school.

Table 37: Average weekly physical education teaching time for each class in S1, S2, S3, S4 and S5

	S1	S2	S3	S4	S5
Average lesson length (minutes)	47.5	42	47	42.5	33.25
Number of lessons in week	2	2	2	2.5	3
Weekly average (minutes)	95	84	94	106	100

The shortest amount of teaching time in S2 can be attributed to two reasons. One was the occasional insistence of writing related theory into a notebook prior to practical activity for the boys. This inevitably reduced their practical time. The other reason was the use of a nearby off-site facility which, when used, involved the girls in a five minute walk each way. Both of these practices drastically reduced the actual time devoted to teaching and if continued over a five-year period would result in approximately seventy hours less teaching when compared with the time allocation in the other schools. As a pupil could reasonably expect sixty hours of contact time in any one year, this represents a substantial proportion of time that is lost in a school career.

The number of periods each day ranged between four and six dependent on the school organization. During the course of a week the most teaching was carried out in S4 with just under eighteen hours, and the least teaching conducted in S2 at exactly fourteen hours. The average teaching time was sixteen hours a week and there were substantial variations about this of approximately 12 per cent. If teaching time allows more time for the teacher to teach and the pupil to learn, then S4 would appear to have the more efficient organization to allow this to happen.

The lessons in S1, S2, S3 and S4 were scheduled to last for at least an hour and were essentially double periods. This was not the case in S5 which had single periods of approximately forty-five minutes. The pace of the lessons was sometimes much brisker in S5 and there was often a greater sense of urgency to begin. Whether this resulted in greater motor activity will be apparent from the ALT-PE analysis, but subjectively it was felt that this could be the case.

Summary

The analysis in this section was not in accord with the original hypothesis that S1 and S2 would emerge as the most efficient schools in relation to the administration of their departments. The evidence was contrary to this and suggested that S4 was the most effective school by virtue of the comprehensive and cohesive way in which the staff had planned and presented their syllabus. S4 could justifiably be described as an integrated department whereas the other schools were either completely separate or in the first stage of coming together.

Consistent with the effectiveness of low ranking schools was the fact that S5 had the poorest facilities, had a few lessons taught by non-physical education staff with little expertise in the area, did not include gymnastics in the boys' curriculum and did not allow the pupils to shower at the end of a lesson.

It is not unreasonable to suggest that the more time that is allocated to the teaching of physical education, the more successful the teachers should be in achieving their aims and objectives. If this is the case, then the fact that S4 and S5 had the longest periods of time devoted to the teaching of the subject was not consistent with the predictions.

Overall, the evidence was only partly supportive of the original hypothesis. In the administration of their departments, S4 emerged as the most effective school which was contrary to the prediction whereas S5 appeared to be the least effective which was a predicted finding.

Consistency of the Observation of Teaching Practice with Pupils' Evaluation

It was difficult to make accurate subjective judgements about qualitative observations on teaching and learning which took place in different locations at different times, but an attempt was made to provide unbiased answers to a number of prepared questions which had been identified in the design of the main study.

Lesson Climate

All the physical education staff in the schools appeared to be effective in their ability to communicate with pupils. There were few instances of confusion which resulted in instructions having to be repeated. This applied to the organizational aspects of lessons as well as to the setting of motor tasks.

One overriding impression was that there was a generally warm, pleasant and supportive working atmosphere. There were occasional exceptions to this, such as the indiscipline in a gymnastic lesson in S1 which led to a strong and formal reaction from the teacher and the fourth years group of girls in S5 who refused to participate in an aerobic class because of the unsuitable nature of the music chosen by the teacher, but these were isolated examples. Usually pupils were interested and motivated to participate. The staff were interested in the children and spoke with pleasant sounding voices. There were many occasions when the teachers smiled at the children, made eye contact, or engaged them in some kind of friendly verbal 'banter.' Placing a hand on a pupil's shoulder or making signs of approval were all indications of friendliness and support that could be seen in many lessons in all the schools. Only in one school (S5) was there antagonism between a teacher and pupils and this was resulting in some indiscipline.

Nearly all the staff appeared to be achieving one of their stated intentions which was to ensure that the pupils enjoyed the lessons and this was mainly being achieved in a warm and supportive environment. With some classes in some schools (for example senior classes in S1), the recreative nature of the work in the Sports Centre was obviously enjoyed by the pupils but was not matched with a corresponding level of worthwhile activity. There did not appear to be any sex differences in the schools, except perhaps in S3 where the girls were possibly more interested and motivated than the boys. This might be attributed to the fact that the female staff had continued with extra–curricular activities throughout the period of industrial action. Teachers in all the schools made many supportive comments which could be loosely placed under the heading of 'feedback' and these certainly helped to motivate pupils and create a pleasant atmosphere.

In this kind of climate, there was a great deal of mutual respect between the teachers and the pupils. Pleasant pupil-teacher relationships were clearly evident in most of the classes taught by the specialist physical education staff. This confidence was only felt to be lacking in two instances where temporary or part-time teachers were involved in S1 and S5. All the schools valued each pupil's contribution and there were several instances when pupils of lower ability were actively encouraged to participate without any risk of embarrassment or fear. Honest endeavour and effort were always encouraged regardless of ability.

In the main, staff were firm yet fair in all their dealings with pupils. Only the public choosing of teams to play competitive games in S2 and S5 seemed to be unfair. So too was the occasion when a teacher in S1 did no teaching in a volleyball lesson and thereby abdicated his responsibility. Quite often the teachers explained why they were making decisions in either the administration or teaching context and these were especially notable in S2 and S4 — procedures consistent with effective teaching.

Summary

Overall there was a pleasant teacher-pupil relationship in all the schools and, on the available evidence, it was not possible to place them in a rank order of effectiveness. The few instances of indiscipline and poor re-lationships were observed in S1 and S5 which were the two schools at opposite ends of the effectiveness range.

173

Organization and Development of Lessons

The organization of pupils either as individuals or groups was usually done efficiently. During the actual lessons the practice of sitting some pupils on the sidelines naturally resulted in a great deal of waiting and this could not be regarded as effective practice. Class organization was generally sound and this sample of staff supported the notion that physical education teachers are generally good organizers.

Logical and related development of the content of lessons is an essential ingredient of good teaching. Without doubt this was most clearly apparent in both the indoor and outdoor work in S4. The majority of lessons in the other schools also progressed logically, but there were several instances where this was not the case. For example, in a gymnastics lesson in S1, pupils spent nearly an hour working on a mat when some progression on to apparatus or a change of activity would have been more appropriate. Some of the warm up practices at the start of games lessons were rather unrelated and this practice was observed in a number of schools. There were a number of static games practices in S2 which made their transfer to the game situation problematical. In the same school a gymnastics lesson which had a theme of locomotion would have some difficulty in justifying head stand practices as a related practice. A basketball lesson in S3 contained no consistent theme and there appeared to be less logical progression in the lessons taught by the male staff. The conclusion of an educational gymnastics lesson with a game was perhaps the most incongruous example in this school. In S5 the small–sided games practices were usually relevant and appropriate but the teaching points that had been stressed at this stage were not followed up in the larger game situations. In the girls' games programme hockey and netball were alternated each week. This did not seem to be entirely logical in the learning and development of motor skills. In the learning stage, there is substantial evidence from the motor skills literature (for example, Drowatzky, 1975; and Schmidt, 1982) that activities which are not well learned and practised in close proximity can produce a negative transfer effect on each other. It would probably have been more effective if the activities had been blocked for at least half a term. It is not suggested that all the progressions in S4 were logical and related. There were instances when this was not the case but they did appear to be less frequent and less marked than in the other schools.

All teachers often used pupils to demonstrate aspects of the practical work and there appeared to be a common philosophy that it was more effective for pupils to see skills performed by their peer group rather than by the teacher. In educational gymnastics in S2 and S4 the value of group demonstrations of apparatus work was questioned since there was never time for pupils to practise what they had observed from the demonstrations. (It is important to note that there was no group work included in educational gymnastics lessons in S3 and no gymnastics observed in S5.)

Question and answer techniques were frequently used to bring out teaching points. Some of the most demanding questioning came during the lessons associated with the 'games for understanding' teaching in S1, S4 and S5. However, not all the teachers in S1 and S5 were completely familiar with the principles underlying this teaching approach. A more thorough understanding was evident with the staff from S4. Questions which probed why, how and when certain activities were carried out encouraged pupils to consider the principles and strategies of games playing appropriate to a number of areas. Overall, the quality of questioning appeared to be sound.

Staff in all the schools did appear to cater for individual differences and differing levels of ability. Most skill practices allowed pupils to contribute to the best of their ability and there were several instances of concern for individual pupils in S2. With so much 'games playing' in S5, some pupils may not have had sufficient levels of skill to compete with more skilful players in full games situations.

Whilst recognizing that the question is a particularly difficult one, the answer to 'were the pupils cognitively, motorically and affectively involved in their physical education lessons?' would be generally affirmative. Most pupils appeared to enjoy the lessons and achieve some measure of success and many stated this to be the case. This type of involvement should have produced positive feelings towards the subject. There were, however, some instances such as the swimming lesson at the Sports Centre in S1 when pupils would have enjoyed the lesson but the content had not aided any personal development. Many of the games for understanding lessons (especially in S4) were encouraging pupils to accept responsibility for their organization and practices in solving problems or tasks and were resulting in feelings of personal satisfaction amongst the pupils. The health-related fitness components in S3, S4 and S5 all contained a related theory element which was linked to the practical work. Nevertheless, there were a number of occasions in all schools when it was felt that more could have been achieved and there could have been more 'time-on-task'.

Summary

The organization and development of most lessons was satisfactory in all the schools. However, there were more instances of consistent and logical related development in the lessons taught by the staff in S4 — a school which the pupils had evaluated as being one of the least effective in the sample. Several examples have been cited of poor progressions and inconsistent development in the other four schools. This is not to suggest that everything was perfect in S4 as there were instances of poor organization. For example, no practice time was available after group apparatus demonstrations in gymnastics and the same criticism also applied to S2. (Only these two schools included apparatus work in the gymnastic lessons.) The quality of question and answer techniques in S4 appeared to be superior to those used in the other schools since the staff were more adept in bringing out the underlying principles. Most pupils appeared to enjoy the lessons and in most instances the teachers were attempting to achieve acceptable educational objectives. Some serious concern was felt for the senior school physical education curriculum in S1 which left many pupils to their own devices in a mainly recreational programme. Again, there was contrary evidence which does not support the original hypothesis. Indeed there appeared to be a reverse effect for S1 and S4, with S4, contrary to the original prediction, being the more effective.

Analysis Using Physical Education 'Learner Report' Factors

As the significant differences between the high and low scoring schools had been made on the basis of the pupils' responses to the 'Learner Report' questionnaire, it was considered valid to conduct part of the 'between schools analysis' through an analysis of the four factors identified by the questionnaire. (It will be recalled that there were statistically significant differences between S1/S2 and S4/S5 on all four factors with S1 and S2 having the more positive scores. Also there were statistically significant differences between the male and female pupils on the technomotor, sociomotor and cognitive-reflective factors with male pupils scoring in a more positive way. There were no pupils' sex differences for the affective factor.) Each of the factors will now be examined in relation to the pupils' evaluation and their consistency with the observation of the teaching in each school.

Technomotor Factor

One reason for the higher scores on this factor which related to the technical and tactical aspects of motor skills might possibly be due to the fact that the length of teaching time varied between the schools. Thus, higher scores would be linked with longer periods of physical education teaching. The data in table 37 did not support this hypothesis. Indeed the reverse trend was apparant as S4 and S5 had the longest periods allocated to teaching each week but with the lowest pupil evaluation scores.

All pupils had reacted positively to learning to play well-known ball games (Q 1) and this reflected the strong games bias in the physical education curriculum in all the schools. There was invariably more games in the boys' programme which generally reflected the expertise of the staff and this may account for the boys' more positive score. Most pupils felt they were able to apply the right techniques (Q 13), but the observations of lessons would not fully support this as there were many occasions when the quality of performance was only average. The same comments also applied to the use of appropriate techniques and tactics (Q 22), as many pupils in all schools were unaware of the principles of play in sport. However, there were a few pupils who were aware of these principles and they seemed to be the better performers in the activity. This qualified support applied to all schools and it was therefore not possible to discriminate between them. It will be interesting to see if the 'games for understanding' courses being taught in S1 and S4 will ultimately produce more positive perceptions of pupils' learning than those pupils who follow a more traditional games teaching programme.

The rules of sport (Q 8) were taught incidentally in all schools during the course of a particular lesson. The exception to this was for the boys in S2 where the rules were also taught in a theoretical context and set out in written form in a notebook. This may partly account for S2 having the most positive score for this question. Also, the CSE course required some understanding of the rules and laws of several sports and this could also have been a contributory factor. The only other school involved in CSE courses was S5 but, contrary to expectations, had recorded the lowest score. Thus these results were consistent with the hypothesis.

All schools appeared to include track and field athletics into their programmes in the summer term and there were good outdoor facilities available to practise the various events. As the observation period was in November and December, no lessons were timetabled for this activity and it was not possible to advance reasons for any differences in pupils' achievements in athletics (Q 6).

The ability to perform on gymnastic apparatus (Q 9) received a negative rating for most pupils in most schools. Only S1 had a positive rating with a mean score of 2.66. Clearly pupils in this sample did not consider they had learnt to use the gymnastic apparatus. The gymnastic programme was probably strongest in S1 where not only was there the advantage of the personal expertise of the male and female staff but also a strong gymnastic component throughout the three years of the common core of activities. In addition there was a flourishing gymnastic extra-curricular programme. The lowest score was recorded in S5 where there was no gymnastics in the boys' programme. In this instance, the scores do appear to reflect the ability and keeness of the staff in gymnastics as well as its importance in the curriculum as reflected by the time allocation.

Summary

Answers to some of the technomotor questions were consistent with the pupils' evaluation of effectiveness. For example, pupils in S2 felt that they had greater understanding of the rules of sport whereas those in S5 had the lowest level of understanding. Also, S1 pupils had the highest and S5 the lowest score in relation to their perceived ability to perform on the gymnastic apparatus. It was not possible to make such a clearcut distinction in the answers to the other questions, but what did emerge was that the boys were more positive in their responses to the playing of well-known ball games which probably reflected the emphasis and preference male staff gave to the playing of games. In addition, there appeared to be a mismatch between pupils' perceptions and the observed behaviours in lessons. For instance, the ability to apply techniques into skilled situations and an understanding of the principles of play in games were both scored positively in the questionnaire but the observations of the pupils in the lessons did not always suggest that there was always a strong link between them. This appeared to be the case in all schools and the fact that it was not possible to discriminate between schools did not support the main hypothesis.

Sociomotor Factor

The development of social and interpersonal skills was a declared aim for all the schools but the pupils perceived them as being more fully achieved in the two high-scoring schools. Adapting ways of playing and cooperating with others of differing levels of ability (Q 10) were all scored positively by all the schools and this was particularly marked in S1, S2 and S3. Encouraging pupils of all levels of ability to participate in the extra-curricular programme inevitably involves considerable adaptation in playing and may have contributed to these positive scores, but it is also necessary to point out that S4 and S5 had a similar policy in operation.

Learning how to play and engage in sport with members of the opposite sex received the more positive scores in S1 and S4. These were the only two schools where there was a definite policy of mixed physical education classes and the scores could well be attributed to this organiz-ational arrangement. One other pointer which also supported this interpre-tation was that the only school with a markedly negative score (S3) probably had the lowest level of integration. Thus the opportunity to play sports with the opposite sex within the curriculum appeared to be a strong contributory factor towards pupils' perception of this item.

Adapting the rules of games to the needs and possibilities of others in the group (Q 14) was scored positively by all schools. A large number of small-sided and/or conditioned games and practices were used in games teaching and this often involved adaptation of the rules. The reasons for differences between the five schools is not clear, especially when the school with the most games teaching on the curriculum (S5) had the lowest score.

Q 16 was concerned with pupils' understanding and acceptance of others in sporting situations. All schools scored this item positively — especially S1 and S2. There was no doubt that the staff in these schools set an example by having a caring attitude towards their pupils and in turn encouraged them to be tolerant towards other pupils. However, the same was also true for all the schools, regardless of the sex of the pupil. There were isolated examples of intolerance. For example, the group of first year girls in S4 who could not agree about the organization of their 'striking game' and the more able boy in the basketball lesson in S5 who was critical of less skilled performers, but these were rare occurrences.

The remaining three questions which contributed to this factor were fulfilling different roles (Q 18), involving weaker players (Q 19) and giving pleasure to all pupils (Q 23). Without exception, S1 and S2 had the more positive scores. The reasons for this are not clear as all schools appeared to encourage pupils to take on different roles such as attack and defence in games, but there may possibly have been a greater likelihood that this was encouraged more for boys. However, this is a purely subjective opinion and further evidence is needed. Classes were never streamed according to physical ability which meant that the weaker and less skilled players were always included. Mixed ability groupings were evident in all schools and all pupils, regardless of ability, were encouraged to attend extra-curricular activities. Occasionally there was some evidence of streaming in team practices, but in the main they were organized to cater for the differing levels of ability. In spite of groups of widely differing capacities, all pupils appeared to derive pleasure from the activities in the curriculum.

Summary

Whilst there are some tentative reasons advanced to account for the significant differences between schools and pupils on this factor, it was not possible to present strong arguments from either the subject philosophies of the teachers or the subject organization, which might fully account for these differences. As it was not possible to identify reasons for these differences, all schools were considered to be similar in the development of sociomotor considerations. Consequently this did not support the original hypothesis which suggested that S1 and S2 would have had superior teaching practices supporting these social elements.

Cognitive-Reflective Factor

The higher scoring schools (S1 and S2) and boys scored significantly higher than the lower scoring schools (S4 and S5) in this sample on this factor. Three of the questions (Q2, Q11 and Q15) were related to health and fitness. As already reported, most of the curriculum work on health-related fitness was being undertaken in S4 and S5, yet these schools had the least positive scores. S1 had only recently started a HRF course and in S2 it was incidental to the other teaching. This meant that pupils in schools with a coherently planned course had less positive perceptions about their learning in the area. All schools had responded positively to their ability to apply the basic principles of endurance training but some element of doubt must be expressed about the pupils' understanding of this concept. Certainly the interviews with pupils suggested there was some vagueness and this was particularly apparent from the reported discussions with the girls in S1 who were using a multi-gym as part of a weight training programme. This contrasted with the understanding shown by two second year classes in S5 who had a sound understanding of the components of fitness and this augered well for the future. Perhaps when all the HRF courses have been in progress over an extended period of time, deeper levels of understanding will become apparent. Nevertheless at this stage it was not possible to account for the more positive scores in S1 and S2 but there were occasional indications from the teaching of lessons that greater levels of understanding were being achieved by boys.

The opportunity to organize sport activities (Q20) was often presented in the 'games for understanding' programmes. However, these courses in S1 and S4 had probably not been in operation long enough to have had any effect on fourth form pupils' opinions. No valid reasons are advanced for the inter-school differences. In respect of the sex differences, a subjective opinion would suggest that boys were more involved in organizational aspects than girls. This was especially true in the organization of games groups and in the decisions about playing positions. This may have been because the male staff gave the pupils greater personal responsibility in this organizational area but this is a speculative reason.

There were no instances of any appraisal of media reports (Q 17) or of any examination of the relationship between sport and politics (Q 17) during the period of observation, nor was there any mention of such topics in any of the syllabuses that were made available. The two schools (S2 and S5) which did operate CSE courses for boys scored towards the higher end for these questions but the lack of any specific reference in the syllabuses made any possible links rather tenuous. However, it could be argued that any subject which involved pupils in an examination at some depth might develop some kind of critical attitude to sport and a wider appreciation of the associated problems. As these courses were only run for male pupils, it might provide some tentative explanation for their higher scores.

Summary

Support for the original hypothesis on this factor was equivocal. It did not prove possible to discriminate between schools with regard to the opportunities given to pupils to organize sporting activities, or their ability to appraise media reports or political aspects. Most surprising was the fact that pupils in schools who were operating a health-related fitness programme (S4 and S5) had lower scores. Although consistent with the main hypothesis it was unexpected to find the lower responses in schools where a prepared and planned programme was in operation.

Affective Factor

All pupils in all schools appeared to derive pleasure from participation in the practical subjects (Q 24) and enjoy physical exercise (Q 7). There were no sex differences in this factor, but there were some statistically significant differences between schools. The enjoyment from participation was particularly marked for S1, S2, S3 and S4. Although still very positive, the mean score for S5 was substantially lower than the rest. The more restricted programme (especially for boys) in rather less good facilities may have contributed to this position. Overall, the contact and relationships between staff and pupils in all the schools was particularly good and the general concern by teachers that they wanted all pupils to enjoy participating in the subject appeared to be achieved in this sample of pupils. Similarly, in their written aims for the subject, all staff attached great importance to physical development and the fact that most pupils expressed reasonably positive feelings towards exercising their bodies again suggested that this aim was being achieved. Why S1 and S2 should score higher than the other schools was not clear.

The ability to cope with sporting potential (Q 3) was again scored quite positively by the pupils. All the children were given substantial encouragement to take part in the activities and pupils' efforts were often rewarded. The reward was either through verbal comments at the time or by means of a written comment on the school report. Such comments applied to pupils of all levels of ability and did not single out the more able. Children particularly gifted in an activity were actively encouraged to join outside clubs where their skills could be developed. In addition, all pupils, regardless of ability, were encouraged to attend extra-curricular clubs and team practices. This philosophy applied to the staff in all the schools and the reasons for the inter-school differences remains obscure.

Pupils in S1 and S2 had a much clearer perception of their favourite sport (Q 5). All schools operated a common core of activities during the first three years followed by an increasing range of options thereafter. Four of the schools used facilities in the local community to extend their programmes in the upper school. As a result, a fairly consistent programme was in operation in all the schools so this would not account for the statistical differences.

Summary

The results for this factor were not supportive of the main hypothesis. It did not prove possible to differentiate between the five schools in the affective areas such as enjoyment and participation in physical exercise. It was clear that the affective factor was a major consideration for all the teachers and was at the forefront of their thinking in the everyday teaching of physical education.

Detailed Observation of Lessons

Bearing in mind the cautions expressed earlier by Anderson (1983) concerning the 'extraordinary reductionism' of representing human inter-action in physical education with a coding system, an attempt is made to analyze the data generated by the application of the ALT-PE system to the seventy-four lessons observed in the five schools.

Each lesson was observed and coded at two levels, viz. the context of the lesson which comprised fourteen categories and the learner involvement with eight categories. As each context behaviour occurred it was coded on the ALT-PE recording sheet in 15-second intervals. In this way a continuous recording was made of the complete lesson. To analyze the raw data, the number of seconds was totalled for each category and the grand total for each lesson was a summation of each category total. Each category total was then converted into a percentage score which enabled some standardization and comparison to take place between lessons.

For the learner involvement, every pupil's behaviour was categorized into one of eight categories once every three minutes. This was done through visual observation. The number of observations in each category were totalled and then expressed as a percentage of the grand total of pupils' behaviours in the lesson. Again this produced a standardization for the purposes of comparison.

All the data for each category at both the context and learner involvement levels was expressed as a percentage score for each lesson. As a result, the data was at an interval level of scaling. By summing the category totals in the lesson in each school and dividing by the number of lessons, mean scores for each category were obtained.

Statistical Procedures

It was necessary to establish whether there were any significant differences between the mean scores for the five schools in each category of ALT-PE. The one-way analysis of variance for independent samples which compares the variability between group measures (means) with the variability between individual scores within the group was considered to be appropriate for this purpose. One of the assumptions of ANOVA is that the variances of the sample populations are equal. This was checked through the homogeneity of variance test. The results showed six of the nine categories in the context level to be significantly different and therefore unequal which made the ANOVA test unsuitable for those six categories. Because of this, it was necessary to consider an alternative test and the non-parametric Kruskal-Wallis one-way ANOVA by ranks was appropriate. Cohen and Holliday (1982) referred to research which suggested that 'the power efficiency of the Kruskal-Wallis test relative to the parametric F test is reported as 95.5 per cent'. Thus this test was considered to be suitable to analyze all the categories. In categories where significance was recorded, it was possible to run a homogeneity of variance test and if the group was homogeneous, a confirmatory F test was also conducted which enabled a more sensitive comparison to be made between the means of the five schools.

Comparison of All Lessons

In the conduct of almost all lessons, a certain proportion of time must be allocated to organization and management, and a reasonable expectation would be that the teachers in the more efficient schools would spent less time in the transition, management and providing equipment categories. In this way, non-movement time would be reduced to a minimum and free time for subject matter related to the development of understanding and skill in physical education. The input of subject knowledge would to some extent be dependent on the nature of the skill being taught as well as on the stage of development of the lessons, but in general terms the application of techniques should predominate and this would suggest a greater proportion of time in the strategy category. With regard to the motor element, because the physical is so central in physical education the expectation would be that the motor element would comprise the major proportion of the lessons. In particular, the opportunity offered to pupils to practise their skills in an applied context (skill/scrimmage category) should predominate.

With this background, an examination of the results from the observation of the seventy-four lessons in the five schools is now undertaken.

Context Level

The mean scores for each school showed the distribution of time in the context level and the Kruskal-Wallis ANOVA indicated the level of statistical significance. These are summarized in table 38.

Examining the general content first, this section identified periods of time when pupils were not intended to be involved in the motor skill element of physical education activities. This largely involved the managerial and organizational time of pupils and equipment, but also included physiological periods of warm up. The break category was not included in the analysis as it was rarely used. No significant differences were reported for the warm-up periods (which were fairly consistent at about 4 per cent) and management categories, although the latter was approaching significance. However, it was a comparatively minor category which was used for only 1 or 2 per cent of the time.

Transition periods devoted to managerial and organizational activities related to instruction showed a significant difference which was almost at the 1 per cent level. S4 had the lowest mean score and was significantly different from S2, S3 and S5. S1 also had a low mean score but was only significantly different from S3. The provision of equipment also contributed to this section and was especially marked when apparatus was

Table 38: All lessons: ALT-PE context level: Mean scores and Kruskal-Wallis one-way ANOVA by category for S1-S5

General content	S1	S2	S3	S4	S5	H	p
	N = 13	N = 13	N = 11	N = 19	N = 18		
Transition	12.9	18.5	20.5	10.5	16.7	13.25	<0.5
Management	1.4	0.1	2.3	1.1	0.5	9.26	N.S.
Break	0.2	0	0.5	0.6	0	—	—
Warm-up	3.8	5.2	4.0	3.5	4.4	0.93	N.S.
Providing equipment	6.4	4.2	4.0	3.5	1.1	17.97	<0.01
PE Knowledge							
Technique	9.8	12.2	9.5	6.8	4.8	7.18	N.S
Strategy	7.7	9.8	16.6	13.8	11.1	2.53	N.S.
Rules	0.1	1.2	0.3	0	0.3	—	—
Social behaviour	0.2	0	0.1	0	0	—	—
Background	0	0.2	1.5	2.4	0.2	—	—
PE Motor							
Practice	18.9	18.0	17.2	9.8	13.5	6.07	N.S.
Skill/scrimmage	20.6	30.5	21.2	44.8	46.7	13.74	<0.01
Game	17.5	0.4	2.5	1.3	0.7	9.37	N.S.
Fitness	0	0	0	2.1	0	—	—

used in the gymnastics lessons in S1, S2 and S4. Not surprisingly, S5 had the lowest mean percentage (1 per cent) and this was probably due to the fact that no gymnastics lessons were included in the sample. At the other extreme, S1 spent more time (6.4 per cent) providing equipment and the difference between these two schools was at the 1 per cent level.

In summary, the results for the categories in the general content section did not provide much support for the main hypothesis. There were no significant differences between the schools for the management and warm-up categories. The two categories which did show significance were equivocal in their support for the hypothesis. For example, in transition, S4 had a significantly lower score and S2 had a high score which were both contrary to the prediction.

Obviously the input of PE knowledge is an essential ingredient of any teaching-learning process and the nature of the input warrants consideration. Two categories were mainly used in this section. One was concerned with the techniques of motor skills and the other, name strategy, was related to the application of these techniques in an applied context. As can be seen from table 38, there were no significant differences between schools in either of these categories. Thus, in spite of the many different activities included in the sample, the teachers in these schools did not differ in the amount of time they devoted to knowledge about either technique or strategy.

All schools allocated the greatest amount of curriculum time to games.

A common teaching method involved the application of techniques into small-sided conditioned games which allowed pupils to appreciate and learn the strategies appropriate to the situation. Thus techniques need to be applied in a large number of different settings. This implies that schools with a greater proportion of 'strategy time' would be more effective and S3, S4 and S5 followed this trend. However, this is a generalization which is difficult to substantiate in this study as some of the schools were just beginning a block of new work after a half-term break. S2 certainly came into this category and time spent on initial explanations of skill learning were essential.

There were comparatively few instances relating to the rules or the background to subject areas and only two brief references to social behaviour concerned with appropriate and acceptable ways of behaving within the context of the activity. Because of this, these three categories were not included in the analysis.

The teachers in this sample allocated an average of just over half the teaching time (54.4 per cent) to occasions when the primary focus was on motor involvement in physical education activities. The three categories which contributed to the PE motor section were practice, skills/scrimmage and game. Without exception all schools devoted greater periods of time practising skills in an applied setting than to the development of pure techniques and this was particularly apparent in S4 and S5 where the proportion was approximately four times greater. There were no significant differences between the schools in the practice category, but significance was reached ($p < 0.01$) in the skill/scrimmage category. S4 and S5 spent significantly more time than S1 and S3 in skill settings whereas S2 was not significant from either group. S5 had the greatest overall motor involvement as well as the most time devoted to applied skills and this may be largely attributed to the 'games playing' emphasis in the school and a teaching method which employed a large number of conditioned games and practices. Also, the sense of urgency that was felt because of the shortness of the lessons seemed to have the effect of making the teachers 'get on with the lesson'.

Games playing in which there was no input from the teacher was minimal in S2, S3, S4 and S5 but rose to 17.5 per cent in S1 and this was very close to the 5 per cent level of significance ($H = 9.37$; $df = 4$). This marked difference was attributed to the badminton and basketball lessons at the sports centre which were largely recreational and the volleyball lesson in the gymnasium when the teacher did not teach but merely watched the pupils play a game. The purely recreational nature of these occasions could only loosely be labelled 'educational'. Again the results were not supporting the main hypothesis that S1 and S2 would be the more

Table 39: ALT-PE context level: Mean scores and Kruskal-Wallis ANOVA by sub-section for S1-S5

Context level	S1	S2	S3	S4	S5	H	p
General content	25.1	28.1	31.3	19.3	22.8	7.74	N.S.
PE knowledge	17.8	23.4	28.0	23.1	16.4	4.10	N.S.
PE motor	57.0	48.9	40.8	58.0	60.9	0.35	N.S.

effective schools. Where levels of significance were reached, they were contrary to the prediction as evidenced by the longer periods of time spent by the teachers in S4 and S5 on the practice of applied skills. Also, the marked trend for S1 to provide little input in a number of games lessons was again contrary to the hypothesis.

The context level had three major sub-sections, namely general content, PE knowledge and PE motor. The distribution of time for each school is portrayed in table 39 through the mean scores and the Kruskal-Wallis H values indicated significance levels.

Whilst general content is an essential element of every physical education lesson, it does not directly contribute to the learning of motor skills or the physical development of pupils — two of the major aims of the subject. Its main purpose is 'preparatory' in preparing the environment or the pupils for physical activity. Providing efficiency is not sacrificed, the most efficient schools will be those with the lowest scores. An ANOVA of all the categories combined which comprised general content revealed no significant difference ($H = 7.74$; $df = 4$) between the five schools. A combination of the two remaining categories in the PE knowledge section did not produce significance ($H = 4.10$; $df = 4$) between the five schools and this lack of differentiation was therefore not supportive of the main hypothesis. The sub-section with the largest time allocation was PE motor but again no significant differences were revealed between the five schools.

Whilst there were some substantial differences between the mean scores, the fact that none of the sections produced statistical significance was attributed to the great amount of variance in the scores in each school. None of these results supported the main hypothesis that S1 and S2 would be the more effective schools.

Learner Involvement

It was clear from the literature review that the greater the amount of time spent in the motor appropriate category, the more opportunity pupils would have to acquire physical skills. Thus high scores in this category could well provide an indication of effective teaching.

The development of understanding about an activity or its órganiz-ation within the lesson was embraced by the cognitive category. A substantial amount of every lesson would be allocated to this type of behaviour as it was essential to ensure progressive development in the motor practices. High scores in this category might suggest that explan-ations and demonstrations could be excessive and long-winded.

Off-task behaviour should be minimal in most lessons and attributed to behaviour outside the set task rather than to bad behaviour. A proportion of each lesson would be spent 'on-task' carrying out non-subject matter tasks. Waiting time is 'dead time' and should be reduced to a minimum wherever possible. The expectancy would be that the more efficient schools would have the lower mean scores in this category.

With this background, the level of learner involvement will inevitably be influenced by the teaching at the context level. On average, pupils spent almost 60 per cent of the lesson in the not motor engaged categories with the remainder in the motor engaged area. The means and levels of significance for ALT-PE at the learner level for all lessons is summarized in table 40.

The interim, motor inappropriate and motor supporting categories were not analyzed as they were rarely used and consequently insufficient data was available. No significant differences were recorded in the waiting, off and on-task categories. Although there were no differences between the schools it was of interest to note that the pupils spent approximately one-sixth of every lesson in the waiting category which involved them in waiting for instructions from the teacher or the opportunity to participate in an activity. There was comparatively little off-task behaviour. When it did occur it was partly attributable to indiscipline but in the main it was due to general off-task behaviour in as much that the pupils were not engaged in the activity they should have been. On-task behaviour which

Table 40: All lessons: ALT-PE learner involvement: Mean scores and Kruskal-Wallis one-way ANOVA by category for S1-S5.

Not motor engaged	S1	S2	S3	S4	S5	H	p
	N = 13	N = 13	N = 11	N = 19	N = 18		
Interim	0.4	0	0.6	0.3	0.6	—	—
Waiting	18.1	22.9	19.1	10.7	14.5	6.93	N.S.
Off-task	0.3	0.1	2.0	0.4	0.2	6.55	N.S.
On-task	19.8	15.9	8.1	13.3	15.6	7.23	N.S.
Cognitive	20.2	28.1	43.0	25.7	21.7	10.80	<0.05
Motor engaged							
Motor appropriate	40.8	32.8	27.2	49.5	47.5	9.47	<0.05
Motor inappropriate	0.2	0	0	0	0.2	—	—
Motor supporting	0.5	0.2	0	0.2	0	—	—

involved pupils carrying out a non-subject matter task (for example, a management, transition or warm-up task) averaged 14.7 per cent.

One of the important categories in this section was named cognitive and involved pupils in cognitive tasks such as listening or watching associated with the organization or learning of movement tasks. Here a difference was apparent ($p < 0.05$) with the teachers in the control school S3 spending significantly more time than the teachers in the other four schools engaging their pupils in cognitive tasks. This did not appear to result in any major differences in pupils' understanding and it was possible that these periods of explanation were too long and involved pupils in excessive amounts of listening to descriptions and instructions. S1 and S2 were significantly different from each other but S1, S4 and S5 showed no significant differences.

The average level of motor engagement was 41.5 per cent and almost all of this time was accounted for by the motor appropriate category which, by definition, suggested that the pupils were involved in motor activity in such a way as to produce a high degree of success. Some reservations must be expressed here about the data collection. A visual sweep was made from left to right by the observer every three minutes and although it was comparatively easy to pick out any pupils who were inappropriately engaged, it would be difficult to substantiate that every pupil in the motor appropriate category was working at an 'easy level of difficulty'. With this reservation, a significant difference was just reached at the 5 per cent level in the motor appropriate category. S4 had the highest mean score and was significantly different from S2 and S3. No significant differences were recorded between S1, S4 and S5.

In relation to the main hypothesis, there was little support from the not motor engaged categories. The preponderance of no significant differences between S1, S2, S4 and S5 suggested the schools were equal in their use of these pupil behaviours. The evidence from the motor appropriate category was equivocal as S1, S4 and S5 were the highest scoring schools with no significant difference between them. If, as the literature review suggested, the pupils' motor involvement is an indicator of effective teaching, then S1 and S2 should have had the higher scores. S1 came into this category, but so too did S4 and S5 and they should have been at the lower end of the continuum if the main hypothesis was to be supported.

The learner involvement level had two sub-sections named not motor engaged and motor engaged. The distribution of time for each section in S1–S5 is summarized in table 41 through the mean scores together with the levels of significance.

When the categories in the not motor engaged section were combined and subjected to a Kruskal-Wallis ANOVA, no significant differences were

Table 41:   *All lessons: ALT-PE learner involvement: Mean scores and Kruskal-Wallis one-way ANOVA by sub-section for S1-S5*

Learner involvement	S1	S2	S3	S4	S5	H	p
Not motor engaged	58.8	67.0	72.9	50.5	52.5	5.69	N.S.
Motor engaged	41.4	33.1	27.2	49.7	47.7	0.70	N.S.

revealed. This result did not support the main hypothesis. The motor engaged section also did not reach significance but this was mainly due to the fact that two of the three categories in this section were rarely used and included a large number of zero recordings. The category which contributed most to this section was motor appropriate and when analyzed separately was statistically significant. (This finding has already been commented on in the previous section.)

Summary

Within the ALT-PE context level, five of the nine categories (viz. management, warm-up, technique, strategy and practice) revealed no significant differences. Of the remaining four categories, S1 and S4 had low scores in the transition phases of the lessons. Whilst the results for S1 support the hypothesis, these are counteracted by S4 also having a low score. In the provision of equipment S1 had a significantly higher recording and the teachers were obviously spending longer periods of time on this behaviour — again a non-supportive conclusion. The application of techniques into applied skills settings is to be welcomed and S4 and S5 appeared to devote longer periods of time to this behaviour. Once again, this is contrary to the prediction. Games playing with no teacher input would expect to be found in the least effective schools, whereas this study showed S1 to use this teaching strategy much more frequently than the other schools.

In the learner involvement section, three of the five categories were not significant and consequently non-supportive of the main hypothesis. The two categories which were statistically significant (viz. cognitive and motor appropriate behaviours) both showed S1 to be efficient in the amount of time spent in listening and watching, as well as in the longer amounts of time pupils spent in motor appropriate activity. Whilst these are in accord with the hypothesis, they must be balanced against the fact that S4 and S5 (supposedly the least effective schools) were not significantly different from S1 and therefore not supportive of the hypothesis.

Apart from the large number of non-significant categories, any apparent trends appeared to be the reverse of those projected. For example, S4 had the lowest transition periods and, with S5, had significantly longer periods of applied skills/scrimmage as well as motor appropriate behaviour.

Comparison of Games Lessons

Bearing in mind the advisability of comparing 'like with like', a separate analysis was conducted on the ALT-PE data for lessons which were common to all schools. The fact that games was the only activity taught in S5 meant that this activity was chosen. It also ensured a substantial number of lessons being included in the sample, viz: thirty lessons taught by males and sixteen by females — a total of forty-six lessons. The sample incorporated the following games: badminton, basketball, hockey, lacrosse, netball, soccer, rugby and volleyball.

Context Level

Summary data of mean scores and significance levels for ALT-PE categories for the games lessons in each school is presented in table 42. (Only those categories which contained sufficient data and had been analysed in the full sample were included in subsequent analyses.)

The results for the games lessons showed a very similar pattern to the analysis for all the lessons in the sample, in that the distribution of time in the same six categories (viz. management, warm-up, technique, strategy,

Table 42: Games lessons – ALT-PE: content level: Mean scores and Kruskal-Wallis one-way ANOVA by category for S1-S5

General content	S1	S2	S3	S4	S5	H	p
	N = 6	N = 9	N = 5	N = 8	N = 18		
Transition	15.3	21.0	27.6	12.3	16.7	11.18	<0.05
Management	0.2	0.1	1.2	1.1	0.5	2.53	N.S.
Warm-up	5.3	4.7	1.2	1.0	4.4	6.39	N.S.
Providing equipment	5.3	2.4	4.0	1.1	1.1	12.04	<0.05
PE knowledge							
Technique	7.0	12.8	11.6	8.9	4.8	6.99	N.S.
Strategy	4.0	6.9	2.0	3.0	11.1	7.02	N.S.
PE motor							
Practice	19.0	21.1	28.0	12.9	13.5	6.78	N.S.
Skill/scrimmage	21.3	28.7	19.0	56.0	46.7	12.53	<0.05
Game	21.7	0.6	4.0	3.0	0.7	2.77	N.S.

practice and game) were not significantly different. In addition, the time distribution in the same three categories (transition, providing equipment and skill/scrimmage) were statistically significant at a slightly lower level.

In the general content section, two of the categories did show levels of statistical significance. First, the transition category ($p < 0.05$) revealed S4 to have the lowest mean score and to be significantly different from S2 and S3. Thus the managerial and organizational efficiency of the teachers in S4 was superior to those in S2 and S3. The mean scores in S1 and S5 were also low and not significantly different from S4. The second category to show significance at the 5 per cent level was providing equipment and S1 had a significantly higher score than S2, S4 and S5. This category had originally been added because the handling of large apparatus in the first pilot study involving videotaped lessons had been so time consuming. With the elimination of gymnastic lessons and the standardization of the sample to the teaching of major games this result was unexpected. Clearly teachers in S1 were not as efficient in the provision of equipment as their colleagues in the other schools. There were no shortages or differences in accessibility to equipment which may have accounted for this. Indeed, the facilities in S1 were in many respects superior.

These results were mainly contrary to the main hypothesis that S1 and S2 were the more effective schools. Although S1 had a low transition score, so too did S4 and S5 which was contrary to the prediction. The fact that S1 was less effective in the provision of equipment was also non-supportive.

No significant differences were found in either the technique or strategy categories which comprised the PE knowledge section. A similar pattern of traditional games teaching was apparent in all the schools. This involving giving the pupils information about the techniques and strategies of the activity and then putting them into practice. Thus teachers in the five schools in this study appeared to devote similar amounts of time to the input of PE knowledge in games lessons.

In the PE motor section, the teachers in the five schools were not significantly different in the manner in which they conducted their practice of techniques or chains of techniques outside the applied context. Neither were they different in the time devoted to the application of skills in a competitive game setting when the pupils played a game without intervention from the teacher. Only when it came to the skill category, concerned with the refinement and extension of skills in an applied setting, were any significant differences apparent. This category is considered to be one of the key areas in the acquisition of motor skills. It is not sufficient to become proficient in techniques such as passing and aiming. They have to be performed in a competitive situation against opponents who will do their utmost to disrupt a performance. Consequently it is essential these

Table 43: Games lessons — ALT-PE context level: Mean scores and Kruskal-Wallis one-way ANOVA by sub-section for S1-S5

Context level	S1	S2	S3	S4	S5	H	p
General content	26.3	28.4	34.4	16.3	22.8	3.94	N.S.
PE knowledge	11.7	21.6	14.4	12.0	16.4	3.29	N.S.
PE motor	62.0	50.3	51.0	71.9	60.9	0.66	N.S.

techniques are practised in situations involving passive and active opposition, and conditioned games which simulate the eventual conditions under which the activity is to be performed. High scores in this category would therefore be regarded as advantageous. S4 and S5 came into this grouping with S4 significantly different from S1, S2 and S3. S5 was significantly different from S1 and S3. This was a trend which was against the prediction of the main hypothesis.

The means and significance levels for the three sub-sections at the context level are set out in table 43.

Clearly none of the sections reached statistical significance which suggested that there were no differences in the proportion of time teachers spent in these three sections in the five schools. These results were therefore not supporting the main hypothesis.

Learner Involvement

With the activity standardized to the major games, none of the categories which described the nature of the pupils' involvement was significantly different between the five schools. This conclusion was substantiated by the statistical analysis presented in table 44.

Thus, regardless of the game being taught, there were no differences in the waiting, off-task, on-task, cognitive and motor appropriate categories.

Table 44: Games lessons — ALT-PE learner involvement: Mean scores and Kruskal-Wallis one-way ANOVA by category for S1-S5

Not motor engaged	S1	S2	S3	S4	S5	H	p
	N = 6	N = 9	N = 5	N = 8	N = 18		
Waiting	21.3	18.9	22.4	13.8	14.5	2.92	N.S.
Off-task	0.2	0	1.2	0.1	0.2	2.51	N.S.
On-task	19.2	16.2	8.2	8.9	15.6	4.62	N.S.
Cognitive	12.8	27.2	32.8	10.6	21.7	9.42	N.S.
Motor engaged							
Motor appropriate	45.8	37.6	34.4	66.3	47.5	6.53	N.S.

Through the narrowing of the range of activities the motor appropriate category, which had shown statistical significance for the complete sample of lessons, had become non-significant. Thus there were no significant differences between the five schools in the time-on-task at an 'easy level of difficulty'. Only the cognitive category showed any marked differences and this was almost at the 5 per cent level of significance. Here the lowest scores were recorded in S1 and S4 and the highest in S2 and S3. As no obvious performance differences had been observed in the lessons, the suggestion would be that the lower scores had been just as efficient in involving pupils in cognitive tasks such as listening and watching. This would then have made more time available for other related activity in S1 and S4.

The overall lack of statistical significance was contrary to the hypothesis prediction.

Similarly the ANOVA analysis of the two sub-sections of the learner involvement level presented in table 45 also did not reach statistical significance.

Of some interest is the fact that S4 was the only school where the mean scores were larger in the motor than the not motor engaged section. However, there was obviously considerable variance within the schools and the results were again not supporting the main hypothesis.

Table 45: Games lessons: ALT-PE learner involvement: Mean scores and Kruskal-Wallis one-way ANOVA by sub-section for S1-S5

Learner Involvement	S1	S2	S3	S4	S5	H	p
Not motor engaged	53.7	62.3	65.6	33.6	52.5	3.84	N.S.
Motor engaged	46.8	37.9	34.4	66.3	47.7	0.29	N.S.

Summary

From the analysis of the games lessons in the ALT-PE context level, only the fact that S1 had a low transition score could be interpreted as favourable to the main hypothesis and even this was counteracted by the fact that S4 and S5 also recorded low scores. Two negative results were revealed. The first was the significantly high recording in the provision of equipment in S1 and the second was the significantly higher scores by S4 and S5 in the skill/scrimmage category. Finally, the lack of any significant differences in the six categories and the three sub-sections was also non-supportive. At the learner involvement level none of the pupils' behaviour categories showed a significant difference between the five schools and therefore did not support the hypothesis.

Comparison of Male and Female Teachers

The review of research associated with the teaching behaviour of male and female teachers had produced some equivocal findings. On the one hand some studies (for example, Hickey, 1985, and Spackman, 1986) had revealed no sex differences in the teaching of physical education, whilst others (for example, Cheffers and Lombardo, 1979; and Varstala *et al*, 1983) suggested that although the content of teaching behaviour was similar, the proportion of time spent in each category might differ. Against this background it was considered appropriate to consider the sex of the teacher as a variable in the teaching of the seventy-four lessons in this investigation.

All Lessons: Context Level

The ALT-PE data was collated and compared for the forty lessons taught by the male and the thirty-four lessons taught by the female physical education teachers in the sample to ascertain the similarities and differences of teaching approaches. The Kruskal-Wallis one way ANOVA was used to determine significance levels between the male and female teachers and the results are set out in table 46.

The interpretation of the results in table 46 is clearly all in the same direction. There were no significant differences between any of the categories subjected to analysis. These results give strong support for the notion that male and female teachers provide similar contextual learning environments.

Table 46: *All Lessons: ALT-PE context level: Mean scores and Kruskal-Wallis one-way ANOVA by category for male and female teachers.*

General content	M N = 40	F N = 34	H	p
Transition	15.5	15.2	0.00	N.S.
Management	1.0	1.0	0.01	N.S.
Warm-up	4.0	4.6	0.55	N.S.
Providing equipment	3.1	4.2	3.30	N.S.
PE knowledge				
Technique	8.3	8.1	0.13	N.S.
Strategy	10.5	13.3	2.47	N.S.
PE motor				
Practice	17.5	11.7	2.17	N.S.
Skill/scrimmage	35.9	34.0	0.10	N.S.
Game	2.9	4.6	0.66	N.S.

All Lessons: Learner Involvement Level

At the learner involvement level, each category was analyzed by means of the Kruskal-Wallis one-way ANOVA by ranks and the H values and their levels of significance together with the mean scores are set out in table 47. The results from table 47 again indicated that there were no significant differences between male and female teachers in any of the categories. Thus the sex of the teacher did not appear to be an important variable in relation to the nature of the pupils' engagement in physical education lessons.

Table 47: All lessons: ALT-PE learner involvement: Mean scores and Kruskal-Wallis one-way ANOVA by category for male and female teachers.

Not motor engaged	M	F	H	p
	N = 40	N = 34		
Waiting	16.2	16.5	0.23	N.S.
Off-task	0.4	0.7	0.15	N.S.
On-task	13.7	15.9	1.79	N.S.
Cognitive	25.5	28.3	0.26	N.S.
Motor engaged				
Motor appropriate	44.1	37.9	0.36	N.S.

Games Lessons: Context Level

Again, because of the diverse activities in the main sample, it was decided to conduct an analysis of the forty-six games lessons (thirty taught by male and sixteen by female teachers) in a further attempt to compare 'like with like' and the mean scores together with the ANOVA results are summarized in table 48.

In eight of the nine categories that had sufficient data for analysis, no significant differences were apparent. The one category that did not fall into this pattern was providing equipment which showed a difference at the 5 per cent level of significance. The mean scores showed that male teachers used this category less than females. As many of the same games were taught by both males and females, for example, badminton, basketball, hockey and volleyball, and the other games in the sample (lacrosse, netball, soccer and rugby) were similar in respect of the amount of equipment necessary to conduct the lesson, it was reasonable to suggest that male teachers were more efficient than female teachers in providing equipment for games lessons.

Table 48: Games lessons: ALT-PE context level: Mean scores and Kruskal-Wallis one-way ANOVA by category for male and female teachers.

General content	M	F	H	p
	N = 30	N = 16		
Transition	16.9	19.4	0.67	N.S.
Management	0.7	0.4	1.60	N.S.
Warm-up	3.5	4.0	0.16	N.S.
Providing equipment	1.7	3.5	6.01	<0.05
PE knowledge				
Technique	8.2	7.9	0.00	N.S.
Strategy	7.5	5.9	0.01	N.S.
PE motor				
Practice	18.7	14.4	0.82	N.S.
Skill/scrimmage	37.5	40.3	0.36	N.S.
Game	4.2	4.2	1.23	N.S.

Games Lessons: Learner Involvement Level

As can be seen from the summary data in table 49, four of the five categories revealed no significant differences.

Thus there were no significant differences in the amount of time pupils devoted to waiting, off-task, cognitive and motor appropriate behaviours regardless of whether they were taught by male or female staff. This suggested that pupils had equal amounts of time in games lessons in which to practise and become proficient in motor skills regardless of the sex of the teacher. The only category which did show a significant difference at the 1 per cent level was in on-task behaviour which involved 'non subject matter' behaviour (a management, transition or warm-up task). Pupils taught by male teachers spent less time in this category which would have

Table 49: Games lessons: ALT-PE learner involvement: Mean scores and Kruskal-Wallis one-way ANOVA by category for male and female teachers.

Not motor engaged	M	F	H	p
	N = 30	N = 16		
Waiting	17.9	15.2	0.90	N.S.
Off-task	0.2	0.3	0.41	N.S.
On-task	11.2	19.9	7.91	<0.01
Cognitive	23.2	16.7	1.21	N.S.
Motor engaged				
Motor appropriate	47.3	46.9	0.32	N.S.

released more time for 'subject matter' behaviour but this was not statistically apparent in the other categories.

Summary

There were no significant differences between male and female teachers in their teaching of physical education lessons as evidenced from the data collected through the ALT–PE analysis. (The only exception to this was in the provision of equipment in games lessons where male teachers appeared to be more effective.) Similarly, pupils' involvement also showed no significant differences in the ALT–PE classifications apart from a lower level of involvement by pupils taught by male teachers in on-task behaviour in games lessons.

Overall, there was overwhelming support for the contention that the sex of the teacher did not appear to be an important variable in the teaching of physical education. Male and female teachers appeared to adopt similar teaching approaches which in turn led to similar levels of pupil involvement in the lessons.

11
Overview

Pupils' Perceptions Revisited

This section provides a possible explanation to account for the differences between the pupils' and the observers' ranking of teaching effectiveness in S1-S5. It will be recalled that the pupils' ranking was determined through the responses of fourth form pupils to the Physical Education 'Learner Report' Questionnaire and the observer ranking was based on qualitative and quantitative data obtained during a week of observation in each school. The rank order for the sample is set out in table 50.

Thus a negligible correlation was revealed which did not support the main hypothesis that S1 and S2 would be the more effective schools. It is therefore necessary to examine some of the possible reasons for this discrepancy.

Table 50: Rank order correlation of pupils' and observers' ranking of teaching effectiveness in S1-S5

School	Pupils' ranking	Observers' ranking
S1	1	4
S2	2	2
S3	3	3
S4	4	1
S5	5	5
Rank order correlation = 0.1		

Validity of Pupils' Assessment

The pupils had assessed the strength of their own learning through responses to twenty-four questions on the 'Learner Report' questionnaire.

The lack of confirmation of the rank ordering of schools based on these responses inevitably poses the question 'Can pupils give an accurate indication of their own learning?' It will be recalled that, when allowed to do exactly as they pleased, many pupils enjoyed their physical education lessons. The free activity in a swimming lesson or the playing of a game of soccer without instruction from the teacher were examples of such lessons which would probably have produced positive feelings towards those particular lessons but would not have reflected the extent of any worthwhile learning that had taken place. Under these circumstances false recordings may have been generated.

There was also some evidence to support the suggestion that many of the more skilful performers were prepared to accept the hard training that was necessary in order to improve, whereas pupils of lower ability levels were less likely to accept this form of challenge. Attainment in any sphere involves considerable effort and hard work but some children in the lower ability band were not prepared to accept this in physical education. As a result, they were happier with easier levels of attainment. Consequently they might not be the best judges of the effectiveness of their own learning environments. The teachers' criteria for learning may well have been different from the pupils as the teachers rarely communicated their aims and objectives. Most of the teachers were, through worthwhile and enjoyable experiences, attempting to bring about learning through changes in a wide range of behaviours in such areas as skill, social and cognitive understanding. On the other hand, some pupils were satisfied if the lesson had been enjoyable regardless of the content. Thus the ability of 14 and 15-year-old children to judge the effectiveness of an educational environment and the extent of their own learning in these circumstances may be open to question. After all it is the responsibility of the teacher to decide the nature of the educational experience to be offered to children. Physical education often incorporates a large element of enjoyment, but enjoyment must be seen as a by-product rather than a prerequisite to learning.

The Physical Education 'Learner Report' Questionnaire

The questionnaire used the terms sport and games in all the questions. This is quite a narrow interpretation of physical education as most school programmes include athletics, educational gymnastics, dance, swimming and outdoor activities. None of these was mentioned by name — other than in Q6 and Q9 which referred to achievements in athletics and to performance on the gymnastic apparatus respectively. When examples were given to illustrate a question, they were invariably taken from the major games. Only Q 10 incorporated the phrase movement situations which is common terminology in many schools and even then the word sport was inserted in brackets after the word movement. In this country, the word sport is often synonymous with major games whereas physical education/movement refers to a much greater range of physical activities which are used in an educational context. The questionnaire had been constructed in the Netherlands and there can sometimes be problems in transferring a questionnaire from one culture or country to another. In this case the cultures are very similar but the content of physical education is slightly different in this country and the various activities are given different emphases. A greater range of examples or an indication of the range of activities embraced by the term physical education/movement could have been made in the introductory statement and this might have alleviated the criticism concerning the narrow focus of activities.

In retrospect, some of the questions may have been a little obscure for some pupils. For example Q 11, which asked how deviations in posture occur and how they can be corrected, might have been better if it had been personalized and within their own experience. Similarly, the ability to appraise critically media reports and how sport related to commerce and politics were probably outside the range of many pupils' experience. This may have accounted for the mainly neutral or negative scores on these items which were all in the cognitive-reflective area.

Concern was also felt about the interpretation of the numerical scores to a question. For example Q 2 asked the pupils if they were able to apply the basic principles of endurance training. The average scores in all schools were positive and ranged from 2.11 to 2.42. It would therefore be reasonable to assume that the majority of the pupils in this sample would know and be able to apply these principles to this fitness component. However, through observation and discussions with senior pupils, it became clear that very few were knowledgeable enough to be able to do this. Consequently the questionnaire score on this question may have given a false reading of the pupils' abilities.

The format of the questionnaire required responses to each question to be made by placing a tick in one of five categories which ranged from 'certainly true,' through 'I don't know' to 'certainly not true'. Thus the first box represented a strongly positive score and the last one a strongly negative score. This order of presentation was the same for every question. This may have led some pupils to keep the majority of their responses in a pattern on the positive side. It might have been advantageous to have reversed the responses to some questions which would have then avoided any tendency to adopt a 'response set'.

The use of a learner report questionnaire is comparatively new and innovatory in attempting to obtain a global impression of the nature and extent of pupils' learning. Whilst some of the initial studies reported by Crum (1986a and 1986b) have been encouraging, the results from this study do question the validity of this method in measuring the effectiveness of a physical education programme in a secondary school. For schools to be classed as significantly different statistically (S1/2 and S4/5) on the basis of learner report scores, and then for S4 to be classed as the most effective school using a different method, seriously undermines the ability of the instrument to accurately differentiate between schools.

One of the problems in attempting to measure the effectiveness of the physical education programme in a school is that there are no ultimate criteria by which the subject can be judged. Unlike many subjects there is no public examination by which national standards can be established. (The advent of a GCSE examination in physical education now allows the establishment of criteria which will provide this kind of comparison.) As has already been indicated, pupils can easily overestimate the extent of their learning and the complex interrelated components of learning in physical education may not be best summarized by a numerical mark. If overestimation is possible, then so too is underestimation and this may have been the case in S4.

In spite of these criticisms, the questionnaire served its purpose, which was to identify schools which were 'significantly different' using an unbiased and objective method. Additionally, it had the advantage of giving insight into the pupils' perceptions of their learning in physical education. However, it would be naive to consider that pupils' evaluations of their own learning in a wide range of activities could be incorporated into a single numerical score. It would be more realistic to examine trends and accept that scores are an approximation of the extent and nature of learning in each school.

Validity of Observer's Assessment

Another reason for the lack of support for the main hypothesis may have been caused through inconsistencies or incorrect interpretations in the observer's rankings. To make an evaluation of a physical education department involves many different components such as planning procedures, subject knowledge of the staff, teaching ability, relationships with children and many other aspects. All these have to be taken into consideration when arriving at an overall ranking. Each school in this study had its own strengths and weaknesses. For instance, in one school the girls' department was considered to be more effective than the boys' department, whilst in another the girls' department had a number of temporary staff problems that were being covered by several part-time teachers. Perhaps the biggest staffing problem was apparent in the school where the head of department had recently left and, at the time of the observation visit, had not been replaced. Apart from the staffing, the documentation available in the five schools was substantially different with one school being particularly outstanding in this respect. Weighing the strengths and weaknesses of one department against another is not easy under these circumstances and is open to some bias in interpretation.

Judgements about each school were made during one week of observation within the department. It could be argued that this was too short a period of time in which to judge the efficiency of a department. Nonetheless considerable insight was gained into the way in which teachers in the five schools taught physical education. The methods of observation in all the schools were standardized wherever possible which allowed valid comparisons to be made. Longer periods of observation time would have been preferable, but within the confines of this study one week in each school was considered to be adequate.

The observers' ranking of the schools did involve an element of subjective evaluation which may have been unconsciously biased. However, this criticism can be counteracted by the fact that an educationist who was familiar with the work in all the schools had proposed a similar ranking. Thus there was some independent confirmation available.

Some support for the revised rankings was also obtained from the quantitative analyses generated from the ALT-PE data. Academic learning time is a reliable and valid instrument, originally developed in the classroom in the mid-1970s. Subsequently it has been applied to the physical education context during the last several years. Thus it is a research technique that has frequently been used by many researchers in several countries. Acceptable levels of reliability were achieved in this study and the results were considered to be a valid representation of teacher and pupil behaviour in the physical education context.

On balance there appeared to be a stronger argument in support of the observer's ranking. The use of the learner report method only gave a general indication of the degree of learning that had taken place and the precise quantification through a numerical score needs to be interpreted with caution. The more reliable observation methods of ALT-PE, a proven research instrument, together with confirmation from an independent source gives greater credence to the rankings of the observer.

Methodology

As stated at the outset, the main aims of this study were to examine ways in which physical education is taught in secondary schools and the effects these teaching strategies might have on pupils' behaviours in lessons. In addition, an attempt was made to investigate pupils' perceptions of their own learning in the subject. The literature review had suggested a number of methodological priorities which were incorporated into the design of the study. It would not have been appropriate to have used a single research strategy to investigate such a complex and wide-ranging area. Thus an eclectic approach was used which utilized a variety of methods to collect relevant data and each of the research strategies contributed to the central theme outlined above.

The study began in schools at the heart of the subject, namely in the gymnasium where physical education is taught. The videotape recordings of six educational gymnastic and six basketball/netball lessons enabled a detailed multi-dimensional analysis to be made of the teachers' and the pupils' behaviour. The opportunity to view the same episode in a lesson on several occasions enabled a very accurate and reliable assessment to be made of these behaviours. This pilot study was a valid springboard for the main study as it incorporated one of the main methodological design recommendations, that is that any study should take place in a naturalistic setting. It also highlighted two of the variables to be considered, namely the sex of the teacher and the nature of the activity being taught.

In order to broaden the scope of the study it was decided to conduct a number of case studies in physical education departments in schools. Through pupils' responses to a Physical Education 'Learner Report' Questionnaire in fourteen schools, five schools were chosen which were suitable for this purpose. Based on the pupils' assessment of their own learning in the subject, two were designated high-scoring schools and two, low-scoring, and both pairs were statistically significantly different from each other. These differences were contained in each of four questionnaire factors named technomotor, sociomotor, cognitive-reflective and affective. In addition a 'control' school which was not statistically different from either pair was also chosen. Thus schools with different levels of effectiveness in their physical education programmes, as measured by the pupils, were objectively identified. Apart from the main purpose of identifying suitable schools, it also had the added advantage of giving insight into whether or not male and female pupils considered they had acquired skills in the motor, social, cognitive and affective domains.

The author spent one week observing the teaching of physical education in each of the five schools. In all, seventy-four lessons were observed and each was analyzed through ALT-PE at the context and learner involvement levels. Inevitably this generated a great deal of quantitative data. This type of data is very revealing and objective in nature but can often be 'barren' and hide quite significant episodes in the teaching-learning environment. Because of this, a number of qualitative evaluations were introduced. During the conduct of the lessons several qualitative areas such as the ability of the teacher to communicate, the working atmosphere and the logical and related development of lessons were also monitored. This provided a balance between the two types of data.

As well as observing the actual teaching of physical education lessons, semi-structured interviews were conducted with the staff in each school as well as with a small number of pupils. Staff interviews were related to their planning procedures and were supplemented with an analysis of the written physical education syllabus. It was only possible to interview a small sample of pupils and four were selected by the staff (one high and one low ability boy and girl) in each school.

Thus a variety of research methods were adopted in this study. None was exclusive as they all combined to give insight into the teaching and learning of physical education in secondary schools. At this stage it is pertinent to ask whether the strategies used in this study achieved what they set out to do. The answer would be unequivocally affirmative. The direct observation methods in both the pilot and the main study provided reliable and valid data about the teaching of physical education. Added to this was the qualitative data which extended and enriched the analysis. Thus the topic was probed in several different ways which produced interrelated information.

This is not to suggest that everything was perfect. The strategy which gave the most cause for concern was the pupils' assessment of their own learning as measured by the PE 'Learner Report' Questionnaire. It became clear that a single numerical score from the questionnaire did not appear to be a valid measure of effective teaching. In spite of this limitation, it did give some insight into pupils' perceptions of physical education and allowed specific areas to be probed further during the observation of the lessons and in the course of the pupils' interviews. The fact that the questionnaire responses and the reality of the pupils' perceptions were sometimes incongruent, merely highlighted the caution which needs to be exercised when interpreting 'Likert-type' responses to a questionnaire.

Overall, it was considered that the eclectic approach had been success-ful in identifying effective teaching and learning in physical education in schools. Although some of the results were inconsistent, this was to be expected in such a complex area of human interaction. Generally, the variety of approaches were complementary to one another.

Main Hypothesis

In relation to the central hypothesis of the thesis that S1/2 were more effective than S4/5, it became clear from the 'Between Schools' analysis that there was no relationship between the pupils' and the observers' assessment of teaching effectiveness.

The qualitative data collected from the direct observation of lessons using the ALT–PE system was firstly analyzed in relation to the complete sample of lessons. Secondly, (following a methodological recommendation), the data was analyzed for those lessons with a similar content activity of major games and finally, a comparison was made between lessons taught by male and female teachers.

As a result of the statistical analyses, a number of statements can be made in relation to the teachers and pupils in the five schools in this study. (Where significance was reached, the schools with the more favourable scores are indicated in brackets.)

At the context level for the full and games sample:

1 There were no significant differences in the distribution of time spent in the management, warm up, technique, strategy, practice and game categories.
2 Significant differences were apparent in the transition (S1 and S4 had low mean scores in both samples and S5 in the games sample), providing equipment (S2, S3, S4 and S5) and skills application (S4 and S5) categories.
3 There were no significant differences in the general content, PE knowledge and PE motor sub-sections.

At the learner involvement level, the following general statements are warranted for the full sample:

1 There were no significant differences between schools in the waiting, off-task and on-task categories.
2 Significant differences were reached in the cognitive and motor appropriate categories (S1, S4 and S5).

For the games lessons:

1 No significant differences were apparent in any of the not motor engaged or motor engaged categories.

For the male and female teachers in the full sample:

1 No significant differences were apparent in any of the categories at the context or learner involvement level.

In the games sample:

1 No significant differences were revealed in the transition, management, warm up, technique, strategy, practice, skills and game categories.
2 Male teachers spent significantly less time in the providing equipment category.
3 No significant differences were recorded in the waiting, off-task, cognitive and motor appropriate categories.
4 Pupils taught by male teachers spent significantly less time in on-task behaviour.

The clearest trend from the above conclusions was that there were no significant differences between the schools in the majority of categories and therefore they did not support the main hypothesis. Where statistical significance was reached, apart from occasional references to S1, S2 and S3 having the more favourable scores, the most frequent mention of schools with favourable scores were S4 and S5 which was contrary to the hypothesis.

With regard to physical education lessons taught by male and female teachers, the vast majority of categories showed no significant differences, which indicated that the male and female teaching strategies were very similar. Only in the teaching of games were any significant differences apparent with the male teachers having the more favourable scores.

The quantitative data generated by ALT-PE observations was supplemented with qualitative data from observations and interviews in the schools. Again the evidence was not in accord with the hypothesis that S1 and S2 would emerge as the most efficient schools. As far as departmental administration was concerned S4 was considered to be the most effective. With regard to teacher-pupil relationships, the teachers in all the schools had concern for their pupils and it was not possible to differentiate between them. In the organization and development of lessons, S4 was considered to be the most effective and S1, particularly in relation to the senior school physical education curriculum, somewhat less effective.

In a post-hoc analysis of pupils' perceptions of physical education, (Underwood, 1987) there was statistical evidence to support the contention that the pupils in the two schools which the observer considered to be the most effective (S4 and S2) were more consistent and showed less variation in their responses to the questions on the Physical Education

'Learner Report' Questionnaire than did those pupils in the least effective schools (S1 and S5). Thus there was greater agreement between pupils in the 'better' schools about the aims and objectives of the subject.

This consensus of pupil opinion will almost certainly be due to a variety of reasons. One may be because of a more coherent subject philosophy in the more effective schools. Presumably if the staff are in agreement about the aims of their teaching then there is a greater likelihood that they will transmit them to the pupils. This agreement might well be apparent through written statements incorporated into a syllabus. As has already been reported, S4 had a particularly impressive and coordinated syllabus presentation. S2 also had a combined syllabus for boys' and girls' physical education with shared aims and objectives. In both schools, schemes of work for the different practical activities had been prepared by different members of staff which meant that several staff had made a substantial input to the syllabus presentation. Another feature common to both schools was the regular monthly or half-termly meetings at which important curriculum issues such as aims and objectives, content, methods and assessment procedures were discussed. These procedures contrasted markedly with the arrangements in the less effective schools. Neither S1 or S5 had a combined syllabus for the boys' and girls' physical education, although the first stage of one had just been produced in S1. At the time of the administration of the questionnaire they were mainly existing as separate departments and did not meet together to discuss subject philosophy or planning. Any discussions or meetings appeared to take place informally and infrequently and were confined to the male or female staff. These differences in planning procedures may go some way to account for a more coherent and coordinated subject philosophy amongst the staff in S4 and S2 and in turn result in a greater consensus of pupils' opinions about their learning in physical education.

Whilst the trends in the quantitative and qualitative analyses were not identical it was clear that there was little which supported the central hypothesis. Much of the evidence was not statistically significant and therefore non-supportive. However, there was considerable support for a revised ranking which would place S4 as the school with the most effective department in the conduct and administration of the physical education curriculum.

Educational Issues

A number of educational issues emerged from the review of literature which were highlighted during the course of the investigation. In the light of the results, these are now given further consideration.

Organization and Administration of a Physical Education Department

It was no accident that S4 was considered to be the best organized department. Perhaps its greatest strength lay in the fact that the boys' and the girls' departments were fully integrated. They still had their own separate identities with a teacher responsible for the day-to-day administration but the overall planning had been carried out by all the staff. This was clearly reflected in the integrated and well-planned syllabus which had been devised, discussed and agreed by all the staff. The major components of curriculum planning, viz. aims and objectives, content, method and evaluation, had all been considered at regular monthly department meetings. This had resulted in a cohesive department with a shared ideology. In either one aspect or another, none of the other schools matched the degree of planning and organization that was apparent in S4. Most had quite separate and autonomous boys' and girls' departments with an administrative head of department. It is difficult to justify this segregation when the aims and content of the subject are so similar. With the advent of mixed physical education in secondary schools, there will be greater pressure and even more justification for a 'coming together' of the male and female staff in the planning and implementation of the physical education curriculum in the future.

The clarity of purpose and planning in S4 had resulted in a greater consensus of pupil opinion about the purposes the subject was trying to achieve. This clarity had resulted in a department in which each separate member was clear in pursuing the same overall aims and objectives — a target all departments should aim for.

Management of Lessons

The study enabled a sizeable sample of lessons ($N = 74$) to be examined in relation to how the teachers structured the context within which the pupils' behaviour occurred. It transpired that the teachers, on average, spent just less than one-quarter of the lesson on general content which referred to time when pupils were not involved in physical education activities, a similar amount of time in the subject knowledge section when the focus was on knowledge related to physical education content and the remaining time (54.4 per cent) on subject motor content when the focus was on motor involvement related to physical education activities. These proportions inevitably influenced the pupils' behaviours in the lesson such that pupils spent almost three-fifths of the lesson in the not motor engaged categories and the remaining two-fifths in the motor engaged section.

The criticism from the literature review that physical education lessons were characterized by a great deal of non-movement would appear to be justified from the results of this investigation. Of course a certain amount of time has to be spent on organizational and knowledge factors and these will vary according to the nature of the subject to be taught and the abilities of the children in the class. However, consideration could profitably be given to reducing this time without losing efficiency. This would have the effect of releasing time for more subject motor content. Similarly the learners' involvement was also characterized by the largest proportion in the not motor engaged section. On average, pupils spent 16 per cent of the lesson either waiting to take part or waiting for instructions. Additionally, an average of 27 per cent was spent in cognitive tasks such as listening or watching an aspect of skill acquisition. Thus it may well be in these areas that the most profitable investigations might be undertaken.

As had already been explained, it was difficult for an observer who was unfamiliar with the skill levels of the pupils to make accurate judgements about whether or not a pupil's motor practice was correctly placed in the motor appropriate category at an 'easy level of difficulty.' Thus the percentage scores are, if anything, an overestimate. It was therefore apparent that the actual amount of time a pupil spent in appropriate and purposeful motor activity was less than might first appear.

Lesson Themes

All lessons should have clearly-defined objectives which the teacher hopes to achieve. In physical education these can sometimes be very objective: for instance the reproduction of a prescribed pattern of motor skill, and sometimes rather subjective such as in the creation of a sequence of movement. Regardless of the nature of the objectives, teachers should adopt a consistent and logical development of a lesson(s) theme in pursuit of their achievement.

Whilst lesson themes and objectives were apparent in most lessons, it was not always clear that these were conveyed to the pupils. Additionally there were occasions when the theme became dissipated as the lesson progressed. For example, the gymnastic themes practised on the floor were sometimes not transferred to the apparatus and under these circumstances the links were not clear. Similarly, the techniques practised in the initial part of games lessons were not always emphasized in the applied skills or games playing section of the lesson. There were also occasions when the progression from the technique to the applied skill was too great for some pupils and as a result the learning opportunities were impaired. Nevertheless there were many lessons when the theme was consistent and clearly related. These occasions not only provided optimum conditions for the acquisition of skill but also enabled pupils to develop confidence in a properly structured learning environment.

Feedback

It did not prove possible to monitor the teachers' feedback to pupils as accurately as had been planned. The overwhelming impression was that almost all the feedback was non-specific and motivational and this was confirmed during the observations in the lessons. Rarely was any reference made to the qualitative nature of the movement. Three categories of feedback were monitored, viz. positive, positive with information and negative. Almost all the recordings that were made were in the positive category, a few positive with some information and hardly any in the negative category. Thus the physical education teachers were nearly always supportive in their comments which helped to foster good working atmospheres. However, it did appear that an opportunity was being missed to provide more specific feedback related to a particular movement. Teachers need to be more aware of the opportunities that exist for providing intrinsic feedback which is informational in nature. Examples would include encouraging pupils to get 'the feel of the movement' and making statements about the quality of performance which enhance feelings of personal worth. Through this, pupils would be encouraged to be self-motivated and personally responsible for their actions.

The teachers in this sample gave a great deal of feedback to the pupils. However, a slight shift in direction which emphasized the intrinsic and informational properties of the movements could enhance the quality of performance as well as personal feelings towards the activity.

Development of Fitness

The recent upsurge to develop personal levels of fitness and healthy living through the physical education curriculum has already been noted. In order to develop cardiorespiratory fitness it is necessary to raise pupils' heart rates to something in excess of 150 beats per minute for extended periods of time. This enables pupils to exercise in the 'training zone' from which maximum benefit is derived. It was not possible to measure heart beats accurately but the overwhelming impression was that the vast majority of pupils in nearly all lessons did not exercise in the training zone — let alone for any length of time. There were two exceptions to this. One involved some of the more able pupils who made a full commitment in the major games lessons. Their activity pattern involved a great deal of running off the ball in support play as well as with the ball. The other exception was in three lessons that were specifically related to the development of endurance. In these lessons, not only was there a high physical workload but the underlying principles and methods of developing different components of fitness were also being explained. This was heartening because in the conversations with pupils in lessons and in the pupil interviews, it became apparent that most pupils did not understand the principles of obtaining and developing fitness levels.

Overall there were few signs that fitness levels were being developed which would suggest that personal fitness was not being enhanced for most pupils through participation in physical education lessons. The underlying philosophy and principles for developing fitness were not understood by most pupils and there was obviously a need to supplement the practice of fitness with related theory.

Enjoyment

Most teachers had an agreeable relationship with the pupils and a good working atmosphere was usually apparent. This coupled with the fact that all teachers considered enjoyment to be an essential ingredient of their teaching produced a pleasant teaching-learning environment.

Considerable emphasis was placed on all pupils experiencing enjoyment regardless of their level of ability. The interviews with high and low ability pupils provided support for this contention when seventeen of the twenty pupils interviewed expressed enthusiasm and enjoyment for the subject. Similar impressions were also gained talking to pupils immediately after a lesson when their feelings were still fresh in their minds.

A measure of pupils' enthusiasm for the subject can sometimes be gauged from their participation in extra-curricular activities. Because of the industrial action at the time it was not possible to form an accurate assessment of pupils' levels of participation. However, pupils will only take part in such voluntary activity if they are experiencing achievement and enjoyment. Where clubs and team practices were in operation they appeared to be well supported. Most teachers welcomed all pupils to extra-curricular activities regardless of their level of ability and were prepared to adapt their practices to cater for the broad ranges of ability.

In the main, teachers in this sample of schools appeared to be succeeding in their attempts to enable pupils to enjoy their participation in physical education.

Future Research

During the course of this investigation, a number of research issues have been raised and these are now considered in a broader perspective for future research.

One obvious main issue is the need to validate learner report methods in physical education. The central question is 'Are pupils able to make an accurate evaluation of their own learning?' If they are capable of making such a judgement then the results from this study suggest that the Physical Education 'Learner Report' Questionnaire developed by Crum (1984) is in need of further validation before it can be used with confidence. Whilst the questionnaire has a certain face validity, further research needs to be undertaken with regard to its construct validity and the factors that have so far been identified. Numerical scores may not be the best way to describe the nature and extent of pupils' learning in a subject and, if they are used, need to be supplemented with additional personalized and qualitative data.

Much of the investigation in this study was undertaken in a naturalistic setting and therefore had a great deal of ecological validity. There is no doubt that the teaching-learning situations in physical education do take place in a complicated and highly interactive environment. Whilst extracting particular issues, such as the value of different teaching styles or the use of feedback, and testing hypotheses in controlled experimental situations is a valid research procedure, there is also a need for more studies that take place 'in the field'. The problem is that it is difficult to control all the variables in such situations, but the global view does place the research in its true perspective.

A reasonable balance has been used between quantitative and qualitative analysis and this eclectic approach is commended for future research strategies. The contrast between the 'hard data' obtained from the questionnaire and ALT-PE observations and the richness of personal observations and interviews which probed issues in some depth, provided a good blend of information.

The pupils' behaviour in physical education lessons does warrant more detailed investigation. Whilst the time-on-task as measured by the motor appropriate category did give an approximation of their motor behaviour, more detailed and accurate evaluations need to be made. In particular, the concepts of 'competent bystander' and 'fringe player' need to be probed.

This could be done by observing such pupil's behaviour in lessons over extended periods of time or by using videotaped recordings.

The interviews with pupils revealed that some pupils had learnt to become inept in physical education and this was described in the literature as 'learned helplessness'. Serious consideration needs to be given to the reasons why pupils have learnt to fail in the subject. This would involve probing the nature of their educational experiences. Situations which embarrass pupils, such as the public choosing of teams by peer group evaluation of ability, would be seriously called into question. Whilst some children have failed, others have succeeded and 'learned excellence'. Physical ability and prowess in an activity will obviously have been an important factor and the extent that the self-fulfilling prophesy had been in operation warrants attention. Do physical education teachers give more time and attention to the more physically gifted, and if so, what form does this take? Not only must the teachers' and the pupils' behaviours be carefully monitored in lessons but the pupils' opinions must also be examined. In this way, suggestions could be made about the formation of opinions and attitudes towards physical education.

In most secondary schools, male and female pupils only work together in some of the optional activities in the senior school. However, there is a strong emerging trend towards mixed physical education for all pupils. At the moment there is no empirical evidence to support such a change from a practice which has been in existence for approximately a century. Would a change of this nature improve levels of performance, enhance social skills and improve personal relationships? These are the kinds of questions to which answers are needed. A longitudinal study which monitored such a curriculum change would be a very worthwhile investigation.

Anderson's Descriptive Category System which analyzed videotaped physical education lessons and the ALT-PE method which enabled codings to be made while the lesson was in progress were both considered to be valid and reliable systems with which to record the teaching-learning environment. As such, they could be used with confidence in future research. Where comparisons between lessons are being considered, the recommendation would be that the activity is standardized. The proportion of time teachers spend in the three sections of the context level of ALT-PE would provide valuable information about teaching behaviours at a personal level. This could then be considered in relation to the objectives of the lesson. Information such as this would raise teachers' understanding and consciousness of their teaching strategies and the potential effects they can have on pupils' learning. Similarly, information provided from the learner involvement categories would indicate some of the links between teaching and learning. At an individual level this would provide realistic and relevant data from which to consider possible strategies with which to improve his or her teaching. Personalized information of this kind would have a much greater impact on a teacher than rather generalized statements and could be used to devise individual intervention strategies to amend teaching styles.

More detailed evaluation of the product of teaching physical education is indicated. Teachers may have very clear objectives about what they hope to achieve, but they cannot always be sure they have attained them. In this investigation, many pupils did not understand the principles of games playing which can be applied in many different games situations. Also, they were very unclear about how to develop the components of physical fitness. The advent of games for understanding and health–related fitness into the curriculum may go some way to bridge the gap in understanding that currently exists, but methods need to be devised to ensure that learning has actually occurred.

The national campaign 'Sport for All' seems to be paralleled with a desire to involve all pupils of all ability levels in physical activity. As a result, pupils are rarely streamed according to ability in lessons and extra-curricular activities are no longer the elitist clubs they were a few years ago. Whilst this is the philosophy underlying the pupils' involvement in physical education, the present investigation did reveal occasions when the pupils organized their own 'selection' procedures. The 'them and us' situations which operated in some games lessons was a particularly vivid example. The frequency and nature of such occurrences needs to be examined in some detail.

Research into the teaching of physical education should help to enhance the quality of the experiences that pupils encounter in their secondary education. The potential for educating through the physical is enormous and it is incumbent on every teacher to plan and teach as efficiently as possible. Research which helps a teacher to improve his or her ability to teach effectively can only be welcomed.

Appendices

1
Anderson's Descriptive Category System. Dimensions and Categories of Teacher Behaviour

The definitions which appear below are simplified and abbreviated versions of the actual definitions. The definitions for categories with self-explanatory titles are omitted.

DIMENSION: INTERACTIVE FUNCTION — identifies the purpose of the teacher's interactive behaviour.
Categories:

1 Preparing for motor activities (games, sports, exercises, exploratory and fundamental movements).

(a) Organizing: providing information to students about their location, position, grouping, role, order of performance etc.
(b) Preparatory instructing: providing information about the activity to be performed, i.e. rules, skills etc.
(c) Providing equipment or readying the environment: interacting to provide equipment or get the environment ready.

2 Guiding the performance of motor activities.

(a) Concurrent instructing: providing instruction to student(s) while they are performing an activity.
(b) Officiating: performing duties of an official such as regulating starting/stopping of activity, enforcing rules, keeping scores.
(c) Spotting: interacting with students for the purpose of protecting them against injury, assisting them and positioning oneself for the above.
(d) Leading exercises: counting cadence, regulating performance of exercises etc.
(e) Intervening instruction: providing instruction to students regarding their past performance of the activity.

3   Observing the performance of motor activities: silently attending to student(s) who are performing motor activities. (Only silent periods of five seconds or more are recorded.)

4   Participating in motor activities: performing as a participant in motor activity (not leading or demonstrating).

5   Other interacting related to motor activities: all other interactions directly related to the motor activities which do not fall in the above categories, for example, history of activity, spectator behaviour, current events related to activity.

6   Other interactive behaviours

(a)   Administering: interacting with students to carry out school/class policies, for example, attendance, dress, schedules, excuses.
(b)   Establishing and enforcing codes of behaviour: interacting to influence student's social/personal conduct, for example, disciplining, commanding appropriate behaviour.
(c)   Other interacting: all other interactive behaviours which do not fall into above categories.

7   Non-interactive intervals: periods of five seconds or more during which no interactive function is being carried out.

(a)   Dealing with equipment.
(b)   Other non-interactive behaviours: tying shoes, looking out of windows, reading etc.

8   Non-discernible intervals: periods of five seconds or more during which you cannot determine whether the teacher's behaviour is interactive or non-interactive.

(a)   Insufficient audio-video
(b)   Absent from gymnasium.

DIMENSION: FUNCTION SUBSCRIPTS — indicates the extent to which the teacher carries out the function himself/herself, or shares it with others.

Categories.

1   Does: the teacher's behaviour carries out the function.

2   Shares: the teacher and student share in carrying out the function.

3   Delegates: the teacher delegates the carrying out of the function to the student(s).

DIMENSION: MODE — Identifies the way(s) in which the teacher interacts with others, i.e. the ways in which he/she conveys messages to others, receives messages from others or acts upon them.

Categories:

1   Talks.
2   Listens.
3   Observes.
4   Demonstrates.
5   Uses student demonstrator.
6   Uses audio-visual aids.
7   Uses signalling devices.
8   Writes or provides written materials.
9   Manually assists.
10   Participates.
11   Performs physical task.

DIMENSION: DIRECTION   — identified the other person(s) toward whom the teacher's behaviour is directed.

Categories:

1   One student.
2   Group/whole class of students.
3   One student and group/whole class.
4   Other persons (other than enrolled students).
5   Other combinations (of above).

2
Academic Learning Time — Physical Education. Learner Involvement

LEARNER INVOLVEMENT LEVEL — CATEGORY DEFINITIONS

This level of decision-making focuses on the individual learner(s) and is designed to describe the nature of the learner(s) involvement in a specific way. There are two major sub-divisions at the learner involvement level — not motor engaged and motor engaged.

Not motor engaged refers to all involvement other than motor involvement with subject matter oriented activities.

Motor engaged refers to motor involvement with subject matter oriented motor activities.

Each of the two main sub-divisions has categories which describe more specifically the nature of the learner's involvement. These categories are defined as follows:

NOT MOTOR ENGAGED CATEGORIES

INTERIM (I) — The student is engaged in a non-instructional aspect of an ongoing activity such as retrieving balls, fixing equipment, retrieving arrows or changing sides of a court in a tennis match.

WAITING (W) — Student has completed a task and is awaiting the next instructions or opportunity to respond such as waiting in line for a turn, having arrived at an assigned space waiting for the next teacher direction, standing on a sideline waiting to get in a game, or having organised into the appropriate formation waiting for an activity to begin.

OFF TASK (OFF) — The student is either not engaged in an activity he/she should be engaged in or is engaged in activity other than the one he/she should be engaged in — behaviour disruptions, mis-behaviour and general off-task behaviour, such as talking when a teacher is explaining a skill, misusing equipment, fooling around, fighting, disrupting a drill through inappropriate behaviour.

ON TASK (ON) — The student is appropriately engaged carrying out an assigned non-subject matter task (a management task, a transition task or a warm up task) such as moving into squads, helping to place equipment, counting off, doing warm up exercises or moving from the gym to a playing field.

COGNITIVE (C) — The student is appropriately involved in a cognitive task such as listening to a teacher describe a game, listening to verbal instructions about how to organize, watching a demonstration, parti-cipating in a discussion or watching a film.

MOTOR ENGAGED CATEGORIES

MOTOR APPROPRIATE (MA) — The student is engaged in a subject matter motor activity in such a way as to produce a high degree of success.

MOTOR INAPPROPRIATE (MI) — The student is engaged in subject matter oriented motor activity but the activity or task is either too difficult for the individual's capabilities or the task is so easy that practising it could not contribute to lesson goals.

MOTOR SUPPORTING (MS) — The student is engaged in subject matter motor activity the purpose of which is to assist others learn or perform the activity such as spotting in gymnastics, feeding balls to a hitter in a tennis lesson, throwing a volleyball to a partner who is practising set up passing or clapping a rhythm for a group of students who are practising a movement pattern.

3
Physical Education 'Learner Report' Questionnaire

Listed on the following pages are some of the statements which are related to your learning in physical education. We are interested in your opinions of these statements on a scale that ranges from 'certainly true' to 'certainly not true'. You are asked to place a tick in the appropriate space that reflects your viewpoint. Please give your own opinion and remember there are no right or wrong answers.

	Certainly true	I think so	I don't know	I don't think so	Certainly not true	Please leave this margin blank
The physical education lessons and sports activities in my secondary school have contributed to my learning the following:						
1. to play well-known ball games (for example, basketball, netball, soccer, hockey)						
2. to be able to apply the basic principles of endurance training						
3. how to cope with my sporting potential or lack thereof						
4. to adapt my way of playing and moving to the level of others						
5. what my favourite sport is						
6. to achieve in athletic activities (running, long and high jump, javelin and discus throwing)						
7. to enjoy exercising my body						
8. to understand the official competition rules of well-known sports						
9. to perform on gymnastic apparatus						
10. how to co-operate with others (stronger or weaker) in movement (sport) situations						
11. how deviations in posture occur and can be corrected						
12. how to play and engage in sports with members of the opposite sex						

	Certainly true	I think so	I don't know	I don't think so	Certainly not true	Please leave this margin blank
13. to be able to apply the right techniques in, for example, basketball or hockey						
14. how game rules can be adapted to the needs and possibilities of the group						
15. how sport can be used to promote health						
16. how to understand and accept others in sport situations						
17. how to critically appraise reports (T.V., radio, newspaper) of major sporting events						
18. how to fulfil different roles (for example, as assistant or as leader) in sport and play situations						
19. how weaker players might be involved in play						
20. how one might oneself organise sport activities						
21. how sport relates to commerce and politics						
22. why a certain technique or tactic is more appropriate in particular sport situations						
23. how it is possible in a group of widely differing capacities to play in a way that gives pleasure to all						
24. to obtain pleasure from sport participation						

226

4
Academic Learning Time — Physical Education. Context Level

CONTEXT LEVEL — CATEGORY DEFINITIONS

This level of decision making focuses on the class as a whole (or a subset of the class) and is designed to describe the context within which student behaviour is occurring. There are three major sub-divisions at the content level — general content, subject matter knowledge content and subject matter motor content.

General content refers to class time when students are not intended to be involved in physical education activities.

PE knowledge content refers to class time when the primary focus is on knowledge related to physical education content.

PE motor content refers to class time when the primary focus is on motor involvement in physical education activities.

Each of the three main sub-divisions at the context level has categories which describe more specifically the nature of the setting within which individual student behaviour is occurring. These categories are defined as follows:

GENERAL CONTENT CATEGORIES

TRANSITION (T) — Time devoted to managerial and organizational activities related to instruction such as team selection, changing equipment, moving from one space to another, changing stations, teacher explanation of an organizational arrangement and changing activities within a lesson.

MANAGEMENT (M) — Time devoted to class business that is unrelated to instructional activity such as taking attendance, discussing a field trip, lecturing about appropriate behaviour in the gymnasium or collecting money for the year book.

BREAK (B) — Time devoted to rest and/or discussion of non-subject matter related issues such as getting a drink of water, talking about last night's ball game, telling jokes, celebrating the birthday of a class member or discussing the result of a student election.

WARM UP (WU) — Time devoted to routine execution of physical activities whose purpose is to prepare the individual for engaging in further activity, but not designed to alter the state of the individual on a long term basis, such as a period of light exercise to begin a class, stretching exercises prior to a lesson or a cooling down activity to terminate a lesson.

PHYSICAL EDUCATION KNOWLEDGE CATEGORIES

TECHNIQUE (TN) — Time devoted to transmitting information concerning the physical form (topography) of a motor skill such as listening to lecture, or watching a demonstration or film.

STRATEGY (ST) — Time devoted to transmitting information concerning plans of action for performing either individually or as a group such as explanation of a zone defence, demonstration of an individual move or discussion of how best to move the ball down a field.

RULES (R) — Time devoted to transmitting information about regulations which govern activity related to the subject matter such as explanation of the rules of a game, demonstration of a specific rule violation, or viewing a film depicting the rules of volleyball.

SOCIAL BEHAVIOUR (SB) — Time devoted to transmitting information about appropriate and inappropriate ways of behaving within the context of the activity such as explanation of what constitutes sportsmanship in soccer, discussion of the ethics of reporting one's own violations in a game, or explanations of proper ways to respond to officials in a game.

BACKGROUND (BK) — Time devoted to transmitting information about a subject matter activity such as its history, traditions, heroes, heroines, records, importance in later life or relationship to fitness.

PHYSICAL EDUCATION MOTOR CATEGORIES

SKILL PRACTICE (P) — Time devoted to practice of skills or chains of skills outside the applied context with the primary goal of skill development, such as a circle drill in passing a volleyball, one against one practice of dribbling a basketball, exploration of movement forms or practising a particular skill on a balance beam.

SKILL/SCRIMMAGE (S) — Time devoted to refinement and extension of skills in an applied setting (in a setting which is like or simulates the setting in which the skill is actually used) and during which there is frequent instruction and feedback for the participants such as a half court 5 v 5 basketball activity, the practice of a complete free exercise routine or 6 v 6 volleyball.

GAME (G) — Time devoted to the application of skills in a game or competitive setting when the participants perform without intervention from the teacher such as a volleyball game, a complete balance beam routine, the performance of a folk dance or running a half mile race.

FITNESS (F) — Time devoted to activities whose major purpose is to alter the physical state of the individual in terms of strength, cardiovascular endurance or flexibility such as aerobic dance, distance running, weight lifting or agility training (the activities should be of sufficient intensity, frequency and duration so as to alter the state of the individual).

5
Academic Learning Time — Physical Education. Coding Sheet 1

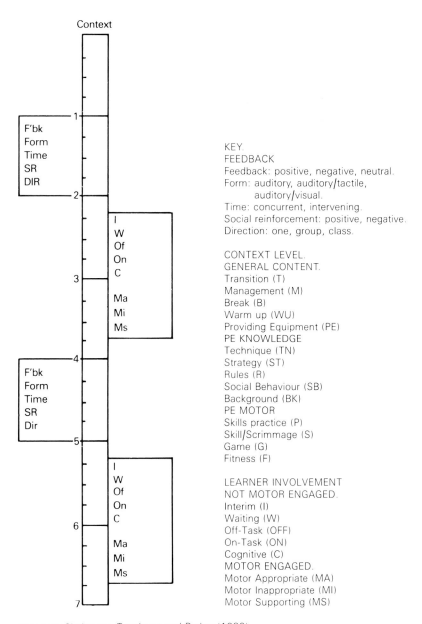

Context

KEY.
FEEDBACK
Feedback: positive, negative, neutral.
Form: auditory, auditory/tactile,
 auditory/visual.
Time: concurrent, intervening.
Social reinforcement: positive, negative.
Direction: one, group, class.

CONTEXT LEVEL.
GENERAL CONTENT.
Transition (T)
Management (M)
Break (B)
Warm up (WU)
Providing Equipment (PE)
PE KNOWLEDGE
Technique (TN)
Strategy (ST)
Rules (R)
Social Behaviour (SB)
Background (BK)
PE MOTOR
Skills practice (P)
Skill/Scrimmage (S)
Game (G)
Fitness (F)

LEARNER INVOLVEMENT
NOT MOTOR ENGAGED.
Interim (I)
Waiting (W)
Off-Task (OFF)
On-Task (ON)
Cognitive (C)
MOTOR ENGAGED.
Motor Appropriate (MA)
Motor Inappropriate (MI)
Motor Supporting (MS)

231

6
Academic Learning Time — Physical Education. Coding Sheet 2

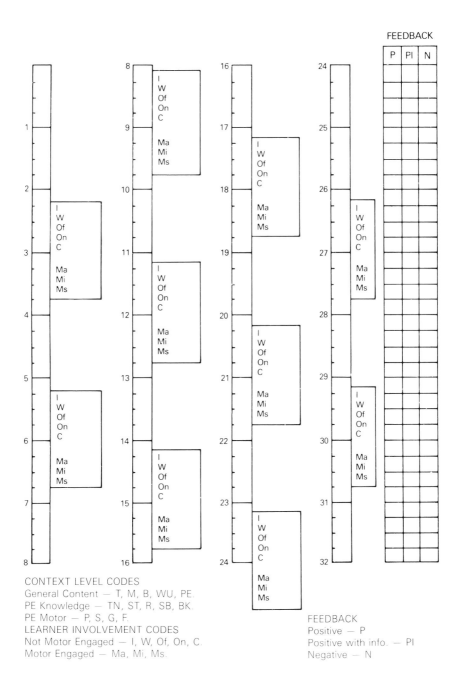

CONTEXT LEVEL CODES
General Content — T, M, B, WU, PE.
PE Knowledge — TN, ST, R, SB, BK.
PE Motor — P, S, G, F.
LEARNER INVOLVEMENT CODES
Not Motor Engaged — I, W, Of, On, C.
Motor Engaged — Ma, Mi, Ms.

FEEDBACK
Positive — P
Positive with info. — PI
Negative — N

233

7
Academic Learning Time — Physical Education: Context Level—Category Percentages for all Lessons in S1–S5 for Male and Female Teachers

ALT-PE DATA SUMMARY
Male teachers: Category percentages for all lessons in S1-S5

GENERAL CONTENT	S1	S2	S3	S4	S5	Av
Transition	15.6	20.8	23.8	9.0	15.4	15.5
Management	2.4	0	1.5	0.6	0.7	1.0
Break	0.3	0.3	0.5	0.5	0	0.3
Warm up	3.0	7.0	1.8	4.6	3.3	4.0
Providing Equipment	8.0	1.5	3.8	4.2	0.2	3.1
Sub section Av.	29.3	29.7	31.3	18.9	19.6	23.8
PE KNOWLEDGE						
Technique	12.6	16.0	5.0	5.4	5.5	8.3
Strategy	4.9	7.0	15.3	12.2	12.5	10.5
Rules	0.1	2.2	0.8	0	0.2	0.5
Social Behaviour	0.4	0	0	0	0	0.1
Background	0	0.3	0	0	0.3	0.2
Sub section Av.	18.0	25.5	21.0	17.7	18.5	19.5
PE MOTOR						
Practice	24.4	28.8	22.8	7.2	14.8	17.5
Skill/Scrimmage	17.6	15.2	19.5	54.4	46.2	35.9
Game	10.7	0.8	5.5	2.4	1.0	2.9
Fitness	0	0	0	0	0	0
Sub section Av.	52.7	44.8	47.5	64.0	62.0	56.9

234

ALT-PE DATA SUMMARY (Continued)

Female teachers: Category percentages for all lessons in S1-S5

GENERAL CONTENT	S1	S2	S3	S4	S5	Av
Transition	9.8	16.6	18.7	12.1	20.2	15.2
Management	0.2	0.1	2.7	1.6	0	1.0
Break	0	0	0.4	0.8	0	0.3
Warm up	5.7	3.6	5.3	2.4	7.4	4.6
Providing Equipment	4.5	6.4	4.1	2.8	3.4	4.2
Sub section Av.	20.2	26.7	31.3	19.7	31.0	25.3
PE KNOWLEDGE						
Technique	6.5	8.9	12.1	8.3	3.0	8.1
Strategy	11.0	12.3	17.4	15.6	7.6	13.3
Rules	0	0.4	0	0	0.4	0.2
Social Behaviour	0	0	0.1	0	0	0
Background	0	0	2.4	5.0	0	1.9
Sub section Av.	17.5	21.6	32.0	29.1	11.0	23.4
PE MOTOR						
Practice	12.5	8.7	14.0	12.7	10.0	11.7
Skill/Scrimmage	24.2	43.7	22.1	34.2	48.2	34.0
Game	25.3	0	0.9	0	0	4.6
Fitness	0	0	0	4.4	0	1.2
Sub section Av.	62.0	52.4	37.0	51.3	58.2	51.5

8
Interviews with Pupils: Discussion Questions

Introduction
What do you think of physical education?
What has happened in physical education to make you feel like this?

Technomotor
Do you have enough time in lessons to practise your physical skills?
Do you think you have learnt to perform on the gymnastic apparatus?
Do you know most of the rules of well-known sports?
(Have they been taught to you?)
Have you been taught any principles of games playing which can be applied to all sports?

Sociomotor
If you are playing with others who are either better or not as good as you, do you find you can still join in and cooperate with them?
Is there any opportunity to play sports with members of the opposite sex?
What is your reaction if there is someone in a group activity who is not good enough and cannot cope?
Do you belong to any physical education clubs and teams? Why?

Cognitive-reflective
Can you give me any examples of sponsorship in sport? What do you think about it?
Which English city recently made a bid for the 1992 Olympics? Why?
How is it possible to develop strength and endurance?
Do you know how deviations in posture can occur?
Are you ever involved in organising any sport?

Affective

Do you get any pleasure from taking part in physical education?

Do you enjoy the physical exercise? Is it challenging enough?

What is your favourite practical activity in physical education?

Do you consider physical education has enabled you to make the most of your talents?

Bibliography

ADAMS, J.A. (1971) 'A closed-loop theory of motor learning', *Journal of Motor Behaviour*, 3, pp 111–50.

ALLARD, R. and RIFE. F. (1980) 'A teacher-directed model of peer supervision in physical education', *Physical Educator*, 37, 2, pp 89–94.

ALTENBERGER, H. and GROSSING. S. (1978) 'Systematic classroom observation as a method of sport pedagogy', *International Journal of Physical Education*, 15, 2, pp 21–4.

AMIDON, E.J. and HOUGH, J.B. (Eds) (1967) *Interaction Analysis: Theory, Research and Application*, Addison Wesley.

ANDERSON, H.H. (1939) 'The measurement of domination and of socially integrative behaviour in teachers' contacts with children', *Child Development*, 10, pp 73–89.

ANDERSON, L. (1981) 'Interaction and time-on-task: A review', *Journal Curriculum Studies*, 13, 4, pp 289–303.

ANDERSON, W.G. (1971) 'Descriptive-analytic research on teaching', *Quest*, Monograph XV, pp 1–8.

ANDERSON, W.G. (1974) 'Teacher behaviour in physical education classes: Part 1: Development of a descriptive system', Unpublished paper, Department of Physical Education, Teachers' College, Columbia University.

ANDERSON, W.G. (1980) *Analysis of Teaching Physical Education*, C.V. Mosby.

ANDERSON, W.G. (1983) 'Observations from outside the system', *Journal of Teaching in Physical Education*, Summer, Monograph 1, pp 53–7.

ANDERSON, W.G. and BARRETTE, G.T. (Eds) (1978) *What's Going On In Gym? Descriptive Studies of Physical Education Classes, Monograph 1 of Motor Skills: Theory into Practice*, Newtown, CT.

AREND, S. and HIGGINS, J.R. (1976) 'A strategy for the classification, subjective analysis and observation of human movement, *Journal of Human Movement Studies*, 2, pp 36–52.

ARMSTRONG, C.W. and HOFFMAN, S.J. (1979) 'Effects of teaching experience, knowledge of performer competence, and knowledge of performance outcome on performance error identification', *Research Quarterly*, 50, 3, pp 318–27.

ARMSTRONG, N. (1984), 'Why implement a health related fitness programme', *British Journal of Physical Education*, 15, 6, pp 173–4.

BAIN, L.L. (1976) 'An instrument for identifying implicit values in physical education programs', *Research Quarterly*, 47, 3, pp 307–15.

BAIN, L.L. (1978) 'Differences in values implicit in teaching and coaching behaviours', *Research Quarterly*, 49, 1, pp 5–11.

BARRETT, K.R. (1979a) 'Observation of movement for teachers — a synthesis and implications', *Motor Skills: Theory into Practice*, 3, 2, pp 67–76.

BARRETT, K.R. (1979b) 'Observation for teaching and coaching', *Journal of Physical Education and Recreation*, January, pp 23–5.

BATCHELDER, A.S. and CHEFFERS, J.T.F. (1976) 'CAFIAS: An interaction analysis instrument for describing student-teaching behaviours in different learning settings', Paper read at International Conference for Physical Acitivity Sciences, Quebec, July.

BERLINNER, D. (1979) 'Tempus educare' in PETERSON, P.L. and WALBERG, H.J. (Eds.) *Research on Teaching: Concepts, Findings and Implications*, McCutchan.

BILODEAU, E.A., BILODEAU, I.McD. and SCHUMSKY, D.A. (1959) 'Some effects of introducing and withdrawing knowledge of results early and late in practice', *Journal of Experimental Psychology*, 58, pp 142–4.

BISCAN, D.V. and HOFFMAN, S.J. (1976) 'Movement analysis as a generic ability of physical education teachers and students', *Research Quarterly*, 47, 2, pp 161–3.

BLOOM, B.S. (1980) 'The new direction in educational research: alterable variables', *Phi Delta Kappan*, February, pp 382–5.

BONDI, J.C. (1970) 'Feedback from interaction analysis: some implications for the improvement of teaching'. *Journal of Teacher Education*, 21, 2, pp 189–96.

BORYS, A.H. (1986) 'Development of a training procedure to increase pupil motor engagement time (MET)', in PIERON, M. and GRAHAM, G. (Eds.) *Sport Pedagogy*, Human Kinetics.

BOYALL, J. (1982) *Suggestions for Teachers Doing Research in Classrooms*, Department of Physical Education and Sports Science, Loughborough University of Technology.

BROWN, G. (1975) *Micro-teaching: A programme of Teaching Skills*, Methuen.

BUCKLAND, D.G. (1965) 'The attitudes of adolescent boys towards physical education'. *Carnegie Research Papers in Physical Education*, 1, pp 22–8.

BUNKER, D. and THORPE, R. (1982), 'A model for the teaching of games in secondary schools', *Bulletin of Physical Education*, 18, 1, pp 5–8.

CARLISLE, C. and PHILLIPS, A.D. (1984) 'The effects of enthusiasm training on selected teacher and student teacher behaviours in pre-service physical education teachers', *Journal of Teaching in Physical Education*, 4, 1, pp 64–75.

CARROLL, B. (1986) 'What's in a name? Pupils' identity in physical education', *Physical Education Review*, 9, 1, pp 19–27.

CARRON, A.V. and BENNETT, B.B. (1977) 'Compatibility in the coach-athlete dyad', *Research Quarterly*, 48, 4, pp 671–9.

CHEFFERS, J.T.F. (1972) 'The validation of an instrument design to expand the Flanders system of interaction analysis to describe non-verbal interaction, different varieties of teacher behaviour and pupil responses', Upublished doctoral dissertation, Temple University.

CHEFFERS, J.T.F. (1977) 'Systematic observation in teaching', Paper presented at the AIESEP International Conference, Madrid, July.

CHEFFERS, J.T.F. and KEILTY, G.C. (1980) 'Developing valid instrumentation for measuring teacher performance', *International Journal of Physical Education*, 17, 2, pp 15–22.

CHEFFERS, J.T.F. and LOMBARDO, B.J. (1979) 'The observation and description of teaching behaviour and interaction of selected physical education teachers', Resources in Education (ERIC) Document ED 173325.

CHEFFERS, J.T.F. and MANCINI, V.H. (1978) 'Teacher-student interaction' in ANDERSON, W.G. and BARRETTE, G.T. (Eds.) *What's Going On in Gym? Descriptive Studies of Physical Education Classes. Monograph 1 of Motor Skills: Theory into Practice.* Newtown, CT.

CHEFFERS, J.T.F., MANCINI, V.H. and ZAICHKOWSKY, L.D. (1976) 'The development of an elementary physical education attitude scale', *Physical Educator*, 33, 1, pp 30–3.

COE, M.J. (1984) 'Children's perceptions of physical education in the middle school', *Physical Education Review*, 7, 2, pp 120–5.

COHEN, L. and HOLLIDAY, M. (1982) *Statistics for Social Scientists*, Harper and Row.

COSTELLO, J. and LAUBACH, S.A. (1978) 'Student behaviour' in ANDERSON, W.G. and BARRETTE, G.T. (Eds) *What's Going On In Gym? Descriptive Studies of Physical Education Classes. Monograph 1 of Motor Skills: Theory into Practice*, Newtown, CT.

CRUM, B.J. (1984) 'The use of learner reports for exploring teacher effectiveness in physical education', Paper presented at the Olympic Scientific Congress, University of Oregon, July.

CRUM, B.J. (1986a) 'The use of learner reports for exploring teacher effectiveness in physical education', in PIERON, M. and GRAHAM, G. (Eds) *Sport Pedagogy*, Human Kinetics.

CRUM, B.J. (1986b) 'Concerning the quality of the development of knowledge in sport pedagogy', *Journal of Teaching in Physical Education*, 5, 4, pp 211–20.

DANIELSON, R.R., ZELHART, P.F. and DRAKE, C.J. (1975) 'Multidimensional scaling and factor analysis of coaching behaviour as perceived by high school hockey players', *Research Quarterly*, 46, 3, pp 323–34.

DARST, P.W. (1976) 'Effects of competency-based intervention on student-teacher and pupil behaviour', *Research Quarterly*, 47, 3, pp 336–45.

DARST, P.W., MANCINI, V.H. and ZAKRAJSEK, D.B. (1983) *Systematic Observation Instrumentation for Physical Education*, Leisure Press.

DARST, P.W. and STEEVES, D. (1980) 'A competency-based approach to secondary student teaching in physical education', *Research Quarterly*, 51, 2, pp 274–85.

DELAMONT, S. and HAMILTON, D. (1976), 'Classroom research: A critique and a new approach' in STUBBS, M. and DELAMONT, S. (Eds) *Explorations in Classroom Observation*, Wiley.

DICKENSON, B. (1986) 'The physical activity patterns of young people — the implications for physical education', *Bulletin of Physcial Education*, 22, 1, pp 36–8.

DODDS, P. (1979) 'A peer assessment model for student teacher supervision', *Research Quarterly*, 50, 1, pp 18–29.

DODDS, P. and RIFE, F. (Eds) (1983) 'Time to learn in physical education: History, completed research and potential future for academic learning time in physical education', *Journal of Teaching in Physical Education*, Monograph 1, summer.

DODDS, P., RIFE, F. and METZLER, M. (1982) 'Academic learning time in physical education: data collection, completed research and future directions' in PIERON, M. and CHEFFERS, J.T.F. (Eds) *Studying the Teaching in Physical Education*, AIESEP

DOUGHERTY, N.J. (1970) 'A comparison of command, task and individual program styles of teaching in the development of physical fitness and motor skills, Unpublished doctoral dissertation, Temple University.

DOUGHERTY, N.J. (1971) 'A plan for the analysis of teacher-pupil interaction in physical education classes', *Quest*, Monograph XV, pp. 39–50.

DROWATZKY, J.N. (1975) *Motor Learning: Principles and Practices*, Burgess.

DWECK, C.S. (1980) 'Learned helplessness in sport' in NADEAU, C.H. (Ed) *Pscyhology of Motor Behaviour in Sport — 1979*, Human Kinetics.

EARLS, N. (1983) 'Research on the immediate effects of instructional variables' in TEMPLIN, T.J. and OLSON, J.K. (Eds) *Teaching in Physical Education*, Human Kinetics.

EVANS, D. (1983) 'Methods of gaining feedback from senior girl pupils in school', *British Journal of Physical Education*, 14, 1, pp 20–1.

EVANS, J. (1984) 'Muscle, sweat and showers. Girls' conceptions of physical education and sport: A challenge for research and curriculum reform, *Physical Education Review*, 7, 1, pp 12–18.

EVANS, J. (Ed) (1986) *Physical Education, Sport and Schooling: Studies in the Sociology of Physical Education*, Falmer Press.

FIGLEY, G.E. (1985), 'Determinants of attitudes towards physical education, *Journal of Teaching in Physical Education*, 4, 4, pp 229–40.

FISHMAN, S. (1978) 'A procedure for recording augmented feedback in physical education classes. Unpublished doctoral dissertation'. Teachers' College, Columbia University.

FISHMAN, S.E. and ANDERSON, W.G. (1971) 'Developing a system for describing teaching', *Quest*, Monograph XV, pp 9–16.

FISHMAN, S.E. and TOBEY, C. (1978) 'Augmented feedback' in ANDERSON, W.G. and BARRETTE, G.T. (Eds) *What's Going On In Gym? Descriptive Studies of Physical Education Classes. Monograph 1 of Motor Skills: Theory into Practice*, Newtown, CT.

FLANAGAN, D. (1985) 'Current issues in physical education — the state of play', *Bulletin of Physical Education*, 21, 3, pp 8–10.

FLANDERS, N.A. (1970) *Analyzing Teacher Behaviour*, Addison Wesley.

FLANDERS., N.A. (1976) 'The problems of observer training and reliability', in AMIDON, E.J. and HOUGH, J.B. (Eds) *Interaction Analysis: Theory, Research and Application*, Addison Wesley.

FOX, C. and POPPLETON, P. (1983) 'Verbal and non-verbal communication in teaching: A study of trainee physical education teachers in the gymnasium', *British Journal of Educational Psychology*, 53, 1, pp 107–20.

FUCHS, A.H. (1962) 'The progression-regression hypothesis in perceptual motor skill learning', *Journal of Experimental Psychololgy*, 63, pp 177–82.

GALTUNG, J. (1967) *Theory and Methods of Social Research*, Allen and Unwin.

GIBSON, D.R. (1970) 'Classroom observation using videotapes', *Bulletin, University of London*, 20, pp 31–4.

GLAISTER, I.K. (Ed) (1976) *Evaluation in Physical education*, NATFHE Physical Education Section Conference Report.

GODBOUT, P. (1983) 'Academic learning time in elementary and secondary physical education classes', *Research Quarterly for Exercise and Sport*, 54, 1, pp 11–19.

GOLDBERGER, M.S. (1974) 'Studying your teaching behaviour', *Journal of Health, Physical Education and Recreation*, 45, 4, pp 33–6.

GOLDBERGER, M.S. and GERNEY, P. (1982) 'The effects of three styles of teaching on the psychomotor performance and social skill development of fifth grade children', *Research Quarterly for Exercise and Sport*, 53, 2, pp 116–24.

GRAHAM, G. (1983) 'Review and implications of physical education experimental teaching unit research', in TEMPLIN, T.J. and OLSON, J.K. (Eds.) *Teaching in Physical Education*, Human Kinetics.

GRAHAM, G. and HEIMERER, E. (1981) 'Research on teacher effectiveness: A summary with implications for teaching', *Quest*, 33, 1, pp 14–25.

GRANT. B. (1980) 'A study of effectiveness in teaching physical education in the elementary school,' Unpublished masters thesis, University of Victoria.

GRIFFEY, D. (1983) 'ALT in context: On the non-linear and interactional characteristics of engaged time', *Journal of Teaching in Physical Education*, Monograph 1, summer.

GRIFFIN, P.S. (1984) 'Girls' participation patterns in a middle school team sports unit', *Journal of Teaching in Physical Education*, 4, 1, pp 30–8.

GRIFFIN, P.S. (1985) 'Boys' participation styles in a middle school physical education team sports unit', *Journal of Teaching in Physical Education*, 4, 2, pp 100–10.

HAWKINS, R.P. and DOTSON, V.A. (1975) 'Reliability scores that delude: An Alice in Wonderland trip through the misleading characteristics of inter-observer agreement scores in interval recording' in RAMP, E. and SEMB. G. (Eds) *Behaviour Analysis: Areas of Research and Application*, Prentice Hall.

HEINILA, L. (1979) 'Analysing systems in the evaluation of the teacher-pupil interaction process in physical education classes' in TAMMIVUORI, T. (Ed.) *Evaluation in the Development of Physical Education*, International Congress of Physical Education, Finnish Society for Research in Sport and Physical Education.

HICKEY, B.J. (1985) 'The interrelationship of teacher experience, student behaviour and effective teaching in secondary school physical education' in HOWE, B.L. and JACKSON, J.J. (Eds) *Teaching Effectiveness Research*, University of Victoria.

HILL, C. (1984) 'Criteria for judging a physical education department', *Bulletin of Physical Education*, 20, 1, pp 13–18.

HOFFMAN, S.J. (1983) 'Clinical diagnosis as a pedagogical skill' in TEMPLIN, T.J. and OLSON, J.K. (Eds.) *Teaching in Physical Education*, Human Kinetics.

HOSTE, R. (1976) 'Evaluating the physical education course' in GLAISTER, I.K. (Ed.) *Evaluation in Physical Education*. NATFHE Physical Education Section, Conference Report.

HOWE, B.L. and JACKSON, J.J. (Eds.) (1985) *Teaching Effectiveness Research*, University of Victoria.

HURWITZ, R.F. (1973) 'The reliability and validity of descriptive-analytic systems for studying classroom behaviours'. *Classroom Interaction Newsletter*, 8, 2, pp 50–9.

HURWITZ, R.F. (1978) 'Review' in ANDERSON, W.G. and BARRETTE, G.T. (Eds.) *What's Going On in Gym? Description Studies of Physical Education Classes, Monograph 1 of Motor Skills: Theory and Practice*, Newtown, CT.

IKULAYO, P.B. (1983) 'Attitudes of girls towards physical education', *Physical Education Review*, 6, 1, pp 24–5

IMWOLD, C.H., RIDER, R.A., TWARDY, B.M., OLIVER, P.S., GRIFFIN, M. and ARSENAULT, D.N. (1984) 'The effect of planning on the teaching behaviour of preservice physical education teachers', *Journal of Teaching in Physical Education*, 4,1, pp 50–6.

JENSEN, M. (1980) 'Teaching: An open skill, implications for teacher training', *Quest*, 32, 1, pp 60–70.

JEWETT, A.E. and BAIN, L.L. (1985) *The Curriculum Process in Physical Education*, Wm. C. Brown.

KANE, J.E. (1974) *Physical Education in Secondary Schools*, Macmillan.

KERLINGER, F.N. (1973) *Foundations of Behavioural Research*, Holt, Rinehart and Winston.

KNEER, M.E. (1986) 'Description of physical education instructional theory/practice gap in selected secondary schools', *Journal of Teaching in Physical Education*, 5, 2, pp 91–106.

KRAFT, R.E. (1980) 'A system for monitoring student behaviour', *Journal of Physical Education and Recreation*, 25, May.

LAUBACH, S.A. (1975) 'The development of a system for coding student behaviour in physical education classes', Unpublished doctoral dissertation, Teachers' College, Columbia University.

LEWIN, K., LIPPITT, R. and WHITE, R.K. (1939) 'Patterns of aggressive behaviour in experimentally created "social climates"', *Journal of Social Psychology*, 10, pp 271–99.

LOCKE, L.F. (1977) 'Research on teaching physical education: new hope for a dismal science', *Quest*, 28, pp 2–28.

LOCKE, L.F. (1979) 'Teaching and learning process in physical activity: The central problem of sport pedagogy, (ERIC) Document ED 171700.

LOCKE, L.F. (1983) 'Research on teacher education for physical education in the USA: Part II: Questions and conclusions' in TELAMA, R. *et al* (Eds.) *Research in School Physical Education*, Foundation for Promotion of Physical Culture and Health, Jyvaskyla.

LOCKE, L.F. and MASSENGALE, J.D. (1978) 'Role conflict in teacher/coaches', *Research Quarterly*, 49, 2, pp 162–74.

LOGSDON, B.J. (Ed.) (1977) *Physical Education for Children: A Focus on the Teaching Process*, Lea and Febiger.

LUFF, I.V. (1980) 'Curriculum evaluation: A neglected process?', *Physical Education Review*, 3, 1, pp 18–33.

MACDONALD, B. and WALKER, R.R. (1975) 'Case-study and the social philosophy of educational research', *Cambridge Journal of Education*, 5, 1, pp 2–11.

MCCONNELL, A. and FAGES, S. (1980) 'Videotaped feedback in physical education methods class', *Journal of Physical Education and Recreation*, May, pp 64–5.

MCINTYRE, D.I. (1980) 'Systematic observation of classroom activites', *Educational Analysis*, 2, 2, pp 3–30.

MCKENZIE, T.L. (1986) 'Analysis of the practice behaviour of elite athletes' in PIERON, M. and GRAHAM, G. (Eds) *Sport Pedagogy*, Human Kinetics.

MCLEISH, J. (1985) 'An overall view' in HOWE, B.L. and JACKSON, J.J. (Eds.) Teaching Effectiveness Research, Melbourne, University of Victoria.

MCNEIL, J.D. and POPHAM, W.J. (1973) 'The assessment of teacher competence' in TRAVERS, R.M.W. (Ed.) *Second Handbook of Research in Teaching*. Rand McNally.

MANCINI, V.H., CHEFFERS, J.T.F. and ZAICHKOWSKY, L.D. (1976) 'Decision making in elementary children: effects on attitudes and interaction', *Research Quarterly*, 47, 1, pp 80–5.

MANCINI, V.H., WUEST, D.A., CLARK, E.K. and RIDOSH, N. (1983) 'A comparison of interaction patterns and ALT-PE of low and high burnout secondary physical educators' in TEMPLIN, T.J. and OLSON, J.K. (Eds.) *Teaching in Physical Education*, Human Kinetics.

MARTENS, R. (1975) *Social Psychology and Physical Activity*, Harper and Row.

MARTINEK, T.J. (1981) 'Pygmalion in the gym: A model for the communication of teacher expectations in physical education', *Research Quarterly*, 52, 1, pp 58–67.

MARTINEK, T.J., CROWE, P.B. and REJESKI, W.J. (1982) *Pygmalion in the Gym*, Leisure Press.

MARTINEK, T.J. and JOHNSON, S.B. (1979) 'Teacher expectations: Effects on dyadic interactions and self-concept in elementary age children', *Research Quarterly*, 50, 1, pp. 60–70.

MARTENIUK, R.G. (1976) *Information Processing in Motor Skill*, Holt, Rinehart and Winston.

MEEK, C. (1986) 'The contribution of physical education to the new curriculum', *Physical Education Review*, 9, 2, pp 73–81.

MELOGRANO, V.J. (1971) 'Effects of teacher personality, teacher choice of educational objectives and teacher behaviour on student achievement', Unpublished doctoral dissertation, Temple University.

METZLER, M. (1983) 'An interval recording system for measuring academic learning time in physical education' in DARST, P., MANCINI, V.H. and ZAKRAJSEK, D.B. (Eds.) *Systematic Observation Instrumentation for Physical Education*, Leisure Press.

METZLER, M., DEPAEPE, J. and REIF, G. (1985) 'Alternative technologies for measuring academic learning time in physical education', *Journal of Teaching in Physical Education*, 4, 4, pp 271–85.

MILLER, C. (1986) 'An investigation into the teaching of netball by secondary school physical education teachers using Anderson's Descriptive Category System, Unpublished dissertation, Nonington College, Kent.

MORGENEGG, B.L. (1978) 'Pedagogical moves' in ANDERSON, W.G. and BARRETTE, G.T. (Eds.) *What's Going On In Gym? Descriptive Studies of Physical Education Classes: Monograph 1 of Motor Skills: Theory into Practice*, Newtown, CT.

MORRISON, A. and MCINTYRE, D. (Eds.) (1972) *Social Psychololgy of Teaching*, Penguin.

MOSSTON, M. (1966) *Teaching Physical Education*, Charles E. Merrill.

MOSSTON, M. (1972) *Teaching: From Command to Discovery*, Wadsworth.

NASH, R. (1973) *Classrooms Observed*, Routledge and Kegan Paul.

NIXON, J.E. and LOCKE, L.F. (1973) 'Research on teaching physical education' in TRAVERS, R.M.W. (Ed.) *Second Handbook of Research on Teaching*, Rand McNally.

NORUSIS, M.J. (1986) *SPSSX User's Guide*, 2nd ed., McGraw Hill.

NYGARD, G. (1975), 'Interaction analysis of physical education classes, *Research Quarterly*, 46, 3, pp 351–7.

O'SULLIVAN, M.M. (1985) 'A descriptive analytical study of student teacher effectiveness and student behaviour in secondary school physical education' in HOWE, B.L. and JACKSON, J.J. (Eds.) *Teaching Effectiveness Research*, Melbourne, University of Victoria.

PAESE, P. (1982) 'The effect of feedback on Academic Learning Time (PE Motor) in student teachers' classes', (ERIC) Document ED 229368.

PAIN, S. (1986) 'Physical education and health in the UK', *British Journal of Physical Education*, 17, 1, pp 4–7.

PARLETT, M. and HAMILTON, D. (1976) 'Evaluation as illumination' in TAWNEY, D. (Ed.) *Curriculum Evaluation To-day: Trends and Implications*, Schools Council, Macmillan.

PECKMAN, G.I., TAINTON, B.E. and HACKER, W.J. (1986) 'Daily physical education in three Brisbane primary schools: An evaluation of the effectiveness of programs implemented by classroom teachers' in PIERON, M. and GRAHAM, G. (Eds.) *Sport Pedagogy*, Human Kinetics.

PHILLIPS, A.D. and CARLISLE, C. (1983) 'A comparison of physical education teachers categorised as most and least effective'. *Journal of Teaching in Physical Education*, 2, 3, pp 55–67.

PHYSICAL EDUCATION ASSOCIATION COMMISSION (1987) *Physical Education in Schools*, Physical Education Association of Great Britain and Northern Ireland.

PIERON, M. (Ed.) (1978) *Towards a Science of Teaching Physical Education: Teaching Analysis*, AIESEP.

PIERON, M. (1982) 'Behaviours of low and high achievers in physical education classes' in PIERON, M. and CHEFFERS, J.T.F. (Eds.) *Studying the Teaching in Physical Education*, AIESEP, pp 53–60.

PIERON, M. (1983) 'Teacher and pupil behaviour and the interaction process in physical education classes' in TELAMA, R. *et al* (Eds.) *Research in School Physical Education*, Foundation for Promotion of Physical Culture and Health, Jyvaskyla.

PIERON, M. (1986) 'Analysis of the research based on observation of the teaching of physical education' in PIERON, M. and GRAHAM, G. (Eds.) *Sport Pedagogy*, Human Kinetics.

PIERON, M. and DELMELLE, R. (1982) 'Augmented feedback in teaching physical education: Responses from the students in PIERON, M. and CHEFFERS, J.T.F. (Eds.) *Studying the Teaching in Physical Education*, AIESEP.

PIERON, M. and DEVILLIERS, C. (1980) 'Multidimensional analysis of informative feedback in teaching physical activities' in SCHILLING, G. and BAUR, W. (Eds.) *Audio-visual Means in Sport*, Birkhauser Verlag.

PIERON, M. and GRAHAM, G. (1984) 'Research of physical education teacher effectiveness: The experimental teaching units', *International Journal of Physical Education*, 21, 3, pp 9–14.

PIERON, M. and GRAHAM, G. (Eds.) (1986) *Sports Pedagogy*, Human Kinetics.

PIERON, M. and HAAN, J.M. (1980) 'Pupils activities, time on task and behaviours in high school physical education teaching', *Bulletin of the International Federation of Physical Education*, 50, 3/4, pp 62–8.

PIERON, M. and HACOURT, J. (1979) 'Teaching behaviours at different levels of physical education teaching', *Bulletin of the International Federation of Physical Education*, 49, 2, pp 3–11.

PLACEK, J.H. (1983) 'Conceptions of success in teaching: Busy, happy and good?' in TEMPLIN, T.J. and OLSON, J.K. (Eds.) *Teaching in Physical Education*, Human Kinetics.

PLACEK, J.H. (1984) 'A multi-case study of teacher planning in physical education', *Journal of Teaching in Physical Education*, 4, 1, pp 39–49.

PLACEK, J.H. and RANDALL, L. (1986) 'Comparison of academic learning time in physical education: Students of specialists and non specialists', *Journal of Teaching in Physical Education*, 5, 3, pp 157–65.

POULTON. E.C. (1957) 'On prediction in skilled movements', *Psychology Bulletin*, 54, 6, pp 467–78.

RANKIN, K.D. (1975) 'Verbal and non-verbal interaction analysis of student teachers with students in elementary physical education', Unpublished doctoral dissertation, University of Kansas.

RANKIN, K. (1978) 'An objective approach to student teacher evaluation', *Physical Educator*, 35, 1, pp 43–6.

RIFE, F. (1979) 'Developing observation instruments for physical education', *Physical Educator*, 36, 1, pp 35–8.

RIFE, F., SHUTE, S. and DODDS, P. (1985) 'ALT-PE Versions I and II: evolution of a student centred observation system in physical education', *Journal of Teaching in Physical Education*, 4, 2, pp 134–42.

ROSENSHINE, B. and FURST, N. (1973) 'The use of direct observation to study teaching' in TRAVERS, R.M.W. (Ed.) *Second Handbook of Research on Teaching*, Rand McNally.

ROTHSTEIN, A.L. (1980) 'Effective use of videotape replay in learning motor skills, *Journal of Physical Education and Recreation*, February, pp 59–60.

RUSHALL, B.S. and MACEACHERN, J.A. (1977) 'The effects of systematic behavioural feedback on teaching behaviours of student physical education teachers'. *Canadian Journal of Applied Sports Sciences*, 2, pp 161–9.

RUSHALL, B.S. and SMITH, K.C. (1979) 'The modification of the quality and quantity of behaviour categories in a swimming coach'. *Journal of Sport Psychology*, 1, pp 138–50.

SALTER, W.B. and GRAHAM, G. (1985) 'The effects of three disparate instructional approaches on skill attempts and student learning in an experimental teaching unit', *Journal of Teaching in Physical Education*, 4, 3, pp 212–8.

SCHMIDT, R.A. (1982) *Motor Control and Learning*, Human Kinetics.

SHUTE, S., DODDS, P., PLACEK, J., RIFE, F., and SILVERMEN, S. (1982) 'Academic learning time (ALT-PE) in elementary school movement education: A descriptive analytic study', *Journal of Teaching in Physical Education*, 1, 2, pp 3–14.

SIEDENTOP, D. (1983) *Developing Teaching Skills in Physical Education*, Mayfield.

SIEDENTOP, D., BIRDWELL, D. and METZLER, M. (1979) 'A process approach to measuring teacher effectiveness in physical education', Paper presented at the AAHPERD National Convention, New Orleans, March.

SIEDENTOP, D., TOUSIGNANT, M. and PARKER, M. (1982) *Academic Learning Time — Physical Education. Coding Manual*, School of Health, Physical Education and Recreation, College of Education, Ohio State University.

SILVA, J.M. and WEINBERG, R.S. (1984) *Psychological Foundations of Sport*, Human Kinetics.

SILVERMAN, S. (1984) Academic learning time in elementary school physical education (ALT-PE) for student subgroups and instructional activity units', *Research Quarterly for Exercise and Sport*, 55, 4, pp 365–70.

SILVERMAN, S. (1985) 'Relationship of engagement and practice trials to student achievement', *Journal of Teaching in Physical Education*, 5, 1, pp 13–21.

SINGER, R.N. (1980) *Motor Learning and Human Performance*, Collier Macmillan.

SINGER, R.N. and DICK, W. (1974) *Teaching Physical Education: A Systems Approach*, Houghton Mifflin.

SINGER, R.N. and GERSON, R.F. (1981) 'Task classification and strategy utilisation in motor skills', *Research Quarterly for Exercise and Sport*, 52, 1, pp 100–16.

SKELTHORNE, A. (1986) 'The development of a profiling system', *Bulletin of Physical Education*, 22, 3, pp 43–7.

SKINSLEY, M. (1986) 'Profiling using the computer', *Bulletin of Physical Education*, 22, 3, pp 48–51.

SMITH. R.E., SMOLL, F.L. and HUNT, E. (1977) 'A system for the behavioural assessment of athletic coaches', *Research Quarterly*, 48, 2, pp 401–7. `

SMOLL, F.L., SMITH, R.E., CURTIS, B. and HUNT, E. (1978) 'Towards a mediational model of coach-player relationships', *Research Quarterly*, 49, 4, pp 528–41.

SNEDECOR, G.W. and COCHRAN, W.G. (1978) *Statistical methods*, Iowa State University Press.

SPACKMAN, L. (1986) 'The systematic observation of teacher behaviour in physical education', *Physical Education Review*, 9, 2, pp 118–34.

STEWART, M.J. (1980) 'Teaching behaviour of physical education teachers in the natural environment', *College Student Journal*, 14, 1, pp 76–82.

TAVECCHIO, L.W.C. (1977) *Quantification of Teaching Behaviour in Physical Education*, VRB drukkerijen.

TAYLOR, J.L. (1979) 'Development of the physical education observation instrument using generalisability study theory', *Research Quarterly*, 50, 3, pp 468–81.

TAYLOR, P.H. (1976) 'Explorations in the concept of evaluation' in GLAISTER, I.K. (ed.) *Evaluation in Physical Education*. NATFHE Physical Education Section. Conference Report.

TELAMA, R. *et al* (Eds) (1983) *Research in School Physical Education*, Foundation for Promotion of Physical Culture and health, Jyvaskyla.

TELAMA, R., PAUKKU, P., VARSTALA, V. and PAANANEN, N. (1982) 'Pupils' physical activity and learning behaviour in physical education classes' in PIERON, M. and CHEFFERS, J.T.F. (Eds.) *Studying the Teaching in Physical Education*, AIESEP.

TEMPLIN, T.J. and OLSON, J,K, (Eds.) (1983) *Teaching in Physical Education*, Human Kinetics.

TINNING, R.I. (1983) 'The use of interaction analysis in describing instructional processes in physical education', (ERIC) Document ED 227081.

TOUSIGNANT, M. and BRUNELLE, J. (1982) 'What we have learned from students and how we can use it to improve curriculum and teaching' in PIERON, M. and CHEFFERS, J.T.F. (Eds.) *Studying the Teaching in Physical Education*, AIESEP.

TRAVERS, R.M.W. (Ed.) (1973) *Second Handbook of Research on Teaching*, Rand McNally.

TRIANDIS, H.C. (1971) *Attitude and Attidue Change*, Wiley.

UNDERWOOD, G.L. (1978) 'An investigation into the teaching of a basketball lesson using interaction analysis techniques' in PIERON, M. (Ed.) *Towards a Science of Teaching Physical Education*, AIESEP.

UNDERWOOD, G.L. (1980) 'A comparison of direct and problem-solving approaches in the teaching of physical education', in SCHILLING, G. and BAUR, W. (Eds.) *Audio-visual Means in Sport*, Birkhauser Verlag.

UNDERWOOD, G.L. (1983) *The Physical Education Curriculum in the Secondary School: Planning and Implementation*, Falmer Press.

UNDERWOOD, G.L. (1986) 'Curriculum theory and practice in physical education in secondary schools in England and Wales' in PIERON, M. and GRAHAM, G. (Eds.) *Sport Pedagogy*, Human Kinetics.

UNDERWOOD, G.L. (1987) 'An investigation into the teaching behaviour of male and female physical education teachers in secondary schools and its effect on pupils' behaviour', Unpublished doctoral thesis, University of Kent at Canterbury.

VARSTALA, V., PAUKKU, P. and TELAMA, R. (1983) 'Teacher and pupil behaviour in physical education classes' in TELAMA R. *et al* (Eds.) *Research in School Physical Education*, Foundation for Promotion of Physical Culture and Health, Jyvaskyla.

VERABIOFF, L.J. (1983) 'Elementary student behaviour and activity intensity during physical educational class' in TELAMA, R. *et al* (Eds.) *Research in School Physical Education*, Foundation for Promotion of Physical Culture and Health. Jyvaskyla.

VOS STRACHE, C. (1979) 'Players' perceptions of leadership qualities for coaches', *Research Quarterly*, 50, 4, pp 679–86.

WALKER, R. and ADELMAN, C. (1975a) *Classroom Observation*, London, Methuen.

WALKER, R. and ADELMAN, C. (1975b) 'Interaction analysis in informal classrooms: A critical comment on the Flanders' system', *British Journal of Educational Psychology*, 45, pp 73–6.

WALKER, R. and ADELMAN, C. (1976) 'Strawberries' in STUBBS, M. and DELAMONT, S. (Eds.) *Explorations in Classroom Observation*, Wiley.

WEBER, M. (1977) 'Physical education teacher role identification instrument', *Research Quarterly* 48, 2, pp 445–51.

WHITING, H.T.A. (1969) *Acquiring Ball Skill*, Bell.

WIDMER, K. (1978) 'The problem of the teacher-pupil relationship in sport instruction' in HAAG, H. (Ed.) *Sport Pedagogy: Content and Methodology*, University Park Press.

WITHALL, J. (1949) 'The development of a technique for the measurement of social-emotional climate in classrooms', *Journal of Experimental Education*, 17, pp 347–61.

WRAGG, E.C. (1970) 'Interaction analysis as a feedback system for student teachers', *Education for Teaching*, 81, pp 38–47.

WUEST, D.A., MANCINI, V.H., van der MARS, H. and TERILLION, K. (1986) 'The ALT-PE of high, average and low-skilled female intercollegiate volleyball players' in PIERON, M. and GRAHAM, G. (Eds.) *Sport Pedagogy*, Human Kinetics.

YERG, B.J. (1977) 'Relationships between teacher behaviours and pupil achievements in the psychomotor domain' Dissertation Abstracts International, 39, 1981A (University Microfilms No.77-22, 229).

YERG, B.J. (1981) 'Reflections on the use of the RTE model in physical education', *Research Quarterly for Exercise and Sport*, 52, 1, pp 38–47.

YERG, B.J. (1982) 'Relationship of specified instructional teacher behaviours to pupil gain on a motor skill task' in PIERON, M. and CHEFFERS, J.T.F. (Eds.) *Studying the Teaching in Physical Education*, AIESEP.

YERG, B.J. (1983) 'Re-Examining the process-product paradigm for research on teaching effectiveness in physical education' in TEMPLIN, T.J. and OLSON, J.K. (Eds.) *Teaching in Physical Education*, Human Kinetics.

Index